Child Soldiers and the Defence of Duress under International Criminal Law

Windell Nortje • Noëlle Quénivet

Child Soldiers and the Defence of Duress under International Criminal Law

palgrave
macmillan

Windell Nortje
Faculty of Law
University of the Western Cape
Cape Town, South Africa

Noëlle Quénivet
Bristol Law School
University of the West of England
Bristol, UK

ISBN 978-3-030-20662-8 ISBN 978-3-030-20663-5 (eBook)
https://doi.org/10.1007/978-3-030-20663-5

This Palgrave Macmillan imprint is published by the registered company Springer Nature Switzerland AG
The registered company address is: Gewerbestrasse 11, 6330 Cham, Switzerland

Preface

The phenomenon of child soldiering is not a new one. From the Crusades in Medieval Europe to the American Civil War and both world wars, children have always been fighting alongside adults. At the time, it was not a controversial issue as the modern conception of childhood being a period of innocence, freedom and playfulness did not exist. Even during the decolonization process, little attention was paid to scores of children fighting with their parents against colonial powers. However, the proliferation of small arms and the increase in forceful recruitment of children by brutal armed opposition groups enmeshed in protracted conflicts have brought to the fore the plight of child soldiers. As scholars painted a gruesome picture of the reality, the international community reacted by adopting a range of international legal instruments. Yet, increasingly a more nuanced portrait of these child soldiers emerged. Whilst they were the victims of horrible crimes at the hands of ruthless armed forces or armed opposition groups, they were also committing crimes, notably against the civilian population. The international community, seemingly unable to conceive that a child could be nothing but innocent, struggled with the fact that they were perpetrators of international crimes. Academic literature followed a similar path, focusing more on the child soldiers as victims than perpetrators. Only recently have more studies (such as the works of Mark Drumbl, Kirsten Fisher and Leonie Steinl) been published on this complex issue of child perpetrators.

Animated by a desire to investigate this situation from a legal viewpoint, we both separately wrote and published in this field. Windell graduated with an LLD (Legum Doctor, or Doctor of Laws) degree at the

University of the Western Cape (South Africa) in 2017 having written a thesis on 'The Accountability of Juveniles for Crimes under International Law', whilst Noëlle published an article entitled 'Does and Should International Law Prohibit the Prosecution of Children for War Crimes' in the European Journal of International Law in 2017. Whilst reading about child soldiers we were both intrigued by what would actually happen to child soldiers if they were to be prosecuted for crimes under international law. Would they indeed be deemed innocent and thus acquitted? Would the judicial system on the national and international level allow them to be primarily considered as victims? Could the judicial system cope with their dual role as victims and perpetrators?

Windell contacted Noëlle exploring the possibility of writing a joint journal article on child soldiers and grounds for excluding criminal responsibility as nothing substantial had been published on the topic. We agreed that as duress was often the defence most mentioned in relation to child soldiers, it should form the basis of our study. As our ideas developed and became more refined, the article became longer and longer to the point where we had to consider turning it into a book. At the annual conference of the British International Studies Association, the authors found out about the possibility to publish shorter books with Palgrave and so seized this amazing opportunity. We have to thank Ms Sarah Roughley for highlighting this innovative feature of Palgrave's publishing options and giving us this chance to print our work! And, as you can see, this is not such a short book!

We hope that, as much as we enjoyed writing this book, you will enjoy reading it.

Cape Town, South Africa — Windell Nortje
Bristol, UK — Noëlle Quénivet

Acknowledgements

Acknowledgements are never easy to write as a book is never just the product of the authors. It would not exist without a myriad of distant and not-so-distant scholars and friends. First, we would like to thank the many scholars who have written on topics such as child soldiers, armed conflict, duress, victims and perpetrators and so inspired us. Second, the book has undoubtedly benefitted from the excellent constructive feedback made on the book proposal by the anonymous reviewers selected by Palgrave and colleagues who have read various drafts. The authors are sincerely grateful for the financial and administrative support of both the University of the Western Cape (South Africa) and the University of the West of England (United Kingdom). This provided the authors with the opportunity to continue discussing their ideas in person and present their work. Last but not least, thank you all, friends and colleagues, for supporting us in so many ways through this journey.

In particular, the authors would like to thank Dr Alison Bisset (University of Reading, UK), Mr Christian Dadomo (University of the West of England), Dr Shane Darcy (National University of Ireland, Galway, Ireland), Ms Sarah Grabham (University of the West of England), Prof Israel Leeman (University of the Western Cape), Prof Nicholas O'Regan (University of the West of England), Dr Suwita Hani Randhawa (University of the West of England) and Ms Shilan Shah-Davis (University of the West of England, UK).

Contents

About the Authors

Windell Nortje received his LLD at the University of the Western Cape in Cape Town, South Africa. His doctoral studies focused on the accountability of juveniles for crimes under international law, with a special emphasis on child soldiers. He was the former project coordinator of the Deutscher Akademischer Austauschdienst (DAAD) South African-German Centre for Transnational Criminal Justice. He is an Associate Lecturer at the Law Faculty of the University of the Western Cape where he teaches constitutional law, criminal law, criminal procedure law and international criminal law. His most recent publications focus on international criminal law, South African criminal procedure and anti-corruption law.

Noëlle Quénivet is an Associate Professor in International Law at the University of the West of England, United Kingdom. She teaches and has taught public international law, international humanitarian law, international criminal law and human rights law to undergraduate and postgraduate students, humanitarian workers and military legal advisers. She has published and edited books as well as written journal articles in the field of international humanitarian law, international criminal law and human rights law, mainly on issues relating to children and women in armed conflict. Her most recent publications focus on the prosecution of child soldiers.

Abbreviations

A.H.R.L.J.	African Human Rights Law Journal
A.J.I.C.L.	African Journal of International and Comparative Law
A.J.I.L.	American Journal of International Law
A.P.J.H.R.L.	Asia-Pacific Journal on Human Rights and the Law
Acta Jr. Hung.	Acta Juridica Hungarica
Afr.J.Confl.Resolut.	African Journal on Conflict Resolution
Afr.Stud.Rev.	African Studies Review
Afr.Yrbk Int'l L.	African Yearbook of International Law
Alb.Gov.L.Rev.	Albany Government Law Review
Am.J. Community Psychol.	American Journal of Community Psychology
Am.U.Int'l L.Rev.	American University International Law Review
Am.U.L.Rev.	American University Law Review
Anthropol.Q.	Anthropological Quarterly
BMC Int. Health Hum. Rights	BMC International Health and Human Rights
Brook.J.Int'l L.	Brooklyn Journal of International Law
C.J.I.C.L.	Cambridge Journal of International and Comparative Law
C.L.Q.	Criminal Law Quarterly
C.L.R.	Criminal Law Review
C.S.L.R.	Cambridge Student Law Review
Cal.W.Int'l L.J.	California Western International Law Journal
Cardozo J.Int'l & Comp.L.	Cardozo Journal of International and Comparative Law
Cardozo L. Rev.	Cardozo Law Review

Child Psychiatry Hum.Dev.	Child Psychiatry and Human Development
Children's Leg. Rights J.	Children's Legal Rights Journal
Chinese J.I.L.	Chinese Journal of International Law
Colum.Hum.Rts.L.Rev.	Columbia Human Rights Law Review
Colum.L.Rev.	Columbia Law Review
Cornell Int'l L.J.	Cornell International Law Journal
Crim.L.F.	Criminal Law Forum
CUP	Cambridge University Press
Duke L.J.	Duke Law Journal
E.J.I.L.	European Journal of International Law
Eur.J.Crime Cr.L.Cr.J.	European Journal of Crime, Criminal Law and Criminal Justice
Eur.J.Int.Relat.	European Journal of International Relations
Ga.J.Int'l & Comp.L.	Georgia Journal of International and Comparative Law
Geo.J.Int'l L.	Georgetown Journal of International Law
H.R.B.	Human Rights Brief
H.R.L.Rev.	Human Rights Law Review
Harv.Int'l L.J.	Harvard International Law Journal
Hum.Rts.Q.	Human Rights Quarterly
HUP	Harvard University Press
I.J.H.R.	International Journal of Human Rights
I.J.T.J.	International Journal of Transitional Justice
I.R.R.C.	International Review of the Red Cross
ICC	International Criminal Court
ICJ	International Court of Justice
ICRC	International Committee of the Red Cross
ICTR	International Criminal Tribunal for Rwanda
ICTY	International Criminal Tribunal for the Former Yugoslavia
ILC	International Law Commission
Ind.Int'l & Comp.L.Rev.	Indiana International and Comparative Law Review
Ind.L.J.	Indiana Law Journal
Int. Political Sociol.	International Political Sociology
Int.C.L.R.	International Criminal Law Review
Int.Crim.J.Rev.	International Criminal Justice Review
Int.J.L.C.	International Journal of Law in Context
Int'l J. Child Rts.	International Journal of Children's Rights
ISIS	Islamic State in Iraq and the Levant
Isr.L.Rev.	Israel Law Review
J. Genocide Res.	Journal of Genocide Research

J.Adolesc.	Journal of Adolescence
J.Affect.Disord.	Journal of Affective Disorders
J.Aggress.Maltreat. Trauma	Journal of Aggression, Maltreatment and Trauma
J.Trauma. Stress	Journal of Traumatic Stress
J.C.L.	Journal of Criminal Law
J.Epidemiol. Community Health	Journal of Epidemiology and Community Health
J.I.C.J.	Journal of International Criminal Justice
J. Marshall L.Rev.	John Marshall Law Review
J.Mod.Afr.Stud.	Journal of Modern African Studies
L.J.I.L.	Leiden Journal of International Law
LLD	Legum Doctor (or Doctor of Laws)
Lond.Rev.Int. Law	London Review of International Law
Merkourios—Utrecht J.Int'l & Eur.L.	Merkourios—Utrecht Journal of International and European Law
Mil.L.Rev.	Military Law Review
MUP	Manchester University Press
N.I.L.Q.	Northern Ireland Legal Quarterly
N.I.L.R.	Netherlands International Law Review
N.S.E.R.	New School Economic Review
N.Z.J.P.I.L.	New Zealand Journal of Public and International Law
New Crim.L.Rev.	New Criminal Law Review
Notre Dame L.Rev.	Notre Dame Law Review
O.J.L.S.	Oxford Journal of Legal Studies
Osgoode Hall Rev.L.Pol'y	Osgood Hall Review of Law and Policy
OUP	Oxford University Press
Pace Int'l L.Rev.	Pace International Law Review
Peace Confl.	Peace and Conflict: Journal of Peace Psychology
Pep.L.Rev.	Pepperdine Law Review
Perth Int'l L.J.	Perth International Law Journal
Psychiatry Res.	Psychiatry Research
Queen's L.J.	Queen's Law Journal
R.G.D.	Revue Générale de Droit
S.Ac.L.J.	Singapore Academy of Law Journal
S.Afr.J.Psychol.	South African Journal of Psychology
S.Cal.L.Rev.	Southern California Law Review
SAIS Review	School of Advanced International Studies Review
SCSL	Special Court for Sierra Leone
St John's L.Rev.	St John's Law Review
Stud.Confl.Terror.	Studies in Conflict and Terrorism
Suffolk Transnat'l L.Rev.	Suffolk Transnational Law Review

SUP	Stanford University Press
Sw.J.Int'l L.	Southwestern Journal of International Law
Syracuse L.Rev.	Syracuse Law Review
T.W.Q.	Third World Quarterly
Temp.Int'l & Comp.L.J.	Temple International and Comparative Law Journal
Terror. Political Violence	Terrorism and Political Violence
TIAS	Texts of International Agreements to which the US is a Party
Trinity C.L.Rev.	Trinity College Law Review
U.C.Davis J.Int'l L. & Pol'y	University of California Davis Journal of International Law and Policy
U. La Verne L.Rev.	University of La Verne Law Review
UCP	University of Chicago Press
UK	United Kingdom of Great Britain and Northern Ireland
UNCRC	United Nations Convention on the Rights of the Child
UNGA	United Nations General Assembly
UNHCR	United Nations High Commissioner for Refugees
UNICEF	United Nations International Children's Emergency Fund
UNSG	United Nations Secretary-General
UNSR	United Nations Special Representative of the Secretary-General on Children and Armed Conflict
UNTAET	United Nations Transitional Administration in East Timor
UNTS	United Nations Treaty Series
US	United States of America
Va.J.Int'l J.	Virginia Journal of International Law
Vand.J.Transnat'l L.	Vanderbilt Journal of Transnational Law
Vill.L.Rev.	Villanova Law Review
Wayne L.Rev.	Wayne Law Review
Willamette J.Int'l L. & Disp.Resol.	Willamette Journal of International Law and Dispute Resolution
Y.I.H.L.	Yearbook of International Humanitarian Law
Yale L.J.	Yale Law Journal
Z.a.ö.R.V.	Zeitschrift für ausländisches und öffentliches Recht und Völkerrecht
Z.St.W.	Zeitschrift für die gesamte Straftrechtswissenschaft

CHAPTER 1

Introduction

It is common cause that children should be shielded from participating in armed conflicts. The reality, however, is that children, defined as persons under the age of 18 years old,[1] actively engage in conflicts across the world and are involved in duties, such as fighting,[2] portering,[3] gathering information,[4] caretaking,[5] cooking,[6] looting,[7] acting as bodyguards or military guards,[8] manning checkpoints,[9] providing medical care[10] and abducting and training other children.[11] Consequently, as some children take a direct part in the hostilities[12] they are likely to commit international crimes.[13] Indeed, child soldiers commit some of the most egregious crimes under international law since they are often used by armed groups at the frontline of armed conflicts.[14] However, they are usually not prosecuted for such crimes and are rehabilitated once they have been disarmed and demobilised.[15] While some child soldiers are rehabilitated when they are still children, many child soldiers are not demobilised and become adult soldiers because often they cannot escape from the armed group or simply decide to stay with the group.[16] Many of these children even become military commanders, such as Dominic Ongwen. In the past few years Ongwen has become the face of a former child soldier turned commander[17]: abducted at a young age and forced to commit horrendous crimes he moved up the ranks of the Lord's Resistance Army headed by the infamous Joseph Kony,[18] and is now facing prosecution before the International Criminal Court (ICC), though for crimes committed as an adult. Another 'poster boy' of this terrible conflict that engulfed northern

W. Nortje, N. Quénivet, *Child Soldiers and the Defence of Duress under International Criminal Law*,
https://doi.org/10.1007/978-3-030-20663-5_1

Uganda for almost 30 years is Thomas Kwoyelo who suffered the same fate as Ongwen as a child but, unlike him, is now being prosecuted on the national level before the High Court of Uganda. It must however be pointed out that whilst they might both be the face of these former child soldiers, they are prosecuted for crimes committed as adults and not as children. Yet, both symbolise the fate of hundreds of thousands of children around the world and have caught the Western world's imagination.[19] Such attitude is partially due to the fact that they epitomise the cross-breed of victims and perpetrators and challenge a number of binary models. Firstly, they blur the established moral norm that divides those caught in an armed conflict between, on the one hand, victims who are innocent and pure and, on the other, perpetrators who are guilty and evil.[20] Secondly, international criminal law (and any criminal law for that matter) is based on this victim-perpetrator dichotomy[21] as 'international courts are meant to deliver messages about the values and norms, which are assumed to characterize humanity'[22]: much of their life story shows that they are both. The victim-perpetrator narrative is an immense disruptive power that, it is argued, the International Criminal Court has recognised.[23] Thirdly, they shatter the binary model of adults-bad and children-good that dominates modern legal discourse.[24] Child soldiers struggle to fit into this idealised vision of childhood as a 'period of play and innocent experimentation'.[25] Although '[c]hild soldiers carry the burden of simultaneously being recipients and perpetrators of violence'[26] they are quintessentially viewed as 'innocent', 'pure' victims.[27] Yet, 'while the perception of young people as victims of forced conscription and unscrupulous warlords might be correct for many of the very young children, the quantitatively more significant number of older child and youth combatants often do not fit this picture.'[28] Indeed, the prosecutions of Ongwen and Kwoyelo irremediably challenge this Western liberal idea that child soldiers should be viewed as victims only. This book provides numerous examples of children having committed crimes, thus supporting a more nuanced and complex understanding of the role that children play in armed conflicts.

Whilst the concept of a child soldier might conjure up in the general public's mind archetypal pictures of very young boys holding AK47s, it is used in law and social sciences to cover a much wider set of individuals, including girls and children who are not fighting. Indeed, although there is no legally binding definition neither in treaty nor in customary law, soft law instruments, such as the 1997 Cape Town Principles, state that child soldiers are '[a]ny person under 18 years of age who is part of any kind of regular or irregular armed force or armed group in any capacity, including but not limited to cooks, porters, messengers and anyone accompanying such groups, other than family members. It includes girls recruited for sexual purposes and forced marriage. It does not, therefore, only refer to a child who is carrying or has carried arms.' The 2007 Paris Principles heavily draw upon this definition too.[29] In addition, Graça Machel[30] who penned the 1996 seminal report 'The Impact of Armed Conflict on Children'[31] and Radhika Coomaraswamy, former Special Representative of the Secretary-General on Children and Armed Conflict,[32] adopt a similar definition. As this book deals with crimes committed by child soldiers, it does not matter in which 'function' these children were acting as long as their acts fall within the scope of an international crime as defined later in this chapter.

The classic position is that children are unable to understand what they are doing. 'It is claimed that their immaturity does not allow them to distinguish right from wrong or to fully comprehend the consequences of their acts; they are pawns in the adult game of war.'[33] Accordingly, the predominant legal position on the international level is that children are not deemed culpable.[34] Secondly, it is argued that their participation in hostilities is forced upon them by adults who see them as 'expendable, less demanding and easier to manipulate than adult soldiers'.[35] Happold notes that '[c]hildren are less socialised, and more docile and malleable than adults, and hence are more easily persuaded or coerced into committing atrocities.'[36] In other words, they are persuaded to commit such crimes.

The predominant, universalist, legal, social and political narrative on the international level frames children as innocent, dependent and in need of protection.[37] They are victims, dragged by evil adults into a conflict they do not understand and into committing acts whose consequences they do not fully appreciate.[38] As Drumbl eloquently explains, the 'dominant vision of the child soldier is that of a faultlessly distraught, prepubescent African boy—barely able to carry weapons and keep his socks up—brutalized by crazed rebel groups.'[39] If that is the case, then, surely, the law, and more specifically criminal law, must recognise this![40] Law, a system of norms that govern the relations between individuals, is premised on the idea that individuals recognise such norms and are able to comply with them. Criminal capacity is defined as 'understanding of the act in its context and its consequences and having a fair opportunity *not* to carry it out'.[41] As Lacey explains in a more comprehensive manner, '[t]his concept of responsibility consists in both a cognitive and a volitional element: a person must both understand the nature of her actions, knowing the relevant circumstances and being aware of possible consequences, and have a genuine opportunity to do otherwise than she does—to exercise control over her actions, by means of choice.'[42] Consequently, if an individual, for example, a child, cannot distinguish right from wrong, is not able to fathom the consequences of his/her act and has no (understanding of the) opportunity to refrain from carrying out the act, such individual should not be punished for violating a norm: he/she does not have criminal capacity.[43] Following this logic, a child cannot commit a crime. As a matter of fact, the law makes express and specific arrangements for children because they are deemed not to be able to have criminal capacity and hence to form a *mens rea* (or mental element)[44] especially for the commission of an international crime,[45] which means that technically no crime has been committed. Children fall within a special category of individuals under criminal law.[46] This legal accommodation is justified on the basis that children are vulnerable, less mature and have a reduced capacity for moral judgement.[47] Also, children under the circumstances of war tend not to ask questions and challenge the authority of their commanders.[48] By virtue of the presumption that children are incapable of evil, *doli incapax*, many national legal systems allow them to avoid criminal liability under a certain age.[49] At this juncture it must be stressed that this is not the case for all individuals under the age of 18. States at national level have specified various ages for criminal responsibility. In other words, they have identified the chronological age from which an individual can be prosecuted for a crime.

Additionally, the law acknowledges that whilst the definitional elements of an offence are present, that is, the *actus reus* (the material conduct of a person) and the *mens rea*, the act might be justified or excused, thereby certainly allowing for children to be deemed blameless.[50] Thus, if children were to be prosecuted, the trial would end with a non-guilty verdict, thereby confirming the generally held view that children are innocent victims. This book fundamentally challenges this idea by demonstrating that the most relevant defence, that of duress, does not work as the ultimate protection against a guilty verdict.

The main legal tool used to prevent children from prosecution is the concept of the minimum age for criminal responsibility.[51] A chronological age is arbitrarily set and it varies from country to country as no universal minimum age for criminal responsibility has ever been agreed upon.[52] It however does not mean that children are innocent; only, that they cannot be prosecuted because they are too young,[53] because they fall under the minimum age established by the legislator. This must be clearly spelled out and the myth of the pure, innocent child busted.

In the specific context of international crimes committed during an armed conflict, the three international legal regimes, that is, human rights law, international humanitarian law and international criminal law, that affect the age of criminal responsibility on the national and international levels do not shield all children from prosecution. Admittedly, although children cannot be prosecuted before the ICC, this is due to a *jurisdictional* limit set under Article 26 of the Rome Statute[54]: 'the Rome Statute has completely avoided confronting the issue of the criminal responsibility of child soldiers.'[55] In contrast, it seems that under international law children above the age of 15 can be prosecuted. Firstly, it is postulated that '[p]rohibiting the child's participation at a specific age [15] indicates a belief that this child does not have the requisite mental, physical, or moral development to make a logical decision regarding his or her participation in the conflict',[56] which in turn indicates that the child is not able to commit related crimes if he/she is under the age of 15 years though he/she is able to do so if he/she is older than 15 years.[57] Secondly, 'the concept of responsible command would not be compatible with a recognition that members of armed groups between 15 and 18 years of age are immune from prosecution.'[58] Thirdly, the Statute of the Special Court for Sierra Leone that was drafted under the aegis of the United Nations allows for the prosecution of individuals aged 15 and above.[59] In other words, the law does not regard them as innocent *per se*. In fact, in 2006 the International Criminal Tribunal for the former Yugoslavia (ICTY) plainly stated that the rule that 'there can be no criminal liability for a war crime committed by an individual below the age of 18' does not 'exist[ ] in conventional or customary international law'.[60] Therefore, the possibility to prosecute children, or, better phrased, individuals who were children aged between 15 and 18 years at the time of the commission of the act, for international crimes in armed conflict remains intact under international law.[61]

So, for which crimes can children be prosecuted? Whilst no definition of international crimes has been agreed upon, they can be identified as a combination of elements.[62] Firstly, all international crimes involve direct individual liability under international law. Secondly, international crimes are violations of an international treaty or customary norm, that is, the norm is part of the body of international law. Thirdly, these norms protect values deemed important by the international community,[63] their violation is a matter of international concern,[64] as a result of which all states and individuals are bound to comply with them. Fourthly, owing to the universality and significance of these values the international community has a profound interest in seeking the repression of international crimes. It is a crime irrespective of whether it has been criminalised on the national level. Fifthly, the prosecution of such crimes is not left within the exclusive competence of a single state,[65] but often attracts universal jurisdiction.[66] To reach the 'status' of an international crime the act is regarded as a crime against humankind; often these are crimes that have been committed since time immemorial.[67] In accordance with this definition, war crimes, crimes against humanity, torture, genocide, aggression and international terrorism qualify as international crimes.[68] Not all these international crimes are the subject of this book though. Rather, this book centres on crimes listed in the statutes of, and investigated and prosecuted by, international and hybrid criminal tribunals and the ICC, that is, war crimes, crimes against humanity, genocide and aggression, crimes that are often considered as 'core crimes'. The list is further narrowed down to war crimes, crimes against humanity and genocide, when committed in an armed conflict as this book deals with 'child *soldiers*'.

Since children aged 15–18 years old can be prosecuted for these international crimes, though not at the ICC but before national jurisdictions and potentially any newly created *ad hoc* tribunal,[69] it is imperative to explore the grounds for excluding criminal responsibility that are available to them, especially as the great majority of child soldiers are adolescents.[70] For the first time in history, the drafters of an international criminal court statute have expressly included a provision, Article 31 ICC Statute, enumerating and defining the grounds for excluding criminal responsibility which permit the court to declare a person not guilty on the basis that he/she, despite having committed the crime, was not criminally responsible for it.[71] Whilst it is clear that the ICC has no jurisdiction in relation to children, this provision is of importance as it can be argued that the ICC articulation of the defences generally reflect customary international law.[72] It should be noted that the concept of 'grounds for excluding criminal responsibility' is specific to international criminal law,[73] for under domestic law the notion of 'defences' is preferred. 'Defences', in a broad sense of the term, covers not only grounds excluding criminal liability leading to an acquittal but also mitigating or extenuating factors leading to a reduction in the sentence.[74] In a narrower meaning, it refers to the former only.[75] Further, the term 'grounds for excluding criminal responsibility' allows distinguishing between pure procedural impediments to prosecution and material defences.[76] Since the objective of this book is to examine whether child soldiers can be acquitted of international crimes on the basis of duress, the concept of defence will be used in its narrower meaning, unless otherwise specified.

Duress features among the grounds for excluding criminal responsibility listed in Article 31 ICC Statute but it is also a defence invoked before previous international criminal tribunals. Generally, duress is viewed as a controversial claim because it tends to blur the neat distinction between victims and perpetrators. As Dressler notes, 'it is unclear which appellation more fairly describes a person who accedes to an unlawful threat.'[77] Against this backdrop, it is unsurprising that duress is mentioned in legal circles as the best or at least most appropriate defence to be invoked by a child soldier, since child soldiers are often forced to commit atrocities and viewed as victims.[78] Their quintessential victimhood makes them the perfect candidate for raising the defence of duress. But is it indeed the case that they can automatically benefit from the defence of duress and be found not guilty?

This book aims to answer this important question and thus fills a number of gaps in contemporary legal literature. Firstly, discussions about the prosecution of children for international crimes often only focus on whether international law allows for the prosecution of children and whether such prosecution would be good policy. Yet, nothing has been written in an extensive manner on what would happen to these children at trial stage. Secondly, studies on the defence of duress so far only centre on a legal analysis of the ICC Statute in light of previous case-law rather than on the concrete application of the legal requirements of duress to situations in which international crimes are committed. In other words, there is no academic literature that applies concretely the law to the reality on the ground. Thirdly, although a plethora of scholars mention (often too briefly) defences such as superior orders and duress in relation to child soldiers[79] they do not apply the legal requirements of these defences to child soldiers. In contrast, this book offers a rigorous and comprehensive insight into how the defence of duress applies (or not) to children who have committed international crimes as children. It is however not the focus of the book to debate at great length the various elements of the defence of duress under international criminal law but rather to discuss such elements in relation to their application to child soldiers. Fourthly, it is often assumed in academic literature that the use of the defence of duress would almost automatically lead to a not-guilty judgement.[80] The simple and unrefined result of this study is that this is not the case; in many instances, child soldiers cannot get away with international crimes by relying on duress. Invoking the defence of duress is not the ultimate shield protecting child soldiers from being found guilty of international crimes.

In carrying out this research the authors have adopted a doctrinal research method accompanied by a socio-legal methodology. In doing so they use the sources of law, notably the ICC Statute as well as the jurisprudence of international and hybrid criminal tribunals and courts to expose the law and analyse the relationship between the relevant rules and principles. This study does not attempt to provide a treatise on the defence of duress under international criminal law. It is aimed at a particular group of offenders, namely child soldiers, and focuses on examining whether the defence of duress under international criminal law can be applied to them. To provide an appropriate and nuanced understanding of the complexity of the application of these legal principles in relation to child soldiers, the authors have applied a socio-legal or law in context methodology. Such a methodology also enables the authors to explore the problematic dichotomy between victims and perpetrators that is so neatly presented in criminal trials and in transitional justice processes more generally.[81] To do so the researchers have supplemented their collection of legal documents with information provided in secondary sources in the field of sociology, anthropology, criminology and psychology. It is in fact this literature that fundamentally questions the binary models child/adult, good/evil and victim/perpetrator.[82] Only by taking a broader view of the true circumstances in which child soldiers are living and interacting is it possible to understand whether the defence of duress, as spelled out in the ICC Statute, can be successfully claimed by them. The authors are however mindful that they rely on secondary sources rather than first-hand empirical research. Although some of the studies are based on surveys and interviews their analysis are undoubtedly tainted by the views of the researchers. An additional limit of this study is that the sources used are generally anglophone though some literature in French and German has been incorporated too.

To fully appreciate the defence of duress, Chap. 2 identifies a normative legal framework that helps to appreciate how the defence of duress is interpreted and applied in international criminal law and enquires into its use as a justification defence by (national and) international criminal tribunals. The theoretical and jurisprudential background helps to understand that because duress has historically been viewed as a justification under international criminal law it is in essence unlikely to be successfully invoked for international crimes,[83] be they committed by children or adults. It is however not the aim of this book to offer a comprehensive theoretical examination of the defence of duress under international criminal law. Chapter 2 further explains the relevance of the ICC Statute in setting standards, and hence the reason for adopting and applying the elements of the definition of duress as encapsulated in Article 31 ICC Statute despite the fact that children cannot be prosecuted by the ICC.

Chapter 3 is dedicated to meticulously applying the requirements of the defence of duress to the particular situation of children aged 15–18 years committing crimes in armed conflict. After all, scholarly endeavours have thus far failed to offer a comprehensive application of the law to child soldiers.[84] The authors aim to fill this critical gap against the backdrop of the vast scholarship on child soldiers in law and social sciences. The book however does not tackle the difficult issue of whether an adult defendant who was a child soldier can raise the defence of duress for crimes committed as an adult.

Chapter 4 explores the limitations placed on the defence of duress, looking at the cases of a special duty to assume danger and the fact that to be able to avail him/herself of the defence of duress a child soldier must demonstrate that he/she is free of fault, that is, that he/she has not placed him/herself in a duress situation. Such an application of the law to child soldiers presents a novelty in legal scholarship.

These two chapters enable the authors to draw the conclusion that in reality the defence of duress does not lead to a 'not guilty' verdict. In analysing the requirements these chapters also provide some concrete recommendations relating to these constraints as applied to child soldiers. Yet, they conclude that even adaptations in the case-law of international criminal courts and tribunals that take into account the idiosyncrasies of children's involvement in armed conflict will not suffice to transform duress into a successful defence. The authors do not argue that a special, distinct law on duress should be created to accommodate the situation of child soldiers. Rather, they wish the law to be interpreted in a child soldier-friendly manner. In other words, the specific circumstances and challenges that child soldiers face must be taken into account when applying the criteria of the defence of duress.

In this light, Chap. 5 suggests that a potential avenue to interpret the defence of duress in a way that more accurately reflects the reality faced by child soldiers is to revisit duress as an excuse rather than a justification. Whilst other authors have argued in favour of such a reformulation, the book supports this approach not on the basis of theory alone but also on the basis of the application of the legal requirements to child soldiers, thereby demonstrating that in fact the defence of duress in the context of mass atrocities, even applied to individuals who epitomise victimhood, does not work automatically. Following the application of the defence of duress to child soldiers and bearing in mind that the authors do not wish to introduce a special law on duress for minors, the authors suggest that duress, viewed as an excuse rather than a justification, is more adapted to such situation though they also acknowledge the flaws of such a position. Indeed, even understood as an excuse, the authors concede that such an interpretation is not a panacea: many child soldiers would still fail the test and be found guilty, thereby stressing that duress, even interpreted in a different light, is not the ultimate defence as so often claimed by scholars.

Notes

1. UNCRC 1989, art. 1. Van Bueren notes that '[t]raditionally a child has been defined as a comparative negative: a child is an individual who is not yet an adult. It is a definition which is laden with religious, cultural, physical and psychological practices and beliefs.' Van Bueren 1998, 33. For a discussion on the concept of a child under international law, see Nair 2017, 41–42.
2. Wessells 2006, 76; ICC *Katanga and Chui* 2008, paras 256–257; ICC *Lubanga* 2012, para. 834.
3. Steinl 2017, 18; Human Rights Watch 1999; Davison 2004, 138.
4. Faulkner 2001, 494.
5. McKay 2004, 23.
6. Save the Children 2005, 11; ICC *Lubanga* 2012, para. 882.
7. Briggs 2005, 18; ICC *Katanga and Chui* 2008, para. 257.
8. ICC *Katanga and Chui* 2008, paras 258 and 261; ICC *Lubanga* 2012, paras 838 and 857.
9. Almohammad 2018, 21.
10. Wessells 2006, 71.
11. Tercier Holst-Roness 2006, 13.
12. Quénivet 2008, 219–235; Yuvaraj 2016, 69–93. For a definition of direct participation, see Sandoz et al. (eds) 1987, para. 1944; ICTR *Rutaganda* 1999, para. 99; Melzer 2009; Wainryb 2011, 274.

13. Lafayette 2012–2013, 298; Happold 2002, 1144; Drumbl 2012, 85.
14. See Briggs 2005, 6; Wessells 2006, 1–2.
15. See Brett 2003, 857; Leveau 2013, 41.
16. See, for example, Klasen et al. 2010, 576; Amone-P'Olak and Ovuga 2017, 156.
17. Much alike Eichmann who became the face of the crimes linked to the Holocaust, Ongwen is that 'person [who] becomes a stand-in for all the perpetrators connected to the same tragedy, and the world stares, hoping to grasp how this nightmare, this stain on humanity, could have happened'. Mohamed 2015, 1160–1161.
18. Branch 2017, 38.
19. See, for example, Branch 2017, 38.
20. Baines 2009, 177. Boyden states that: 'Ultimately, the categories "civilian" and "combatant" become fused, with children, their families, and communities emerging as both victims and perpetrators of violence.' Boyden 2003, 344.
21. Mohamed 2015, 1165; Cryer et al. 2014, 37; Schabas 2016, 42–43. Fletcher notes that '[j]ustice in criminal law is invariably *ex post*. The facts are always asymmetrical. Someone is an aggressor and someone else is a victim.' Fletcher 2007, 183.
22. Rauschenbach 2018, 294.
23. Branch 2017, 39 and 41.
24. Hinton 2008, 288.
25. Fisher 2013, 73.
26. Klasen et al. 2015, 181.
27. Nagle 2011, 4; Schmidt 2007, 54; Maystre 2014, 977.
28. Schmidt 2007, 54. See Derluyn et al. 2015, 29.
29. UNICEF Paris Principles 2007.
30. '[A] child soldier is any child—boy or girl—under the age of 18, who is [...] recruited or used in hostilities by armed forces. [...] Child soldiers are used for forced sexual services, as combatants, messengers, porters and cooks [...]. The majority are boys, but a significant proportion overall are girls.' Machel 2001, 7.
31. UNGA 1996.
32. ICC *Lubanga* 2008, paras 17–26.
33. Quénivet 2017, 435. See Leveau 2013, 38; McDiarmid 2006, 86. Fisher poignantly asks whether 'child soldiers [are] simply tools of adult architects of atrocity, morally equivalent to guns or landmines'. Fisher 2013, 64.
34. It is however different on the national level as the great majority of legal systems provide for criminal responsibility of those under the age of 18.
35. Fonseka 2001, 69–89; Happold 2008, 62; Boyden 2003, 347–348. See Swart and Hassen for a discussion of the role of duress in child soldier marriages. Swart and Hassen 2016, 471–475.

36. Happold 2006, 70; see Nair 2017, 44.
37. Moynagh 2014, 660.
38. See, for example, the 'coerced youth' model as discussed in Murphy 2003, 64; Stahn 2019, 314.
39. Drumbl 2015.
40. Drumbl 2014–2015, 626.
41. McDiarmid 2016, 329 (italics in original).
42. Lacey 1988, 63. See Fisher 2013, 62.
43. Nortje 2017, 193. See Goldson 2009, 515.
44. Leveau 2013, 64.
45. Happold 2008, 72.
46. See, for example, Singer 2005, 154; Musila 2005, 330; Wessells 2006, 219–221.
47. Konge 2010, 55.
48. Singh 2007, 211.
49. Happold 2002, 1147; Davison 2004, 129; Fisher 2013, 62.
50. See, for example, Singer 2005, 155.
51. McDiarmid 2006, 85. See Nagle 2011, 35–37.
52. Although a universal minimum age of criminal responsibility does not exist, General Comment No. 10 to the Convention on the Rights of the Child, at para. 32, provides that an age of criminal responsibility below the age of 12 is not an acceptable international standard. See Cipriani 2009, 58; Grossman 2007, 339; Nagle 2011, 35.
53. See Ursini 2015, 1023–1048.
54. ICC Statute 1998; ICTY *Orić* 2006, fn 1177. See Moreno-Ocampo 2006, 113; Aptel 2010, 105; Drumbl 2012, 119.
55. Freeland 2005, 324. See Ambos 1999, 22; Drumbl 2012, 119–120.
56. Lafayette 2012–2013, 303. See ICC *Lubanga* 2012, para. 613. In contrast, Sampaio and McEvoy argue that the current international legal framework does not consider children aged 15 or older to be legally able to have the intent to participate in the hostilities. Sampaio and McEvoy 2016, 61–64.
57. Ursini 2015, 1042–1044; Akakpo 2012, 36.
58. Cassese et al. 2013, 227.
59. SCSL Statute 2002, art. 7(1).
60. ICTY *Orić* 2006, para. 400. See Schabas 2016, 592. Triffterer and Clark commenting on article 26 of the ICC Statute posit that 'Only the jurisdiction of the ICC is excluded. As can be seen from the historical development of this article, criminal responsibility may not be excluded for persons under eighteen in general.' Triffterer and Clark 2016, 1036.
61. See Quénivet 2017; Achton Thomas 2013, fn 12; Maystre 2014, 989. See Schabas 2016, 592–593; Triffterer and Clark 2016, 1036. It is important

to note that under customary international law states might allow for the prosecution of children at an even lower age.

62. For a list of various elements, see, for example, Cassese et al. 2013, 20–21; Werle and Jessberger 2014, 32 and Naqvi 2010, 31. For a short review of some definitions, see Scaliotti 2001, 113–114. For a comprehensive discussion of the definition and development of crimes under international law, generally see Heller 2017.
63. See ICTY *Tadić* 1995, para. 57.
64. See, for example, US *Hostages Trial* 1948, 1241.
65. See, for example, US *Hostages Trial* 1948, 1241.
66. In the case of international crimes defined in a narrow sense, see below, 'universal jurisdiction [is] nowadays acknowledged in the case of international crimes'. ICTY *Tadić* 1995, para. 62.
67. Freeland 2005, 317. Ambos notes that 'Crimes against the basic principles of humanity are nothing new to the history of mankind.' Ambos 2013, 1.
68. Cassese et al. 2013, 21; Ambos 2013, 2–4.
69. For example, the UNGA 2016 (para. 4) was created with a view to collect evidence to be preserved for a future tribunal.
70. Drumbl 2015. An accused aged 18 who committed offences shortly after reaching the age of 18 could raise immaturity as a mitigating factor, but not as a defence. See Triffterer and Clark 2016, 1035.
71. Article 31 is not without criticism. For example, Knoops notes that 'The absence of a general part of ICL is not remedied by the provisio of Article 31 of the ICC Statute, whose heading misleadingly suggests a complete compilation of all defences. Apart from its clear supplementary function-stemming from its starting text "in addition to other grounds for excluding criminal responsibility" several major defences are not included in the provisio, such as consent of the victim.' See Knoops 2008, 23–24.
72. See Cryer et al. 2014, 400; Werle and Jessberger 2014, 236, 240; Scaliotti 2001, 111; Cassese et al. 2013, 216.
73. It was chosen to accommodate a variety of legal traditions. Gilbert 2006, 144. Schabas notes that 'The *Rome Statute* uses the label "grounds for excluding criminal responsibility" out of a sense of cultural neutrality.' Schabas 2016, 636.
74. See Robinson 1997, 11–12; Ambos 2013, 354; Knoops 2008, 291–294.
75. See Scaliotti 2001, 111.
76. Merkel 2002, 441.
77. Dressler 1988–1989, 1332.
78. Manirakiza 2008–2009, 752–753; Wessells 2006, 79; Yarbrough 2014, 538 and 559; Grover 2005, 234; Lafayette 2012–2013, 312; Ursini 2015, 1047; Akakpo 2012, 37–44; Fisher 2013, 65–76.
79. Ibidem.

80. Ibidem.
81. Rauschenbach 2018, 292–296.
82. See Derluyn et al. 2015, 35.
83. See Cassese et al. 2013, 219; Eser 2016, 1151.
84. Some attempts, though not comprehensive, are made by Achton Thomas 2013; Akakpo 2012, 37–44 and Happold 2002 (through the prism of refugee law).

References

Achton Thomas, M., 2013, 'Malice Supplies the Age? Assessing the Culpability of Adolescent Soldiers', 44 *Cal.W.Int'l L.J.* 1–38.

Akakpo, L., 2012, '*Procureur c. X*: les enseignements à tirer de la poursuite des enfants soldats pour crimes contre l'humanité', 42 *R.G.D.* 9–56.

Almohammad, A., 2018, *ISIS Child Soldiers in Syria: The Structural and Predatory Recruitment, Enlistment, Pre-training Indoctrination, Training, and Deployment*, International Centre for Counter-Terrorism, Research Paper, February 2018.

Ambos, K., 1999, 'General Principles of Criminal Law in the Rome Statute', 10 *Crim.L.F.* 1–32.

Ambos, K., 2013, *Treatise on International Criminal Law: Volume I: Foundations and General Part* (OUP).

Amone-P'Olak, K. and E. Ovuga, 2017, 'The Influence of Types of War Experiences on Conduct Problems in War-Affected Youth in Northern Ugandan: Findings from the WAYS Study', 251 *Psychiatry Res.* 14–19.

Aptel, C., 2010, 'International Criminal Justice and Child Protection', in Parmar, S., et al. (eds), *Children and Transitional Justice: Truth-Telling, Accountability and Reconciliation* (Human Rights Program at Harvard Law School) 67–113.

Baines, E., 2009, 'Complex Political Perpetrators: Reflections on Dominic Ongwen', 47 *J.Mod.Afr.Stud.* 163–191.

Boyden, B., 2003, 'The Moral Development of Child Soldiers: What Do Adults Have to Fear?', 9 *Peace Confl.* 343–362.

Branch, A., 2017, 'Dominic Ongwen on Trial: The ICC's African Dilemmas', 11 *I.J.T.J.* 30–49.

Brett, R., 2003, 'Adolescents Volunteering for Armed Forces or Armed Groups', 85 *I.R.R.C.* 857–866.

Briggs, J., 2005, *Innocents Lost: When Child Soldiers Go to War* (Basic Books).

Cassese, A., et al., 2013, *Cassese's International Criminal Law* (3rd edn., OUP).

Cipriani, D., 2009, *Children's Rights and the Minimum Age of Criminal Responsibility: A Global Perspective* (Ashgate).

Cryer, C., et al., 2014, *An Introduction to International Criminal Law and Procedure* (3rd edn., CUP).

Davison, A., 2004, 'Child Soldiers: No Longer a Minor Incident', 12 *Willamette J.Int'l L. & Disp.Resol.* 124–157.

Derluyn, I., et al., 2015, 'Victims and/or Perpetrators? Towards an Interdisciplinary Dialogue on Child Soldiers', 15 *BMC Int. Health Hum. Rights* 28–40.

Dressler, J., 1988–1989, 'Exegesis of the Law of Duress: Justifying the Excuse and Searching for its Proper Limits', 62 *S.Cal.L.Rev.* 1331–1386.

Drumbl, M., 2012, *Reimagining Child Soldiers in International Law and Policy* (OUP).

Drumbl, M., 2014–2015, 'Children, Armed Violence and Transition: Challenges for International Law and Policy', 43 *Ga.J.Int'l. & Comp.L.* 623–627.

Drumbl, M.A., 2015, 'The Ongwen Trial at the ICC: Tough Questions on Child Soldiers', *Open Democracy*, 14 April 2015, available at https://www.opendemocracy.net/openglobalrights/mark-drumbl/ongwen-trial-at-icc-tough-questions-on-child-soldiers (last visited 2 September 2018).

Eser, E., 2016, 'Article 31: Grounds for Excluding Criminal Responsibility', in Triffterer, O. and K. Ambos (eds), *The Rome Statute of the International Criminal Court: A Commentary* (3rd edn., Beck) 1125–1160.

Faulkner, F., 2001, 'Kindergarten Killers: Morality, Murder and the Child Soldier Problem', 22 *T.W.Q.* 491–504.

Fisher, K.J., 2013, *Transitional Justice for Child Soldiers. Accountability and Social Reconstruction in Post-Conflict Contexts* (Palgrave).

Fletcher, G.P., 2007, *The Grammar of Criminal Law* (OUP).

Fonseka, F., 2001, 'The Protection of Child Soldiers in International Law', 2 *A.P.J.H.R.L.* 69–89.

Freeland, S., 2005, 'Child Soldiers and International Crimes—How Should International Law Be Applied?', 3 *N.Z.J.P.I.L.* 303–328.

Gilbert, J., 2006, 'Justice Not Revenge: The International Criminal Court and the "Grounds to Exclude Criminal Responsibility"—Defences or Negation of Criminality?', 10 *I.J.H.R.* 143–160.

Goldson, B., 2009, 'Counterblast: "Difficult to Understand of Defend": A Reasoned Case for Raising the Age of Criminal Responsibility', 48 *Howard Journal* 514–521.

Grossman, N., 2007, 'Rehabilitation or Revenge: Prosecuting Child Soldiers for Human Rights Violations', 38 *Geo.J.Int'l L.* 323–362.

Grover, L., 2005, 'Trial of the Child Soldier: Protecting the Rights of the Accused', 65 *Z.a.ö.R.V.* 217–238.

Happold, M., 2002, 'Excluding Children from Refugee Status: Child Soldiers and Article 1F of the Refugee Convention', 24 *Am.U.Int'l L.Rev.* 1131–1176.

Happold, M., 2006, 'The Age of Criminal Responsibility for International Crimes under International Law' in Arts, K. and V. Popovski (eds), *International Criminal Accountability and the Rights of Children* (Asser Press) 69–84.

Happold, M., 2008, 'Child Soldiers: Victims or Perpetrators?', 29 *U.La Verne L.Rev.* 56–87.

Heller, K.J., 2017, 'What is an International Crime? (A Revisionist History)', 58 *Harv.Int'l L.J.* 353–420.

Hinton, R., 2008, 'Children's Participation and Good Governance: Limitations of the Theoretical Literature', 16 *Int'l J. Child Rts* 285–300.

Human Rights Watch, 1999, *Promises Broken*, December 1999.

ICC *Katanga and Chui*, 2008, *Situation in the Democratic Republic of the Congo in the Case of The Prosecutor v. Katanga and Ngudjolo Chui*, International Criminal Court, Decision on the Confirmation of Charges, Case No. ICC-01/04-01/07, 30 September 2008.

ICC *Lubanga*, 2008, *Situation in the Democratic Republic of the Congo in the Case of the Prosecutor v. Lubanga Dyilo*, International Criminal Court, Written Submissions of the United Nations Special Representative of the Secretary-General on Children and Armed Conflict, Submitted in Application of Rule 103 of the Rules of Procedure and Evidence, Case No. ICC-01/04-01/06-1229-AnxA (EVD-CHM-00007), 18 March 2008.

ICC *Lubanga*, 2012, *Situation in the Democratic Republic of the Congo in the Case of the Prosecutor v. Lubanga Dyilo*, International Criminal Court, Judgment Pursuant to Article 74 of the Statute, Case No. ICC-01/04-01/06, 14 March 2012.

ICC Statute, 1998, Statute of the International Criminal Court, U.N. Doc. A/CONF.183/9, (1998) 2187 UNTS 90.

ICTR *Rutaganda*, 1999, *Prosecutor v. Rutaganda*, International Criminal Tribunal for Rwanda, Judgment and Sentence, Case No. ICTR-96-3-T, 6 December 1999.

ICTY *Orić*, 2006, *Prosecutor v. Orić*, International Criminal Tribunal for the Former Yugoslavia, Judgment, Case No. IT-03-68-T, 30 June 2006.

ICTY *Tadić*, 1995, *Prosecutor v. Tadić*, International Criminal Tribunal for the Former Yugoslavia, Decision on the Defence Motion for Interlocutory Appeal on Jurisdiction, Case No. IT-94-1, 2 October 1995.

Klasen, F., et al., 2010, 'Multiple Trauma and Mental Health in Former Ugandan Child Soldiers', 23 *J.Trauma. Stress* 573–581.

Klasen, F., et al., 2015, 'The Guiltless Guilty: Trauma-Related Guilt and Psychopathology in Former Ugandan Child Soldiers', 46 *Child Psychiatry Hum.Dev.* 180–193.

Knoops, G.A., 2008, *Defenses in Contemporary International Criminal Law* (Martinus Nijhoff).

Konge, P., 2010, 'International Crimes & Child Soldiers', 16 *Sw.J.Int'l L.* 41–74.

Lacey, N., 1988, *State Punishment: Political Principles and Community Values* (Routledge).

Lafayette, E., 2012–2013, 'The Prosecution of Child Soldiers: Balancing Accountability with Justice', 63 *Syracuse L.Rev.* 297–325.

Leveau, F., 2013, 'Liability of Child Soldiers under International Criminal Law', 4 *Osgoode Hall Rev.L.Pol'y* 36–66.

Machel, G., 2001, *The Impact of War on Children: A Review of Progress since the 1996 United Nations Report on the Impact of Armed Conflict on Children* (Hurst and Company).

Manirakiza, P., 2008–2009, 'Les enfants face au système international de justice: à la recherche d'un modèle de justice pénale internationale pour les délinquants mineurs', 34 *Queen's L.J.* 719–768.

Maystre, M., 2014, 'The Interaction between International Refugee Law and International Criminal Law with Respect to Child Soldiers', 12 *J.Int'l Crim. Just.* 975–996.

McDiarmid, C., 2006, 'What Do they Know? Child-Defendants and the Age of Criminal Responsibility: A National Perspective' in Arts, K. and V. Popovski (eds), *International Criminal Accountability and the Rights of Children* (Asser Press) 85–95.

McDiarmid, D., 2016, 'After the Age of Criminal Responsibility: A Defence for Children who Offend', 67 *N.I.L.Q.* 327–341.

McKay, S., 2004, 'Reconstructing Fragile Lives: Girls' Social Reintegration in Northern Uganda and Sierra Leone', 12 *Gender and Development* 19–30.

Melzer, N., 2009, *Interpretive Guide on the Notion of Direct Participation in Hostilities under International Humanitarian Law*.

Merkel, R., 2002, 'Gründe für den Ausschluss der Strafbarkeit im Völkerstrafrecht', 2 *Z.St.W.* 437–454.

Mohamed, S., 2015, 'Of Monsters and Men: Perpetrator Trauma and Mass Atrocity', 115 *Colum.L.Rev.* 1157–1216.

Moreno-Ocampo, L., 2006, 'The Rights of Children and the International Criminal Court' in Arts, K. and V. Popovski (eds), *International Criminal Accountability and the Rights of Children* (Asser Press) 111–117.

Moynagh, M., 2014, 'Political Futurity and the Child-Soldier Figure', 16 *Interventions* 655–674.

Murphy, W.P., 2003, 'Military Patrimonialism and Child Soldier Clientalism in the Liberian and Sierra Leonean Civil Wars', 46 *Afr.Stud.Rev.* 61–87.

Musila, G., 2005, 'Challenges in Establishing the Accountability of Child Soldiers for Human Rights Violations: Restorative Justice as an Option', 5 *A.H.R.L.J.* 321–334.

Nagle, L.E., 2011, 'Child Soldiers and the Duty of Nations to Protect Children from Participation in Armed Conflict', 19 *Cardozo J.Int'l & Comp.L.* 1–58.

Nair, S., 2017, 'Child Soldiers and International Criminal Law: Is the Existing Legal Framework Adequate to Prohibit the Use of Children in Conflict?', 2 *Perth Int'l L.J.* 40–54.

Naqvi, Y.Q., 2010, *Impediments to Exercising Jurisdiction over International Crimes* (Asser Press).

Nortje, W., 2017, 'Victim or Villain: Exploring the Possible Bases of a Defence in the *Ongwen* Case at the International Criminal Court', 17 *Int.C.L.R.* 186–207.

Quénivet, N., 2008, 'Girl Soldiers and Participation in Hostilities', 16 *A.J.I.C.L.* 219–235.
Quénivet, N., 2017, 'Does and Should International Law Prohibit the Prosecution of Children for War Crimes?', 28 *E.J.I.L.* 433–455.
Rauschenbach, M., 2018, 'Individuals Accused of International Crimes as Delegitimized Agents of Truth', 28 *Int.Crim.J.Rev.* 291–316.
Robinson, P.H., 1997, *Structure and Function in Criminal Law* (OUP).
Sampaio A.A. and M. McEvoy, 2016, 'Little Weapons of War: Reasons for and Consequences of Treating Child Soldiers as Victims', 63 *N.I.L.R.* 51–73.
Sandoz, Y., et al. (eds), 1987, *Commentary on the Additional Protocols to the Geneva Conventions* (Martinus Nijhoff).
Save the Children, 2005, *Forgotten Casualties of War: Girls in Armed Conflict.*
Scaliotti, M., 2001, 'Defences before the International Criminal Court: Substantive Grounds for Excluding Criminal Responsibility—Part 1', 1 *Int.C.L.R.* 111–172.
Schabas, W.A., 2016, *The International Criminal Court: A Commentary on the Rome Statute* (2nd edn., OUP).
Schmidt, A., 2007, 'Volunteer Child Soldiers as Reality: A Development Issue for Africa', 2 *N.S.E.R.* 49–76.
SCSL Statute, 2002, Statute of the Special Court for Sierra Leone, Enclosure to the Report of the Secretary-General on the Establishment of a Special Court for Sierra Leone, U.N. Doc. S/2000/915, 2178 UNTS 138, 16 January 2002.
Singer, P., 2005, *Children at War* (Pantheon Books).
Singh, D., 2007, 'When a Child is Not a Child: The Scourge of Child Soldiering in Africa', 7 *A.H.R.L.J.* 206–224.
Stahn, C., 2019, *A Critical Introduction to International Criminal Law* (CUP).
Steinl, L., 2017, *Child Soldiers as Agents of War and Peace: A Restorative Transitional Justice Approach to Accountability for Crimes under International Law* (Asser Press).
Swart, M. and S. Hassen, 2016, 'A Comparison Between the Position of Child Marriage "Victims" and Child Soldiers: Towards a Nuanced Approach', 16 *A.H.R.L.J.* 458–475.
Tercier Holst-Roness, F., 2006, *Violence against Girls in Africa during Armed Conflicts and Crises*, Second International Policy Conference on the African Child: Violence against Girls in Africa, International Committee of the Red Cross, Addis Ababa, 11–12 May 2006.
Triffterer, O. and R.S. Clark, 2016, 'Article 26: Exclusion of Jurisdiction over Persons under Eighteen', in Triffterer, O. and K. Ambos, *The Rome Statute of the International Criminal Court: A Commentary* (3rd edn., Beck) 1030–1036.
UNCRC, 1989, United Nations Convention on the Rights of the Child, 1577 UNTS 3, 20 November 1989.
UNGA, 1996, *Impact of Armed Conflict on Children*, U.N. Doc. A/51/306, 26 August 1996.

UNGA, 2016, Resolution of 21 December 2016: 'International, Impartial and Independent Mechanism to Assist in the Investigation and Prosecution of Those Responsible for the Most Serious Crimes under International Law Committed in the Syrian Arab Republic since March 2011', U.N. Doc. A/RES/71/248, 11 January 2017.

UNICEF Paris Principles, 2007, UNICEF, *Principles and Guidelines on Children Associated with Armed Forces or Armed Groups*, February 2007, available at https://www.unicef.org/emerg/files/ParisPrinciples310107English.pdf (last visited 12 March 2019).

United Nations Committee on the Rights of the Child, 2007, *General Comment No. 10: Children's Rights in Juvenile Justice*, U.N. Doc. CRC/C/GC.10, 25 April 2007.

Ursini, B., 2015, 'Prosecuting Child Soldiers: The Call for an International Minimum Age of Criminal Responsibility', 89 *St John's L.Rev.* 1023–1048.

US *Hostages Trial*, 1948, *United States of America v. List and Others*, Military Tribunal, Judgment, Case No. 47, 8 July 1947–19 February 1948, available at http://www.worldcourts.com/imt/eng/decisions/1948.02.19_United_States_v_List2.pdf (last visited 12 March 2019).

Van Bueren, G., 1998, *The International Law on the Rights of the Child* (Martinus Nijhoff).

Wainryb, C., 2011, '"And so they Ordered Me to Kill a Person": Conceptualizing the Impacts of Child Soldiering on the Development of Moral Agency', 54 *Human Development* 273–300.

Werle, G. and F. Jessberger, 2014, *Principles of International Criminal Law* (3rd edn., OUP).

Wessells, M., 2006, *Child Soldiers: From Violence to Protection* (HUP).

Yarbrough, S., 2014, 'Amnesty or Accountability: The Fate of High-Ranking Child Soldiers in Uganda's Lord Resistance Army', 47 *Vand.J.Transnat'l L.* 531–568.

Yuvaraj, J., 2016, 'When Does a Child "Participate Actively in Hostilities" under the Rome Statute? Protecting Children from Use in Hostilities after *Lubanga*', 32 *Merkourios—Utrecht J.Int'l & Eur.L.* 69–93.

CHAPTER 2

Duress as a Defence Under International Criminal Law

1 Introduction

Defences are undoubtedly an important component of international criminal law. After all, as Happold explains, '[a] crime consists of three elements: the *actus reus* (the conduct element), the *mens rea* (the mental element), and the absence of any available defence.'[1] Although one might be tempted to believe that there cannot possibly be a defence to international crimes, such as war crimes, crimes against humanity and genocide,[2] the reality is that international criminal law does provide for a variety of potential defences. Three points must be clearly stressed. Firstly, the possibility to use defences should be welcomed as a sign that international criminal justice is not about victor's justice, about revenge; it is there to determine a person's responsibility for a certain crime. Defences are sometimes not acknowledged due to a tendency to show a lack of sympathy for individuals who have committed grave atrocities.[3] Secondly, the importance of defences is confirmed in the application of human rights standards and the principle of fairness in international justice,[4] as 'defences serve to ensure that an accused person benefits not only from a fair trial in the procedural sense, but also one that is fair in a substantive sense'.[5] Thirdly, it should be borne in mind that 'to allow a defence to crime is not to express approval of the action of the accused but only to declare that it does not merit condemnation and punishment'.[6]

W. Nortje, N. Quénivet, *Child Soldiers and the Defence of Duress under International Criminal Law*,
https://doi.org/10.1007/978-3-030-20663-5_2

Duress is but one of a range of defences available to alleged perpetrators being hauled before the International Criminal Court (ICC). To date, no cases involving the defence of duress have been dealt with by the ICC at the trial stage. That being said, the defence of duress (much related to the individual being a former child soldier) was pleaded at the pre-trial stage, though rather summarily addressed by the court itself, in *Ongwen*.[7] However, the dearth of ICC case-law can partially be complemented by recourse to case-law of the International Criminal Tribunal for the Former Yugoslavia (ICTY) which itself is imbued with Anglo-American law, hence warranting an investigation into the latter too. Therefore, to provide an improved appreciation of the defence of duress, it is necessary, first, to acknowledge the aims and purposes of defences in international criminal law, then, to delve into the defence theories of justification and excuse as they tend to undergird present day international criminal law and to explore how duress has been interpreted by international and hybrid criminal courts and tribunals. Finally, the authors justify the use and application of Article 31 ICC Statute to child soldiers despite its lack of jurisdictional applicability to children.

2 Defences in International Criminal Law

The statutes of neither the international criminal tribunals set up to handle international crimes committed during World War II (WWII)[8] nor the *ad hoc* international criminal tribunals established by the United Nations Security Council to examine crimes perpetrated in the former Republic of Yugoslavia (ICTY)[9] and Rwanda (ICTR)[10] specifically refer to defences or grounds excluding responsibility.[11] The silence should however not be interpreted as negating the possibility for defendants to avail themselves of defences,[12] for, as the ICTY stated, defences 'form part of the general principles of criminal law which the International Tribunals must take into account in deciding the cases before it'.[13] Schabas points out that '[w]hy codifiers would focus on eliminating defences rather than defining them is probably explained by a lingering unease with respect to the whole subject, reflected in occasional comments during the drafting of various instruments by those who think there can be no defence to such serious crimes.'[14] Consequently, international law relating to defences, much like the general part of international criminal law,[15] heavily relies on judicial input and has developed rather haphazardly.[16] In stark contrast, the ICC Statute contains a detailed list[17] of admissible 'grounds for excluding criminal responsibility',[18] whilst allowing for further defences to be raised.[19]

The prominence of the judicial imprimatur in the definition of defences and requirements thereof is essential to bear in mind, notably because all criminal law is based on a certain ethical and philosophical *Weltanschauung* of the society in which criminal law is created, applied and enforced.[20] Concomitantly, defences, defined as 'any set of identifiable conditions of circumstances which may prevent a conviction for an offense',[21] are value-laden; they irresistibly depend on which acts society condemns,[22] permits and tolerates. Simply put, defences are 'a fundamental part of criminal law, and reflect important limitations on the proper scope of punishable conduct'.[23] In the absence of an agreed upon list of defences under international criminal law until the establishment of the ICC, one might have rightfully questioned why some defences were admitted at the international level whilst others were not, and how they came to be defined. Undoubtedly, in creating this list judges have relied on their own national experience and understanding of these defences and their suitability in the context of international crimes.[24] The defence of duress does not escape this rule: it is inextricably defined by how society judges the behaviour of an individual put under duress. Wall rightly notes that '[a]t its core, the debate over duress is a moral division of opinion', which is clearly illustrated by the international jurisprudence pertaining to duress.[25]

Generally, duress in (international) criminal law is understood as the compulsion of a perpetrator to commit a crime because he/she fears for his/her life and limb due to the threats made by another person.[26] The perpetrator is placed in a position where his/her freedom of will and decision-making abilities are severely restricted to the extent that the perpetrator is not able to make a moral choice.[27] That being said, as Bassiouni points out, whilst the defence is recognised in most legal systems, it 'varies with respect to certain crimes, the nature and type of threats, the immediacy of the harm likely to occur to the actor, the reasonableness of the belief, and the harm inflicted upon others'.[28]

At this stage it must be noted that duress and necessity are often lumbered together especially in older, post-WWII, jurisprudence.[29] Necessity is broader than duress as it includes threats that emanate from not only individuals but also more general situations ('this inexorable threat is the result of natural circumstances',[30] such as famine and forest fire) as long as the threat is to life and limb.[31] The difference relates to the source of the threat.[32] In this book the focus is on duress rather than on necessity though at times, as elements of duress and necessity are similar and/or a court does not appear to distinguish between the two concepts, recourse may be had to jurisprudence on necessity.

The ICC Statute defines duress in Article 31(1)(d) as

> The conduct which is alleged to constitute a crime within the jurisdiction of the Court has been caused by duress resulting from a threat of imminent death or of continuing or imminent serious bodily harm against that person or another person, and the person acts necessarily and reasonably to avoid this threat, provided that the person does not intend to cause a greater harm than the one sought to be avoided. Such a threat may either be:
>
> (i) Made by other persons; or
> (ii) Constituted by other circumstances beyond that person's control.

To understand the separate elements of this defence and how they have been interpreted, one needs to take a step back because international judges have been influenced mainly by the Anglo-American common law tradition.[33] As a result of this influence and as observed by Scaliotti, '[t]he common law attitude not to allow the defence of duress for the most serious crimes had a certain impact on international law.'[34]

3 Duress: Justification or Excuse in National Criminal Law

In national criminal law defences are often subdivided into a number of categories, including justifications and excuses, which are distinguished by their rationales and consequences.[35] Such division, whilst often discussed in great depth in the literature in common law countries, is however not unknown to civil law countries[36] (e.g., Germany, France and the Netherlands[37]). It stems from an understanding that the 'law should signal the boundaries of morally correct conduct',[38] and thereby distinguishes between wrongfulness and blameworthiness. Basically, '[a] justified action is not *criminal*, whereas an excused defendant has committed a crime but is not *punishable*.'[39]

Justification 'is a circumstance that makes the accused's conduct preferable to even worse alternatives'.[40] Here the conduct, although unlawful, is deemed appropriate, or at least permissible, because 'its benefits outweigh the harm or evil of the offense'.[41] It is correct behaviour in the sense that in the given circumstances it is encouraged or at least tolerated[42]: they are 'acts that produce morally preferred states of affairs'.[43] In other words, the act of the perpetrator is deemed to exclude criminal responsibility not because of a distinctive attribute of the perpetrator but because the act is considered to be justifiable[44]: 'this violation was the right thing to do under the circumstances.'[45] The act, not the actor, is at the heart of this type of defence.[46] This also means that the actor is likely to claim that his/her behaviour was fully warranted.[47] As Robinson underlines, '[a]ll justification defences have the same internal structure: *triggering conditions* permit a *necessary* and *proportional* response.'[48] This enlightens why justification defences are often perceived as a balance of, or choice between, harms or evils.[49]

Excuse 'involves an action that, while voluntary, nevertheless was produced by an impairment of a person's autonomy to such a degree as to negate their blameworthiness'.[50] Here, the focus is on the actor and not the act,[51] as the '[b]lame arises not from engaging in conduct that in fact constitutes a criminal harm or evil, but rather from choosing to engage in such conduct'.[52] Consequentially, an excuse does not negate the unlawfulness of the act but concedes that it would be unjust or inappropriate to hold the perpetrator responsible.[53] The individual is likely to admit to 'the harm or evil but nonetheless claims an absence of personal culpability'.[54] He/she did not have the opportunity to choose how to act.[55] Put simply, the act might be wrongful but it is not morally blameworthy, and thus not punishable. As Olusanya explains, 'the critical issue is not the heinousness of the crime nor is it the role of the victim; instead it is whether, based on a unique set of facts, a reasonable person would have responded in the same way as the accused.'[56]

There are two key differences between justifications and excuses. Firstly, the basic distinction is between warranted and unwarranted conduct[57]: excuses do not grant permission to act in a certain manner whereas justifications do. They tolerate the act. Excuses 'tell judges when persons who have acted without permission ought not to be punished'.[58] Secondly, an element of proportionality is needed for justifications.[59] If the act leads to a less evil outcome it becomes a justification; if it was the product of psychological coercion it is then regarded as an excuse.

This neat separation makes little sense with regard to duress which sits uneasily in one or the other category. After all, duress could be considered a justification since a justification is a choice between two evils under the adage 'either… or else…'. Yet, concomitantly, since making the better choice is a constraint on the individual it can also be viewed as an excuse especially if the perpetrator's decision power and will are impaired in the given circumstances.[60] It could therefore be argued that duress is an excuse because the actor does not have a 'true' choice.[61]

The application of both perspectives on this defence appears to send the message to society that such acts are allowed. In the long run acquittals on these bases might in fact jeopardise the criminality of the conduct, conveying the impression that there is no rightful and wrongful conduct.[62] After all, the person is found to be not guilty and it seems that the distinction does not matter.[63] However, a difference between justification and excuse is noticeable. The acquittal of a person based on a justification defence lends credence to the view that the act was not condemnable; in fact such behaviour might 'be desired and encouraged' even though it has engendered harm.[64] For a defence of excuse, it is clear that such behaviour is neither desired nor encouraged but the frailty of the perpetrator is taken into account. The granting of an excuse does not weaken the prohibition as such.[65] As Robinson stresses, '[s]ociety will continue to condemn and seek to deter such conduct even in identical circumstances.'[66] Overall, 'justifications function as exceptions to the prohibitory norms contained in the criminal law whereas excuses function as exceptions to the attribution of just punishment.'[67] In the case of children caught up in armed conflict, undoubtedly the international society would want to stress that the acts with which children are stained, for example, killing and maiming, are prohibited. However, the specific situation in which they are put reveals their human frailty. As a consequence, looking at duress as an excuse appears to be *prima facie* best suited in relation to children alleged to have committed international crimes.

4 Duress: Justification or Excuse in the Jurisprudence of International Criminal and Hybrid Tribunals

Duress remains a highly controversial defence in international criminal law,[68] notably because it is debatable under which circumstances it can be used (is it a justification or an excuse?[69]) and whether it constitutes a full or partial defence.[70] An analysis of the case-law of the International Military Tribunal of Nuremberg and the Allied courts as well as national law reveals that the law is rather unsettled.[71] Firstly, common law countries and an array of scholars[72] contemplate duress as a justification, whilst duress is usually viewed as an excuse in Romano-Germanic (civil law) systems.[73]

Moreover, whilst common law countries do not admit duress as a full defence, it is acknowledged in civil (Romano-Germanic) law countries[74] not only in respect of 'ordinary' but also international crimes.[75] All these debates have culminated in the ICC Statute, which it is argued 'partially codifies available defences',[76] such as duress, and thus represents the current state of the law.

The ICTY Statute[77] is silent on whether duress can be invoked as a defence and the matter was as a consequence left to the judges to decide.[78] Based on the *Erdemović* Case it appears that the ICTY adopted a common law approach towards the defence of duress by denying its applicability to cases of murder.[79] Indeed, common law prescribes that the killing of a person is punishable irrespective of duress: 'there is no doubt [...] that compulsion is a defence when the crime is not of a heinous character. But the killing of an innocent can never be *justified*.'[80] Such an approach can only be rationalised by common law seemingly viewing duress as a justification,[81] a choice between two evils[82] and the position that '[i]n such a case a reasonable man might reflect that one innocent human life is at least as valuable as his own or that of his loved one'.[83]

The Appeals Chamber of the ICTY clearly stated in the *Erdemović* Case that the defence of duress could not be accepted if it led to the death of other persons: '[d]uress does not afford a complete defense to a soldier charged with a crime against humanity and/or a war crime involving the killing of innocent human beings.'[84] Following the common law approach, the majority judges ignored the common state practice of the defence of duress, drawing the conclusion that there was no consensus as to the exceptions to the application of duress at the time.[85] By espousing the common law approach the ICTY unmistakably chose to deny any possibility of using the defence of duress in international criminal law,[86] for '[i]f national law denies duress as a defence even in a case in which a single innocent life is extinguished due to action under duress, international law, in our view, cannot admit duress in cases which involve the slaughter of innocent human beings on a large scale.'[87] As Greenawalt explains, by allowing Erdemović to raise the defence of duress successfully, it would have looked as if the court had endorsed his behaviour.[88] Furthermore, Wiener observes that the majority's opinion can be explained in utilitarian terms: the harm caused by punishing the accused, even if s/he had no choice but to participate in the murder, is less than the harm that will be caused by others who will be able to exploit this defence (if it is recognised), and therefore policy requires that we find him/her guilty.[89] A similar reasoning for denying duress in the case of killing was given by the House of Lords in *R. v Howe and others*.[90] What matters here is the message sent to society: killing can never be justified. Certain behaviour is simply too wrongful.[91]

At first glance, such a stance appears to contradict the fundamental proposition that duress is a justification. Killing can never be justified, so duress for killing must be an excuse since the act (killing) is inherently wrongful but the actor has given in to his/her frailty in the given circumstances. Such proposition appears to be supported by the fact that the court took Erdemović's situation into account when delivering sentence.[92] In the *Blaškić* Case, the ICTY held that '[d]uress, where established, does mitigate the criminal responsibility of the accused when he had no choice or moral freedom in committing the crime. This must consequently entail the passing of a lighter sentence if he cannot be completely exonerated of responsibility. The Trial Chamber points out that over the periods covered by the present indictment Tihomir Blaškić did not act under duress whilst in his post. Accordingly, he does not enjoy any mitigating circumstances.'[93] After all, as Colvin explains, '[e]xcuses [...] can usually be handled through the exercise of sentencing discretion.'[94] Yet, the court has firmly rejected to view duress as an excuse.[95] On the one hand, one might be able to side with some authors who maintain that in this case the choice between duress as a defence and duress as extenuating/mitigating circumstances appraised at the sentencing stage is one tainted by policy considerations.[96] On the other, it might be submitted that the court simply repudiates the 'neat' justification/excuse dichotomy when applying duress as a defence. Nevertheless such a claim would be incorrect, too, as the court required Erdemović 'to do the "right thing" in the circumstances'[97] and thus to justify his behaviour. Also, it might be contended that '[c]ommitting the *actus reus* is justified when it results in the lesser harm; committing the *actus reus* is excused, when, although exculpation is merited, the ensuing harm is equal to or greater than that of not committing the *actus reus*.'[98] In other words, whether the defence of duress is a justification or an excuse depends on where the balance of harm is struck. This would give currency to Judge Cassese's dissenting opinion in Erdemović as his proposal to apply a strict test of proportionality to the defence of duress leads to a similar outcome: duress can only be a defence to killing if the harm caused is less than the one averted. Unfortunately, given the lack of further cases examined by the ICTY, duress does not appear to be recognised under international criminal law as a complete defence, since the majority judges in *Erdemović* ruled that duress should not be a complete defence for the killing of civilians.[99] If one were to follow this jurisprudence, which has however been pushed aside by the ICC Statute (see discussion below), a child soldier could not successfully claim duress if he/she were to be charged with the murder of, for example, civilians during a conflict, but could probably use it for other acts, provided he/she meets specific conditions. Under this case-law, '[w]hat is clear is that they could at least invoke duress as a mitigating factor.'[100]

In contrast, duress is more likely to be accepted as a complete defence in international and hybrid tribunals imbued with a Romano-Germanic (civil law) system approach to defences. For example, duress is a complete defence under section 19(d) UNTAET Regulation 2000/15[101] that established the United Nations Special Panels for East Timor. In the case of X the 'Presiding Judge…pointed out that duress could be raised in trial as a form of defence and not just as mitigation.'[102] However, in this case, as the right to life is a fundamental human right, the requirements for duress (see Chap. 3) must be applied scrupulously.[103] The Court thus followed the *Wetzling* approach: '[i]t is only in cases involving the most serious duress that a legal order (*Rechtsordnung*) can approve of an interference in the right to life, which is the most important protected value (*das höchste Rechtsgut*).'[104]

During the drafting of the Rome Statute heated debates ensued as to whether duress should be regarded as a justification or an excuse, and whether it is a full or partial defence.[105] This division amongst the drafters revealing a deep rift amongst lawyers from various legal traditions was however settled and so it is possible to speak of the crystallisation of the norm. Article 31(1)(d) of the ICC Statute seems to follow a civil law tradition, acknowledging[106] that duress is a ground excluding responsibility and, since the provision applies in relation to all crimes and does not stipulate that it cannot be pleaded when taking a person's life,[107] it follows that 'killing a person out of duress or necessity as a last resort can go unpunished'.[108] The silence on the matter has led authors to claim that the drafters of the ICC Statute overruled the *Erdemović* jurisprudence that precluded the availability of the claim of duress in situations of murder[109] and reinstated the defence of duress.[110]

However, Article 31 of the ICC Statute does not distinguish between justifications and excuses[111] because the drafters 'decided to disregard the issue and agreed to use the term "exclusion of criminal responsibility", not using a word to distinguish between the two types of defences'.[112] In other words, under the concept of 'grounds for excluding responsibility' the distinction between justification and excuse has disappeared.[113] It was, as Schabas stresses, 'an attempt to address conceptual differences to the issue in national criminal justice systems'.[114] Whereas one must commend the drafters for bridging the differences between the various legal approaches to the defence, the problem is that it is unclear whether duress is a justification or excuse.[115] It does not mean that the issue has been brushed under the carpet though as scholars like Ambos have called for this distinction between justifications and excuses to be maintained.[116] Furthermore, the criteria for duress and necessity (usually viewed as a justification) have been amalgamated in a single provision,[117] thereby 'creating a hybrid defense that serves as both a justification and an excuse',[118] and which does not sit well with jurists from common law and Romano-Germanic backgrounds used to keeping duress and necessity separate.[119]

Prima facie duress seems to be a justification inasmuch as it requires the actor to carry out a lesser evil test.[120] If it is a justification (or a 'justificatory necessity defense'[121] as Chiesa calls it), then it might be inappropriate to maintain that it is a full defence: in the balance of harm, death is unlikely to be considered as the better alternative unless the reasoning of *Wetzling and Others* is espoused or the situation is such that the death of a multiplicity of individuals is averted by the death of fewer individuals. It might also be an excuse since it 'appears to excuse the accused even in the extreme case of the death of a third person'.[122] That being said, even though the defence is included in the ICC Statute and scholars appear to believe that it could act as a full defence, it still needs to be tested by the ICC which can adopt either a common law, a civil law or its own *sui generis* approach.[123] In any case, as Fournet explains, ICC judges 'are likely to depart from the failed attempt at judicial lawmaking by the majority in the *Erdemović* Appeals Chamber'.[124]

5 The Relevance of the ICC Statute in Ascertaining the Requirements of Duress Under International Criminal Law

It should be remembered that individuals under the age of 18 years, such as child soldiers, cannot be prosecuted by the ICC. They have been removed from the ambit of the jurisdiction of the court. As Freeland points out, '[i]t is almost as if the drafters of the Rome Statute would prefer that a consideration of this important aspect of the shameful problem of child soldiers to be delegated elsewhere.'[125] That however does not mean that the ICC Statute and its related jurisprudence are irrelevant to the question of the responsibility of child soldiers under international criminal law.

A first justification for the use of ICC Statute provisions in relation to the prosecution of child soldiers is that the ICC Statute represents the first ever comprehensive codification of international law.[126] This combined with the argument that treaties can 'give rise to general international rules, at least when a large number of States take part in them'[127] seems to indicate that the ICC Statute has created legal norms. Ambos posits that the ICC Statute 'provides for the first codification of ICL with a potentially universal reach'.[128] Part III is no doubt an attempt to provide a coherent set of rules and principles established through the statutes and the jurisprudence of international criminal tribunals,[129] though there it 'is still "a work in progress"'.[130] As Degan stresses, 'for the first time in the history of international criminal tribunals, the Rome Statute provides, in its part 3, the General Principles of Criminal Law in written form and in advance.'[131] In relation to the defences under Article 31, Schabas explains that, after much resistance to their codification, the drafters gave in and agreed to list them in Article 31(1),[132] providing much needed legal certainty. With regard to duress in particular, Bond and Fougere explain that it 'represents both the most recent and the most influential articulation of duress in the international sphere'.[133] One could thus argue that the defences as spelled out in the ICC Statute have created legal norms. Such a legal stance is however difficult to support as it is generally accepted that treaties can only indirectly impose norms on non-state parties if the provisions of the treaties reflect previous general principles or customary law (codification/crystallisation process) or if after the ratification of the treaty a consistent number of states customarily abide by it (subsequent consolidation).[134]

It can be argued that Article 31(1)(d) reflects general principles of criminal law and/or customary international law and so must be complied with by states. Classic textbooks in international criminal law authored by Werle and Jessberger and by Cassese et al. posit that the defence provision 'is no doubt an expression of a general principle of law and of customary international law'.[135] Other authors, in particular Happold and Knoops, argue that Article 31(1)(d) in particular 'reflects a rule of customary international law'.[136] Such a position is tenable as Schabas highlights that little time was spent on discussing the defence of duress,[137] thereby indicating that a consensus had already been reached on the definition of duress and so the defence and its elements were already well established in customary law. If such a view is disputed, it still might be contended that the defence of duress as provided in the ICC Statute is a crystallisation of customary international law in the sense that whilst prior to the negotiations there might have been disagreement between states as to the definition of duress these differences were settled in the negotiation process.[138] Bassiouni attacks such a position by contending that fundamentally 'international law is not customarily practiced with regard to the general part of the criminal law of domestic criminal justice systems' and thus it is not possible to view the norms enshrined in the Rome Statute to have effect beyond the state parties.[139] In his opinion, '[t]he finding that a given general principle exists requires substantial similarity as to any given issue between the world's major criminal justice systems.'[140] Likewise Ambos believes that international criminal law can only be based on comparative criminal law.[141] Applying to the defence of duress this would require an in-depth investigation into such criminal justice systems, a task so far never undertaken and beyond the scope of this book. Given that it is such a contentious issue for some scholars, other possibilities must also be scrutinised.

Although the Statute is a treaty, and for that reason only binds those states that have ratified it, it remains the only codified source of the general part of international criminal law. It would thus make sense for national courts to use or emulate from the ICC Statute when dealing with international crimes. A number of reasons can be adduced to support this position. Firstly, there exists a general unease about the way in which national courts deal with international crimes.[142] This unease could be reduced by adopting a common approach towards the prosecution of international crimes. Secondly, more consistency in the application of international criminal law is warranted by the fact that national courts when adjudicating international crimes act 'as agents of the international community'.[143] Thirdly, as Ambos explains, 'a state-centred approach does not do justice to the complexities of the international order and the international criminal justice system'[144] and in fact perpetuates inconsistencies in the application of international criminal law.[145]

Yet, the problem until the drafting of the ICC Statute was that the general part in criminal law, that is, the sum of all rules relating to the personal criminal liability of an individual, *mens rea*, the different forms of perpetration and the defences,[146] was (and still is) different in all states and so led to different outcomes. At the time no general part for international criminal law had been agreed upon because it was assumed that the general part of domestic criminal law would apply when implemented at the national level.[147] However, crimes committed under international law are complex, as are the conflict or war in which they are committed and this poses serious questions for any domestic court as to whether it is capable of hearing such matters on the basis of the domestic law of the country.[148] The general part of any domestic criminal law framework therefore needs to be well-developed to deal with the unique nature of international criminal law and usually it is not. In contrast, the various international criminal tribunals have over the last century provided the international legal order with a multitude of statutes and case-law necessary to deal with the adjudication of crimes under international law.[149] The ICC Statute is the culmination of these efforts and represents a truly remarkable achievement in the progressive realisation of international criminal law[150] which could thus be used by national courts as a benchmark. Of course, national courts cannot simply use the wording of the ICC Statute. However, they might be able to interpret national law relating to the defence of duress in such a way that it mirrors Article 31(1)(d) of the ICC Statute especially if it is accompanied by international jurisprudence. After all, national judicial bodies tend to view decisions of international courts as carrying persuasive value and are influenced by them although they are not formally binding.[151] Therefore, we argue that the codification of duress, and its future subsequent interpretation, plays a significant role in the adjudication of cases where individuals, including child soldiers, have been forced to commit crimes under international law. Although children have not been prosecuted by any international tribunals or courts, they have been prosecuted in domestic courts, and this leaves the door open for the defence of duress, as spelled out in the ICC Statute, to be raised in such instances, depending on the facts of each case.[152]

The defence of duress might also reach national judicial (and other) bodies not via international criminal law but via refugee law. The importance of Article 31(1)(d) as a rule of customary international law is evident in the event that a child soldier applies for asylum.[153] Asylum is usually granted to individuals who can prove that they have been persecuted in their country; thus child soldiers present a group of asylum seekers that can be viewed as both the persecutors and the persecuted, when they have committed a crime. Article 1F(a) of the 1951 Refugee Convention[154] provides that asylum will not be granted to an individual where there are serious reasons that the person has committed an international crime.[155] Since Article 1F(a) requires the exclusion to be grounded in international criminal law, national bodies, when determining whether an individual has committed an international crime, must seek guidance in international criminal law instruments[156] such as the ICC Statute. After all, the relevant UNHCR guidelines specify that recourse must be had to, amongst others, the ICC Statute to interpret Article 1F of the Refugee Convention.[157] Likewise national bodies will use such instruments not only in relation to the definition of the crimes but also to the *mens rea* and the defences to such crimes.[158] The UNHCR Background Note on the Application of the Exclusion Clauses specifically refers to Article 31(1)(d) of the ICC Statute in relation to the defence of duress.[159] Therefore, Happold explains that child soldiers should be able to raise duress as a defence in order to prove that they did not commit an international crime which would provide them with the opportunity to be granted asylum.[160] It is in this specific context that national bodies determining refugee status might be looking at the concept of duress under the ICC Statute. Again, this demonstrates the relevance of Article 31(1)(d) in relation to child soldiers despite the ICC Statute not being directly applicable to them.

6 Conclusion

Since the inception of the ICC, the defence of duress has not received much attention at the Court. The prosecution of Ongwen before the ICC has, however, undoubtedly revitalised the academic debate on whether duress can be used as a defence to international crimes. The case 'represents the opportunity for an important development in the interpretation of duress at the international level and in setting a precedent on the prosecution of child soldiers'.[161] The plain wording of the ICC Statute signals that it could be used as a full defence, but that it is likely to be a justification since an element of proportionality appears to be required for the claim of duress to be satisfied. Is that a step in the right direction? As explained earlier, as the ICC codifies or crystallises the grounds for excluding responsibility in international criminal law, it is thus going to dictate the future of national and international criminal prosecutions.

Would child soldiers benefit from the definition adopted by the drafters of the Rome Statute? Whilst the authors understand that the ICC cannot prosecute individuals for crimes committed as a child, both its Statute and jurisprudence remain of paramount importance as they are likely to fashion the way the defence will be understood and interpreted at the national level (or by any other potential *ad hoc* court or tribunal established with the purpose of prosecuting crimes committed on a specific territory). In this light, the next chapter aims to find out what the exact legal requirements are that need to be fulfilled to invoke duress successfully, and whether such requirements can be met by child soldiers.

Notes

1. Happold 2002, 1146. See Robinson 1997, 4; Mousourakis 2003, 67.
2. Fournet 2008, 510.
3. Cryer et al. 2014, 398; Xavier 2016, 793–794.
4. Fournet 2008, 510; Knoops 2008, 2. See Van Sliedregt 2006, 104.
5. Schabas 2016, 637; Nagle 2011, 41.
6. UK *Lynch* 1975. See Smith 1989, 13; Olusanya 2010, fn 23.
7. ICC *Ongwen* 2016, paras 150–156.
8. Charter of the International Military Tribunal 1945; Charter of the International Military Tribunal for the Far East 1946. See Control Council Law No. 10, 1945 and Schabas 2016, 637.
9. ICTY Statute 1993.
10. ICTR Statute 1994.
11. See generally Bassiouni 2013, 403; Schabas 2016, 637; Cryer et al. 2014, 399–400; Kittichaisaree 2001, 263.
12. See Fournet 2010, 229–230.
13. ICTY *Kordic and Cerkez* 2001, para. 449. See Schabas 2016, 637.
14. Schabas 2016, 637. See Cryer et al. 2014, 398.
15. Bassiouni 2013, 285. See Schabas 2016, 637.
16. As Ambos explains, international criminal law 'consisted of a spontaneous and improvised set of rules, driven by the moral and political imperative, not to leave unpunished atrocities on a scale unknown until then'. Ambos 2006, 661.
17. It must also be noted here that the list of defences contained in the ICC Statute is not praised by everyone. Fletcher, one of the most prolific criminal law scholars in the world, posits that the defence system at the ICC is still incomplete and needs to be reconsidered. Fletcher 2007, 110.
18. ICC Statute 1998, Arts 31–33.
19. ICC Statute 1998, Art. 31(3).
20. See discussion in Bassiouni 2013, 285.
21. Robinson 1982, 203.
22. Fletcher poses the question '[c]an we expect that individuals, even those suffering from mental illness or those caught under circumstances of overwhelming pressure, always abstain from doing the wrong thing?' Fletcher 1998, 83.

23. Cryer et al. 2014, 398.
24. See, for example, ICTY *Erdemović* 1997b and ICTY *Erdemović* 1997a. More generally Bassiouni explains that '[e]ach judge was made to rely on precedent and concepts native to their national systems and, in many cases, the information available in their native languages.' Bassiouni 2013, 286.
25. Wall 2006, 737. See Stahn 2019, 147.
26. Werle and Jessberger 2014, 239. See Eser 2016, 1149–1155; Duress is also referred to in different legal systems as compulsion and coercion. See Bassiouni 2013, 438.
27. Eser 2016, 1150; Bassiouni 2013, 438; Schabas 2016, 645; Knoops 2003, 71; Dinstein 2000, 373.
28. Bassiouni 2013, 440. See Wiener 2014, 90; Neumann 2014, 593.
29. See Cryer et al. 2014, 407; Werle and Jessberger 2014, 239; Krebs 2013, 407.
30. Schabas 2011, 228; Bassiouni 2013, 438.
31. Linton and Reiger 2001, 172. See Schabas 2016, 645; Eser 2016, 1151; Knoops 2008, 83; Bassiouni 2013, 438; Fletcher 2000, 820.
32. Merkel 2002, 450; Bassiouni 2013, 438.
33. Boumghar 2009, 131; Fletcher 2007, 46.
34. Scaliotti 2001, 145; Boumghar 2009, 131. For a comprehensive overview of duress in common law and civil law jurisdictions, see Ambos 2013, 342–348.
35. See Holder 2016, 215; Cryer et al. 2014, 399; Ambos 2013, 304; Schabas 2016, 636; Knoops 2008, 202.
36. Ambos 2011, 300; Cryer et al. 2014, 398–399; Krebs 2013, 383–384.
37. Bond and Fougere 2014, fn 489.
38. Colvin 1990, 382. See Bassiouni 2013, 438.
39. Berman 2003, 4. See Knoops 2008, 202.
40. Cassese et al. 2013, 209.
41. Robinson 1982, 203; Knoops 2008, 202; Cryer et al. 2014, 399.
42. Rosen 1986, 22. See Knoops 2008, 202; Burchell 2016, 164 and 184; Byrd 1987, 1293.
43. Kahan and Nussbaum 1996, 318.
44. Wiener 2014, 97. See Colvin 1990, 384; Chiesa 2008, 752.
45. Byrd 1987, 1290.
46. Robinson 1982, 229. See Cryer et al. 2014, 399.
47. Greenawalt 1984, 1900.
48. Robinson 1982, 216.
49. Colvin 1990, 387; Wiener 2014, 97; Fletcher 1998, 138.

50. Cassese et al. 2013, 209. See Ambos 2013, 305.
51. Scaliotti 2001, 118; Ambos 2013, 305; Robinson 1997, 81.
52. Robinson 1997, 81. See Byrd 1987, 1290.
53. Robinson 1982, 229; Chiesa 2008, 753; Ambos 2013, 305; Knoops 2008, 202; Byrd 1987, 1301.
54. Robinson 1982, 203. See Knoops 2008, 202; Krebs 2013, 405–406.
55. Rosen 1986, 22. See Ambos 2013, 305.
56. Olusanya 2010, 28–29. See Ambos 2013, 359.
57. Byrd 1987, 1294.
58. Berman 2003, 33.
59. Wiener 2014, 124. See Ambos 2013, 305; Robinson 1997, 95; Kittichaisaree 2001, 264.
60. Fletcher, as cited in Colvin 1990, 387.
61. Colvin 1990, 387. See Paciocco 2010, 244.
62. See Colvin 1990, 385.
63. Krebs 2013, 384.
64. Robinson 1982, 245. See Chiesa 2008, 752.
65. See Berman 2003, 20.
66. Robinson 1982, 246. See Fletcher 1998, 83.
67. Byrd 1987, 1295. See Krebs 2013, 385.
68. Fournet 2010, 238; Stahn 2019, 152.
69. Wiener 2014, 90; Fletcher 2007, 310.
70. In fact, international criminal law has inherited the drawbacks of Anglo-American criminal law. As Colvin explains in relation to Anglo-American courts '[t]he historical uncertainty about the scope of the defences of duress [...] may be due in substantial measure to the courts drifting back and forward between excusatory and justificatory ideas.' Colvin 1990, 400–401. See Mcalhone and Wortley, 2016, 522; Risacher 2013–2014, 1409.
71. See ICTY *Erdemović* 1997a; Akakpo 2012, 40–43; Scaliotti 2001, 145–150. Cryer et al. 2014, 398, alluding to defences under international criminal law, note that '[j]urisprudence from the international criminal tribunals (including the ICC) on the matter is sparse, and not always satisfactory.'
72. See review in Heim 2013, 168.
73. Scaliotti 2001, 143. See Fletcher 2000, 830–831; Weigend 2011, 274.
74. Linton and Reiger 2001, 172; Risacher 2013–2014, 1408; Happold 2002, 1164; Achton Thomas 2013, 31; Gilbert 2006, 151; Fisher 2013, 68.
75. In the *Priebke* Case the court accepted that duress could be used as complete defence, however, *in casu* the court disputed the version of the facts

presented by the defendant. Italy *Priebke* 1955. See discussion in ICTY *Erdemović* 1997a, fn 69 and Bassiouni 2013, 448–449.

76. Schabas 2011, 238.
77. ICTY Statute 1993.
78. Yee 1997, 287; Knoops 2003, 72.
79. Ehrenreich Brooks 2002–2003, 868. On the availability of the defence of duress for murder under common law, see Risacher 2013–2014, 1406–1408; Bassiouni 2013, 440.
80. *Hölzer*, United Nations War Crimes Commission, LRTWC, Vol. XV, at 173 as cited in Gilbert 2006, 152 (emphasis added).
81. Chiesa observes that it appears that the ICTY 'assumed that the defense raised was a justification'. Chiesa 2008, 743.
82. See UK *Howe* 1987.
83. UK *Howe* 1987, 12.
84. ICTY *Erdemović* 1997c, para. 19. It should be noted that this seminal case was followed by the ICTR in ICTR *Rutaganira* 2005, para. 161. See discussion in Bassiouni 2013, 451; Ambos 2013, 352–355; Knoops 2003, 72–74; Cassese et al. 2011, 36; 476–487.
85. Wiener 2014, 120. In contrast, Judge Cassese concluded that 'the customary rule of international law on duress, as evolved on the basis of case-law and the military regulations of some States, does not exclude the applicability of duress to war crimes and crimes against humanity whose underlying offence is murder or unlawful killing.' ICTY *Erdemović* 1997a, para. 44.
86. Krebs 2013, 402. This common law approach is severely criticised in Oellers-Frahm and Specht 1998, 407–408.
87. ICTY *Erdemović* 1997b, para. 75.
88. Greenawalt 2011, 1118.
89. Wiener 2014, 121.
90. See UK *Howe* 1987. See Harris 1997, 54–55; Knoops 2008, 211; Rosenthal 1990, 213; Naylor 2006, 27–28; Krebs 2013, 402.
91. See discussion in Wiener 2014, 97.
92. See Bassiouni 2013, 451.
93. ICTY *Blaškić* 2000, para. 769.
94. Colvin 1990, 384.
95. Merkel 2002, 450. See discussion in Knoops 2008, 202–204.
96. Cassese et al. 2013, 218. See Wiener 2014, 120; Bassiouni 2013, 440.
97. Joyce 2015, 625.
98. Colvin 1990, 387.
99. ICTY *Erdemović* 1997c, paras 77–78. See Knoops 2008, 209–210; Stahn 2019, 152.
100. Leveau 2013, 65. See Bassiouni 2013, 440; Stahn 2019, 152.

101. UNTAET 2000.
102. Judicial System Monitoring Programme 2005. Duress was however not used during the trial because the accused's guilty plea was accepted.
103. Cassese et al. 2013, 219. 'However, as the right to life is the most fundamental human right, the rule demands that the general requirements for duress be applied particularly strictly in the case of killing of innocent persons.' ICTY *Erdemović* 1997a, para. 44.
104. Nemitz 2009, 972. See ICTY *Erdemović* 1997a, para. 38; Oellers-Frahm and Specht 1998, 395.
105. Eser 2016, 1149–1150. For a presentation of the negotiation history, see Scaliotti 2001, 150–155.
106. ICC Statute 1998, Art. 31(1)(d). See Happold 2005, 156–158.
107. Fletcher 2007, 89–90. See Ambos 2006–2007, 2660; Happold 2002, 1169;
108. Werle and Jessberger 2014, 242. See Achton Thomas 2013, 32; Wall 2006, 728; Ambos 2006, 666–667.
109. See, for example, Bond and Fougere 2014, fn 54; Grant 2016, 5; Happold 2002, 1169; Greenawalt 2011, 1119.
110. Schabas 2011, 242; Ambos 1999, 28.
111. Ambos 2006–2007, 2669.
112. Scaliotti 2001, 118.
113. Merkel 2002, 441.
114. Schabas 2011, 238. See Cryer et al. 2014, 398–399. Schabas 2016, 640 explains that this lack of distinction was purposefully adopted after a proposal by Singapore.
115. Fletcher 2007, 90; Ambos 2010, 14; Bond and Fougere 2014, 489; Cryer et al. 2014, 399.
116. Ambos 2006, 666; Ambos 2013, 306–307. See Krebs 2013, 409–410.
117. Werle and Jessberger 2014, 239. See Eser 2016, 1149–1150; Risacher 2013–2014, 1417; Weigend 2012, 1223; Scaliotti 2001, 15; Grant 2016, 17; Ambos 1999, 27. For a discussion on the common law perspective on necessity and duress, see Arenson 2014, 67.
118. Heim 2013, 178; Krebs 2013, 407.
119. Merkel 2002, 448; Ambos 2013, 347. However, Merkel explains that he does not believe this lack of distinction to be problematic. Merkel 2002, 453.
120. Risacher 2013–2014, 1404; Wiener 2014, 13; Ambos 2006, 667.
121. Chiesa 2008, 751.
122. Ambos 2006, 667.
123. As Scaliotti observes 'the common law approach may re-emerge.' Scaliotti 2001, 157.
124. Fournet 2010, 241.
125. Freeland 2005, 324.

126. Werle and Jessberger 2014, 2; Knoops 2003, 78. Schabas calls the ICC 'the missing link in the international legal system'. See Schabas 2016, 57; Zgaga 2014, 153.
127. See discussion in Quirico 2009, 155.
128. Ambos 2013, 55. See Horovitz et al. 2014, 252. Werle and Jessberger call the ICC Statute 'the final milestone in the development of international criminal law'. Werle and Jessberger 2014, 17.
129. Quirico 2009, 148.
130. Ambos 2006, 662.
131. Degan 2005, 79; Boumghar 2009, 98.
132. Schabas 2016, 647.
133. Bond and Fougere 2014, 481. Cryer et al. 2014 (400) note that the ICC is the first treaty to deal with the defences under international criminal law in any systematic way.
134. ICJ *North Sea Continental Shelf* 1969, paras 61 and 74. See discussion in Quirico 2009, 155–156.
135. Werle and Jessberger 2014, 240. See Cassese et al. 2013, 216.
136. Happold 2002, 1169. See Knoops 2008, 46.
137. Schabas 2016, 646.
138. A contrario, Greenawalt argues that '[t]he Statute's relative detail need not represent universal norms but may instead reflect agreements and compromises among states necessary to attract support for that particular tribunal.' Greenawalt 2011, 1124.
139. Bassiouni 2013, 322. As Bassiouni explains, experts in comparative criminal law have copiously criticised the general part of the ICC Statute (324).
140. Bassiouni 2013, 293.
141. Ambos 2006, 662.
142. Cryer et al. 2014, 74. This is also evident where state parties to the ICC have agreed to prosecute their own nationals with the ulterior intention to shield these individuals from prosecution. See Schabas 2016, 467.
143. Happold 2006, 71.
144. Ambos 2013, 57.
145. Greenawalt 2011, 1101.
146. Degan 2005, 55.
147. Bassiouni 2013, 296. Another reason why international criminal law is less codified is because states are reluctant to let other states interfere with their sovereignty. See Werle and Jessberger 2014, 1. See Ambos 2013, 60; Schabas 2016, 57.
148. See Ambos 2013, 57. See Cryer et al. 2014, 74.
149. See Werle and Jessberger 2014, 2.

150. For a comprehensive review of the ICC after 10 years in existence, generally see Schabas 2011, 493–509.
151. Darcy 2014, 35.
152. See Siegrist 2006, 55; Happold 2005, 141. Courts in Rwanda, Colombia and the United States of America have recognised that child soldiers can be held responsible for their actions, see Steinl 2017, 412.
153. Happold 2002, 1143; Dankoff 2011, 48. Drumbl explains that a number of former child soldiers were in fact denied refugee status. Drumbl 2012, 131.
154. Convention Relating to the Status of Refugees 1951.
155. See Happold 2002, 1172; Dankoff 2011, 48.
156. See Maystre 2014, 987.
157. UNHCR 2003a. See Creedon 2015, 86–87.
158. UNHCR 2003b, paras 64–71. See Maystre 2014, 988.
159. UNHCR 2003b, para. 69.
160. See generally Happold 2002, 1158–1172; Dankoff 2011, 50.
161. Grant 2016, 3 and 20.

References

Achton Thomas, M., 2013, 'Malice Supplies the Age? Assessing the Culpability of Adolescent Soldiers', 44 *Cal.W.Int'l L.J.* 1–38.

Akakpo, L., 2012, 'Procureur c. X: les enseignements à tirer de la poursuite des enfants soldats pour crimes contre l'humanité', 42 *R.G.D.* 9–56.

Ambos, K., 1999, 'General Principles of Criminal Law in the Rome Statute', 10 *Crim.L.F.* 1–32.

Ambos, K., 2006, 'Remarks on the General Part of International Criminal Law', 4 *J.I.C.J.* 660–673.

Ambos, K., 2006–2007, 'Toward a Universal System of Crime: Comments on George Fletcher's Grammar of Criminal Law', 28 *Cardozo L.Rev.* 2647–2673.

Ambos, K., 2010, 'Rettungsfolter und (Völker-)Strafrecht', in Koriath, H., et al. (eds), *Grundfragen des Strafrechts, Rechtsphilosophie und die Reform der Juristenausbildung* (Universitätsverlag Göttingen) 5–15.

Ambos, K., 2011, 'Defences in International Criminal Law', in Brown, B.S. (ed.), *Research Handbook on International Criminal Law* (Edward Elgar) 299–329.

Ambos, K., 2013, *Treatise on International Criminal Law: Volume I: Foundations and General Part* (OUP).

Arenson, K.J., 2014, 'The Paradox of Disallowing Duress as a Defence to Murder', 78 *J.C.L.* 65–79.

Bassiouni, M.C., 2013, *Introduction to International Criminal Law* (2nd edn., Martinus Nijhoff).

Berman, M.N., 2003, 'Justification and Excuse, Law and Morality', 53 *Duke L.J.* 1–77.

Bond, J. and M. Fougere, 2014, 'Omnipresent Threats: A Comment on the Defence of Duress in International Criminal Law', 14 *Int.C.L.R.* 471–512.

Boumghar, M., 2009, 'Quelques utilisations des principes généraux du droit international et des principes généraux de droit en droit international penal', 17 *Afr. Yrbk Int'l L.* 97–137.

Burchell, J., 2016, *Principles of Criminal Law* (5th edn., Juta).

Byrd, B.S., 1987, 'Wrongdoing and Attribution: Implications beyond the Justification-Excuse Distinction', 33 *Wayne L.Rev.* 1289–1342.

Cassese, A., et al., 2011, *International Criminal Law: Cases and Commentary* (OUP).

Cassese, A., et al., 2013, *Cassese's International Criminal Law* (3rd edn., OUP).

Charter of the International Military Tribunal, 1945, in Agreement for the Prosecution and Punishment of the Major War Criminals of the European Axis (London Agreement), 82 UNTS 280, 8 August 1945.

Charter of the International Military Tribunal for the Far East, 1946, Special Proclamation by the Supreme Commander for the Allied Powers at Tokyo, TIAS No. 1589, 19 January 1946.

Chiesa, L.E., 2008, 'Duress, Demanding Heroism and Proportionality', 41 *Vand.J.Transnat'l L.* 714–773.

Colvin, E., 1990, 'Exculpatory Defences in Criminal Law', 10 *O.J.L.S.* 381–407.

Control Council Law No. 10, 1945, 'Punishment of Persons Guilty of War Crimes, Crimes Against Peace and Against Humanity, 20 December 1945', 3 *Official Gazette Control Council for Germany* 50–55.

Convention Relating to the Status of Refugees, 1951, 189 UNTS 137, 28 July 1951.

Creedon, S., 2015, '"The Exclusion Clause" and the Intersection of International Criminal Law and the Refugee Convention', 18 *Trinity C.L.Rev.* 84–109.

Cryer, C., et al., 2014, *An Introduction to International Criminal Law and Procedure* (3rd edn., CUP).

Dankoff, J., 2011, 'Advocating Duress and Infancy Exceptions to the Persecutor Bar to Asylum for Former Child Soldiers', 31 *Children's Leg.Rights J.* 43–60.

Darcy, S., 2014, *Judges, Law and War. The Judicial Development of International Humanitarian Law* (CUP).

Degan, V.-D., 2005, 'On the Sources of International Criminal Law', 4 *Chinese J.I.L.* 45–83.

Dinstein, Y., 2000, 'Defences' in McDonald, G.K. and O. Swaak-Goldman (eds), *Substantive and Procedural Aspects of International Criminal Law: The Experience of International and National Courts*, Volume I: Commentary (Kluwer) 371–388.

Drumbl, M., 2012, *Reimagining Child Soldiers in International Law and Policy* (OUP).

Ehrenreich Brooks, R., 2002–2003, 'Law in the Heart of Darkness: Atrocity & Duress', 43 *Va.J.Int'l J.* 861–888.

Eser, E., 2016, 'Article 31: Grounds for Excluding Criminal Responsibility', in Triffterer, O. and K. Ambos (eds), *The Rome Statute of the International Criminal Court: A Commentary* (3rd edn., Beck) 1125–1160.

Fisher, K.J., 2013, *Transitional Justice for Child Soldiers. Accountability and Social Reconstruction in Post-Conflict Contexts* (Palgrave).

Fletcher, G.P., 1998, *Basic Concepts of Criminal Law* (OUP).

Fletcher, G.P., 2000, *Rethinking Criminal Law* (OUP).

Fletcher, G.P., 2007, *The Grammar of Criminal Law* (OUP).

Fournet, C., 2008, 'When the Child Surpasses the Father—Admissible Defences in International Criminal Law', 8 *Int.C.L.R.* 509–532.

Fournet, C., 2010, 'Judicial Development of the Law of Defences by the International Criminal Tribunals' in Darcy, S. and J. Powderly (eds), *Judicial Creativity at the International Criminal Tribunals* (OUP) 229–251.

Freeland, S., 2005, 'Child Soldiers and International Crimes—How Should International Law Be Applied?', 3 *N.Z.J.P.I.L.* 303–328.

Gilbert, J., 2006, 'Justice Not Revenge: The International Criminal Court and the "Grounds to Exclude Criminal Responsibility"—Defences or Negation of Criminality?', 10 *I.J.H.R.* 143–160.

Grant, N., 2016, *Duress as a Defence for Former Child Soldiers? Dominic Ongwen and the International Criminal Court*, International Crimes Database Brief 21, December 2016.

Greenawalt, K., 1984, 'The Perplexing Borders of Justification and Excuse', 84 *Colum.L.Rev.* 1897–1927.

Greenawalt, K., 2011, 'The Pluralism of International Criminal Law', 86 *Ind.L.J.* 1063–1130.

Happold, M., 2002, 'Excluding Children from Refugee Status: Child Soldiers and Article 1F of the Refugee Convention', 24 *Am.U.Int'l L.Rev.* 1131–1176.

Happold, M., 2005, *Child Soldiers in International Law* (MUP).

Happold, M., 2006, 'The Age of Criminal Responsibility for International Crimes Under International Law' in Arts, K. and V. Popovski (eds), *International Criminal Accountability and the Rights of Children* (Asser Press) 69–84.

Harris, J.W., 1997, *Legal Philosophies* (2nd edn., Butterworths).

Heim, S.J., 2013, 'The Applicability of the Duress Defense to the Killing of Innocent Persons by Civilians' 46 *Cornell Int'l L.J.* 165–190.

Holder, J., 2016, *Ashworth's Principles of Criminal Law* (8th edn., OUP).

Horovitz, S., et al., 2014, 'The International Criminal Court', in Shany, Y. (ed), *Assessing the Effectiveness of International Courts* (OUP) 223–252.

ICC *Ongwen*, 2016, *Situation in Uganda in the Case of Prosecutor v. Ongwen*, International Criminal Court, Decision on the Confirmation of Charges against Dominic Ongwen (Public Redacted), Case No. ICC-02/04-01/15, 23 March 2016.

ICC Statute, 1998, Statute of the International Criminal Court, U.N. Doc. A/CONF.183/9, (1998) 2187 UNTS 90.

ICJ *North Sea Continental Shelf*, 1969, International Court of Justice, *North Sea Continental Shelf* (Federal Republic of Germany/Denmark and Federal Republic of Germany/The Netherlands), 1969, ICJ Rep. 3.

ICTR *Rutaganira*, 2005, *Prosecutor v. Rutaganira*, International Criminal Tribunal for Rwanda, Judgement and Sentence, Case No. ICTR-95-1C-T, 14 March 2005.

ICTR Statute, 1994, Statute of the International Criminal Tribunal for Rwanda, United Nations Security Council, U.N. Doc. S/RES/955 (1994), 8 November 1994.

ICTY *Blaškić*, 2000, *Prosecutor v. Blaškić*, International Criminal Court for the Former Yugoslavia, Judgment, Case No. IT-95-14, 3 March 2000.

ICTY *Erdemović*, 1997a, *Prosecutor v. Erdemović*, International Criminal Tribunal for the Former Yugoslavia, Judgment, Case No. IT-96-22-A, Dissenting Opinion of Judge Cassese, 7 October 1997.

ICTY *Erdemović*, 1997b, *Prosecutor v. Erdemović*, International Criminal Tribunal for the Former Yugoslavia, Judgment, Case No. IT-96-22-A, Joint Separate Opinion of Judges McDonald and Vohrah, 7 October 1997.

ICTY *Erdemović*, 1997c, *Prosecutor v. Erdemović*, International Criminal Tribunal for the Former Yugoslavia, Judgment, Case No. IT-96-22-T, 7 October 1997.

ICTY *Kordic and Cerkez*, 2001, *Prosecutor v. Kordic and Cerkez*, International Criminal Tribunal for the Former Yugoslavia, Judgment, Case No. IT-95-14/2-T, 26 February 2001.

ICTY Statute, 1993, Statute of the International Criminal Tribunal for the Former Yugoslavia, United Nations Security Council, U.N. Doc. S/RES/827, 25 May 1993.

Italy *Priebke*, 1955, *Priebke* Case, Military Tribunal, Ordinanza del Giudice per l'Udienza Preliminare presso il Tribunale Militare di Roma, 7 December 1995, available at http://www.asser.nl/upload/documents/DomCLIC/Docs/NLP/Italy/Priebke_OrderPreliminaryAudience_7-12-1995.pdf (last visited 2 September 2018).

Joyce, M., 2015, 'Duress: From Nuremberg to the International Criminal Court, Finding the Balance between Justification and Excuse', 28 *L.J.I.L.* 623–642.

Judicial System Monitoring Programme, 2005, *The Case of X: A Child Prosecuted for Crimes against Humanity*, Dili, Timor Leste, available at https://www1.essex.ac.uk/armedcon/story_id/000386.pdf (last visited 10 February 2019).

Kahan, D.M. and M.C. Nussbaum, 1996, 'Two Conceptions of Emotion in Criminal Law', 96 *Colum.L.Rev.* 269–374.

Kittichaisaree, K., 2001, *International Criminal Law* (OUP).

Knoops, G.A., 2003, *An Introduction to the Law of International Criminal Tribunals: A Comparative Study* (Transnational Publishers).

Knoops, G.A., 2008, *Defenses in Contemporary International Criminal Law* (Martinus Nijhoff).

Krebs, B., 2013, 'Justification and Excuse in Article 31(1) of the Rome Statute', 2 *C.J.I.C.L.* 382–410.

Leveau, F., 2013, 'Liability of Child Soldiers Under International Criminal Law', 4 *Osgoode Hall Review of Law and Policy* 36–66.

Linton, S. and C. Reiger, 2001, 'The Evolving Jurisprudence and Practice of East Timor's Special Panels for Serious Crimes on Admissions of Guilt, Duress and Superior Orders', 4 *Y.I.H.L.* 167–212.

Maystre, M., 2014, 'The Interaction between International Refugee Law and International Criminal Law with Respect to Child Soldiers', 12 *J.I.C.J.* 975–996.

Mcalhone, C. and N. Wortley, 2016, *Criminal Law* (4th edn., Sweet and Maxwell).

Merkel, R., 2002, 'Gründe für den Ausschluss der Strafbarkeit im Völkerstrafrecht', 2 *Z.St.W.* 437–454.

Mousourakis, G., 2003, 'Wrongdoing, Culpability and the Logic of Criminal Law Defences', 44 *Acta Jr.Hung.* 67–87.

Nagle, L.E., 2011, 'Child Soldiers and the Duty of Nations to Protect Children from Participation in Armed Conflict', 19 *Cardozo J.Int'l & Comp.L.* 1–58.

Naylor, M., 2006, 'Resistance is Futile: Duress as a Defence to Intentional Killing', 2 *C.S.L.R.* 24–32.

Nemitz, J., 2009, 'Wetzling and Others', in Cassese, A. (ed), *Oxford Companion to International Criminal Justice* (OUP) 972–972.

Neumann, U., 2014, 'Necessity/Duress', in Dubber, M.D. and T. Hörnle, *The Oxford Handbook of Criminal Law* (OUP) 583–606.

Oellers-Frahm, K. and B. Specht, 1998, 'Die Erdemovic-Rechtsprechung des Jugoslawientribunals: Probleme bei der Entwicklung eines internationalen Strafrechts, dargestellt am Beispiel des Notstands', 58 *Z.a.ö.R.V.* 389–414.

Olusanya, O., 2010, 'Excuse and Mitigation under International Criminal Law: Redrawing Conceptual Boundaries', 13 *New Crim.L.Rev.* 23–89.

Paciocco, D.M., 2010, 'No-One Wants to Be Eaten: The Logic and Experience of the Law of Necessity and Duress', 56 *C.L.Q.* 240–293.

Quirico, O., 2009, 'General Principles of International Criminal Law and their Relevance to Africa', 17 *Afr. Yrbk Int'l L.* 139–163.

Risacher, B.J., 2013–2014, 'No Excuse: The Failure of the ICC's Article 31 "Duress" Definition', 89 *Notre Dame L.Rev.* 1403–1426.

Robinson, P.H., 1982, 'Criminal Law Defenses: A Systematic Analysis', 82 *Colum.L.Rev.* 199–291.

Robinson, P.H., 1997, *Structure and Function in Criminal Law* (OUP).

Rosen, C.J., 1986, 'The Excuse of Self-Defense: Correcting a Historical Accident on Behalf of Battered Women Who Kill', 36 *Am.U.L.Rev.* 11–56.

Rosenthal, P., 1990, 'Duress in the Criminal Law', 32 *C.L.Q.* 199–226.

Scaliotti, M., 2001, 'Defences before the International Criminal Court: Substantive Grounds for Excluding Criminal Responsibility—Part 1', 1 *Int.C.L.R.* 111–172.

Schabas, W.A., 2011, 'The International Criminal Court at Ten', 22 *Crim.L.F.* 493–509.

Schabas, W.A., 2016, *The International Criminal Court: A Commentary on the Rome Statute* (2nd edn., OUP).

Siegrist, S., 2006, 'Child Participation in International Criminal Accountability Mechanisms: The Case of the Sierra Leone Truth and Reconciliation Commission' in Arts, K. and V. Popovski (eds), *International Criminal Accountability and the Rights of Children* (Asser Press) 53–66.

Smith, J.C., 1989, *The Hamlyn Lectures: Justification and Excuse in the Criminal Law* (40th series, Stevens and Sons).

Stahn, C., 2019, *A Critical Introduction to International Criminal Law* (CUP).

Steinl, L., 2017, *Child Soldiers as Agents of War and Peace: A Restorative Transitional Justice Approach to Accountability for Crimes Under International Law* (Asser Press).

UK *Howe*, 1987, *R. v. Howe and others*, House of Lords, [1987] 1 ALL ER 771.

UK *Lynch*, 1975, *Lynch v. D.P.P. for Northern Ireland*, Appeals Court, [1975] AC 643.

UNHCR, 2003a, *Guidelines on International Protection No. 5: Application of the Exclusion Clauses: Article 1F of the 1951 Convention Relating to the Status of Refugees*, U.N. Doc. HCR/GIP/03/05, 2003.

UNHCR, 2003b, *Background Note on the Application of the Exclusion Clauses: Article 1F of the 1951 Convention Relating to the Status of Refugees*, 4 September 2003, available at https://www.refworld.org/docid/3f5857d24.html (last visited 10 February 2019).

UNTAET, 2000, Regulation No. 2000/15 On the Establishment of Panels with Exclusive Jurisdiction over Serious Criminal Offences, United Nations Transitional Administration in East Timor, U.N. Doc. UNTAET/REG/2000/15, 6 June 2000.

Van Sliedregt, E., 2006, 'Criminal Responsibility in International Law: Liability Shaped by Policy Goals and Moral Outrage', 14 *Eur.J.Crime Cr.LCr.J.* 81–114.

Wall, I.R., 2006, 'Duress, International Criminal Law and Literature', 4 *J.I.C.J.* 724–744.

Weigend, T., 2011, 'Germany', in Heller K.J. and M.D. Dubber (eds), *The Handbook of Comparative Criminal Law* (SUP) 252–287.

Weigend, T., 2012, 'Kill or Be Killed. Another Look at Erdemović', 10 *J.I.C.J.* 1219–1237.

Werle, G. and F. Jessberger, 2014, *Principles of International Criminal Law* (3rd edn., OUP).

Wiener, N., 2014, 'Excuses, Justifications, and Duress at the International Criminal Tribunals', 26 *Pace Int'l L.Rev.* 88–131.

Xavier, I., 2016, 'The Incongruity of the Rome Statute Insanity Defence and International Crime', 14 *J.I.C.J.* 793–814.

Yee, S., 1997, 'The Erdemovic Sentencing Judgement: A Questionable Milestone for the International Criminal Tribunal for the Former Yugoslavia', 26 *Ga.J.Int'l & Comp.L.* 263–309.

Zgaga, S., 2014, 'Intoxication and Criminal Liability in International Criminal Law', 2 *Law Journal of the Higher School of Economics* 149–161.

CHAPTER 3

The Application of the Requirements of Duress to Child Soldiers

1 Introduction

The defence of duress has been pleaded on numerous occasions in an array of trials before international tribunals, such as the post-World War II (WWII) tribunals and the International Criminal Tribunal for the Former Yugoslavia (ICTY), yet its requirements were never fulfilled.[1] Duress, in contrast to other defences, is not a defence easily accepted by international tribunals.[2] This is partially due to the fact that usually the individuals who are prosecuted are commanders and thus unlikely to be in a position of being forced to act under duress. Moreover, the requirements of the defence plea appear too stringent to be met against the background of mass atrocities. Also, the idea that an accused who has committed atrocious crimes can be acquitted for such acts if duress is raised successfully does not resonate well with the international legal community as a whole. Yet, both the rights of the victims and the community to justice, as opposed to the fair trial rights of the accused, need to be considered to give legitimacy to the development of international criminal law in the twenty-first century. However, this has not always been the case. International criminal courts and tribunals have followed a victim-centred approach mainly due to the injustices that were committed against millions of victims since the advent of World War I.[3] In addition, international criminal justice and in particular the right of an accused to a defence were largely underdeveloped during the Cold War. As a result, international criminal

W. Nortje, N. Quénivet, *Child Soldiers and the Defence of Duress under International Criminal Law*,
https://doi.org/10.1007/978-3-030-20663-5_3

jurisprudence has been criticised for having tilted 'in an unacceptably pro-prosecution direction'.[4] The ICC Statute attempts to correct this imbalance. On the one hand, the Preamble of the ICC Statute explains the importance of victims in that the court is '[m]indful that during this century millions of children, women and men have been victims of unimaginable atrocities that deeply shock the conscience of humanity'.[5] Yet, on the other, the drafters of the Rome Statute included various grounds excluding responsibility in order to address the right of an accused to raise a defence.

It must be underlined that previous international courts used differing requirements for the plea of duress and it was not until the adoption of Article 31(1)(d) of the Rome Statute that this ground for excluding criminal responsibility was given a unified definition under international criminal law. It is against this standard that the authors will appraise whether children accused of international crimes can successfully claim the defence of duress. As mentioned earlier, defences in relation to crimes under international law have been rather slow to develop throughout the last few decades, considering the fact that the ICTY and the ICTR did not even include duress in their respective statutes.[6] Although duress is included in the ICC Statute it has not yet been properly interpreted by the ICC despite the fact that the defence team of Ongwen raised the issue at the stage of the confirmation of the charges.[7] Whilst the court responded to the defence team's argument, it did so very briefly[8] and hence only some elements of the defence of duress were elaborated upon. Due to this lack of a comprehensive examination of the defence, recourse must be had to previous national and international jurisprudence to elucidate the conditions spelled out in the provisions of the ICC Statute.

In concordance with Article 31(1)(d) of the ICC Statute, to avail oneself of the defence of duress,[9] an individual must demonstrate that his/her acts were committed in order to avoid the threat (4) of imminent (3) death or of continuing or imminent (3) serious bodily harm (2) and that such acts were necessary and reasonable (5) to avoid this threat. Furthermore, the person did not intend to cause a greater harm than the one sought to be avoided (5). Examining each requirement one by one,[10] this chapter seeks to ascertain whether children who have committed international crimes are able to successfully invoke the defence of duress. That being said, it must be borne in mind that prosecutions are about individuals and not collectives. Also, the individual experience of children which is shaped by diversity and difference need to be recognised in light of the increasing homogenisation of viewing children as a homogenous group demarcated from adults by biological and psychosocial characteristics.[11] Hence, although comments can be made about the group 'child soldiers' at large, it is important to look at each case on a case-by-case basis to determine whether a child will be able to raise the defence of duress under international law.[12] Such a case-by-case analysis is based on examining the specific factual and legal circumstances of each case[13] as well as the social characteristics of the individual. In applying the requirements to the situation of child soldiers, the authors, as mentioned in Chap. 1, rely on secondary sources rather than first-hand empirical research on the plight of child soldiers and their involvement in the commission of crimes under international law.

At first glance, it is not immediately clear why child soldiers should be treated differently with regard to duress as opposed to other perpetrators. After all, every juvenile justice system has general legal principles applicable to juveniles who commit crimes, which include various defences applicable to adults and juveniles alike. At a theoretical level nobody would say that there should be a different duress rule for juvenile offenders. However, questions about the application of legal principles appear in specific cases, such as that of Dominic Ongwen at the ICC and those of ex-child soldiers found in empirical studies conducted by researchers mentioned throughout this book. Child soldiers cannot be compared to adult perpetrators. Their cases need special consideration. After all, it is in the best interests of every child soldier to provide him/her with an opportunity to raise the defence of duress for crimes committed under international law and interpret the law in a child-friendly manner in pursuance of Article 3 UNCRC.[14]

This chapter draws the conclusion that under the current requirements set out in Article 31(1)(d) child soldiers cannot successfully raise the defence of duress. More generally, the application of the defence of duress to the ultimate victim-perpetrator archetype, that is, the child soldier, reveals that the defence of duress as expounded in the ICC Statute is unlikely to be invoked successfully by any alleged perpetrator in its current form and interpretation.[15] The authors argue that we need a more nuanced understanding of perpetrators and the unique circumstances under which they act to ensure that domestic courts and international courts are able to apply the defence of duress to child soldiers.

2 Death or Serious Bodily—Physical, and Not Psychological, Harm

The first requirement is that the perpetrator is placed in such a situation that he/she may die or suffer serious bodily harm if he/she does not carry out a certain criminal act. The requirement is limited to a threat of serious bodily harm, that is, a threat to the physical integrity of the body of the perpetrator or another person (danger to other interests may not be averted on this ground).[16] Accordingly, 'blackmail or other threats not involving imminent serious violence will not suffice.'[17] 'Demotion' for failing to carry out the act[18] or a threat to deprive an individual of food and water is not admitted as a valid element of the defence.[19] A German court however explained that long-lasting deprivation of liberty leading to serious impairment of one's health can be seen as endangerment of one's life.[20] This means that circumstances/cases of psychological coercion can only be included under duress if they include a physical component in the harm to be suffered.[21]

Applied to the situation of children, this requirement is rarely ever fulfilled as children tend to react to a wide swathe of elements rather than one specific threat. Moreover, the threats are often of a psychological nature. It is submitted that the defence plea is more likely to work for children in the wake of their recruitment, that is, if they have committed a crime under international law during that time, but not at a later stage (this however does not mean that later children are precluded from raising the defence of duress). The reason for this is that the defence of duress focuses on physical rather than psychological harm, even if the latter can be of extremely high intensity. As a matter of fact, children are often, especially in the days and weeks immediately following their recruitment, threatened with death if they refuse to fight.[22] Initiation rituals during which children are made to commit crimes 'or else' are commonplace amongst armed groups in Africa.[23] As the fear is physical inasmuch as it is directed towards the perpetrator and/or a third-party duress can be claimed.

At first, the initial harm is indisputably physical, for example, but not limited to forcing children to join an armed group, threatening to kill their community members or school teachers if they refuse to join the armed group, but it is also psychological considering the mental immaturity of children.[24] Happold notes that '[t]he move from the care of one's family to the closed environment of an armed force or group is disturbing, particularly when it is accompanied by physical abuse, bullying and harassment.'[25] Child soldiers are therefore served a dangerous cocktail of physical and psychological harm which ultimately disrupts their moral development.[26] However, as children familiarise themselves with the armed group, they tend to avoid physical abuse partly by the execution of the orders of their superiors[27]: they have learned the hard way to conform or else. Although the physical element might disappear after a while, it remains extremely difficult for any child soldier to forget about the possibility of being killed or physically harmed. Children live in the constant, inculcated, deep-seated fear that physical harm will be done to them and/or others.[28] Also, they are aware that if they do not comply some of their rights and privileges might be removed from them. All this happens whilst they are simultaneously subjected to various kinds of mind-numbing indoctrination by their superiors.[29] In the Lord's Resistance Army (LRA) child soldiers were made to believe in the spiritual cult of Kony that fostered a social cohesion grounded in violence and terror.[30] Former Revolutionary United Front (RUF) child soldiers recount 'an aura of menace, repeatedly manifested through verbal abuse and acts of wanton cruelty [that] served as a basis of authority and social cohesion'.[31] In short 'children [are] subjected to a process of psychological and physical abuse and duress which has transformed them from victims into perpetrators.'[32] For example, Thomas Kwoyelo and Dominic Ongwen, two former child soldiers in the LRA, were forced to commit atrocities and subsequently became rebel commanders in the same army.[33] It is often argued that trapped in a world of sustained and orchestrated violence many children turn into merciless killers.[34] Notwithstanding the fact that children may make these choices (see Chap. 3, Sect. 4 for further details), constant fear of physical and psychological harm is internalised and no doubt bears on a child's decision to obey orders even though he/she is not threatened with physical harm at the moment of the commission of the crime.[35] In other words, there is no need for a threat of physical harm to be specifically uttered repeatedly in this situation.

According to the current state of the law, unless child soldiers are threatened with physical harm they cannot use the defence of duress. Indeed, the law does not match the reality which is that there might be no physical harm as such. This incongruence is partially vindicated by the fact that duress is still understood as a justification, and that the focus is on the act rather than on the actor who may have appraised the harm in a different light.

3 Immediacy of the Harm

The second requirement for duress relates to the immediacy of the harm. Duress can only be raised as an exclusionary ground for a particular act.[36] A literal interpretation of Article 31(1)(c) indisputably suggests both a link between the threat and the act as well as temporal proximity between the issuance of the threat and its execution. That being said, Article 31(1)(d) of the ICC Statute does not stipulate that the threat must be the only reason why the individual is committing the crime.[37] A combination of reasons can also be present, although previous case-law seems to specify that the crime must be connected to a clear demand (i.e., the issuance of a threat) and that the threat must be of 'imminent' harm.

Cryer et al.[38] and Ambos[39] view this requirement as objective as the harm must exist in reality and not just in the defendant's mind. The threat must be considered real: a mere abstract danger or an elevated probability of danger would not suffice.[40] The ICC definition no doubt reflects that adopted in common law as '[t]hreats of future injury are not sufficient'.[41] However, the test also has a subjective element because the court should determine whether the defendant realised the immediacy of the harm and not whether objectively, a reasonable person, a standard familiar to common law lawyers, would have realised it. The individual must act in the understanding that a real danger is present and this means that subjective standards are used to determine the 'actual bona fide belief'.[42] Put otherwise, the 'actual bona fide belief' looks at whether the defendant subjectively foresaw that he would be harmed and that this harm was clear, present and immediate. The test is not whether the defendant mistakenly believed that he was going to be immediately harmed, but that he actually knew or foresaw that he was going to be harmed. The test is different to those of self-defence and necessity where the requirements are generally objective.[43] Smith has even ventured so far as to say that '[t]he better view is that the subjective principle should apply to the definitional elements of a defense just as it does to the definitional elements of a crime.'[44] That being said, what is pivotal is that a court should look at the unique set of facts in each case, and whether the defendant was able to realise that the harm was immediate.

As a result of this test, a causal link between the act and the threat must undoubtedly be established. In other words, the threat is of such imminence that 'the fear caused by the threat must be operating on the mind of the actor at the time of the criminal act'.[45] After all, the underlying justification for this defence is that the threat was inescapable, that the perpetrator had no free choice.[46] Nonetheless, in keeping with the *Einsatzgruppen* Case, the peril might not be as imminent as that of a loaded pistol at the head of the perpetrator.[47] In this case, 24 Nazi defendants were charged with the murder of Jews as a crime against humanity and a war crime amongst other charges.[48] Some of the defendants admitted that they committed the offences but pleaded lack of guilt as they were following the superior orders of their commanders.[49] In relation to duress and superior orders, the US Military Court in Nuremberg held that duress could not be pleaded in this instance since all the defendants justified the killings of each and every Jew despite the fact that they might have been forced to commit the murders.[50] Thus, there cannot be a threat if the defendant justifies the killing.

The first stumbling block in applying this condition is that it is acknowledged that child soldiers do not need to be told what to do and to be threatened as they have been conditioned to comply. The ICC has recognised that a way to secure control over child soldiers is via 'intensive, strict and violence [sic] training regimes' during which children 'are taught to shoot, pillage, rape and kill'.[51] Children are easily malleable and simply obey orders,[52] the more so as '[t]hey can generally be intimidated'.[53] They are also loyal to their commanders whom they view as protectors or surrogate fathers.[54] This, in the court's words, 'may be an effective means for automatic compliance with leaders' orders to commit such acts'.[55] Also, cruel forms of punishment are common.[56] A general atmosphere of fear and violence ensures obedience to the hierarchy.[57] It might thus not be possible to claim a correlation between the act carried out by the child and the specific threat of harm, since for the children there might be no threat as such.

Secondly, whilst children are threatened with death and beatings should they disobey the orders, such threats tend to be uttered in a general maelstrom of violence, rather than in the concrete context of an act. For child soldiers, it is the background of their recruitment and current situation that is most likely to dictate how they will react to an order. Research shows that children have been exposed to a wide range of violent acts, such as seeing someone killed (including members of their family), killing someone, being forced to participate in fights without any military training, being beaten, being exposed to air raids and bomb explosions, being used as human shields and so on.[58] The decision to act will be taken in the light of their previous experiences and a general climate of fear and violence, that is, continuous rather than future harm. As a former child soldier recalls:

> It takes time, about six months, to brainwash the new abductees totally. What they do first is, when you are still new, beat you about 500 times. But if you are lucky it is only 200. Then they force you to watch horrible things. We were abducted as a group of students. One of us was brought in front of us and killed there so that we could see. Those are the things they do. They force us to do it. Then, second, anyone among you who tries to escape will be killed the same way. So, as this might be the first time you see a person being killed, this will traumatise you and make you very afraid.[59]

Simply put, in the words of another former child soldier: 'You never refuse to kill, otherwise they will kill you.'[60] The message sent to the children is unambiguous.[61] Here a close correlation between the act and the threat is not essential in practice. Moreover, whilst the threat plays on the mind of the perpetrator no temporal sequencing between the two is required. The threat is in fact omnipresent and it is not possible to pinpoint the direct link between the threat and the act which means that this requirement cannot be fulfilled.

As a result, unless once concedes that continuing threats give rise to duress, child soldiers are unlikely to fulfil the requirement of immediacy of the threat. Some scholars argue that continuing threats might be (notably due to the conflation of duress and necessity in the ICC Statute, see Chap. 2) accepted.[62] In particular, some contend that Article 31(1)(d) of the ICC Statute refers to 'a threat of [...] continuing or imminent serious bodily harm', thereby expressly recognising that 'the continuing coercive and threatening environment in which some child soldiers are kept'[63] could fall under that definition. Yet, under the ICC Statute it is the harm and not the threat that is continuous and so it might not be able to consider that a coercive environment be accepted by the ICC. Some authors, such as Bond and Fougere, go a step further, cogently contending that threats that are implied or indirect, that is, that stem from the broader environment, can inform a person's understanding of the consequences of abstaining to act in a certain manner.[64] Therefore, the probing of whether the requirement is fulfilled should be both objective and subjective, that is, did the perpetrator genuinely believe there was a threat and, given all relevant circumstances, was his/her belief reasonable?[65] However, the case-law of international criminal tribunals plainly sunders the possibility of claiming duress in cases of a generalised atmosphere of fear and the apparent impossibility to disobey orders.[66] In other words, duress is only available to someone 'who has actually tried not to obey an order'.[67] The case of *Mrđa* reveals that the plea of duress, formulated as general, psychological coercion, even combined with the youth and low rank of the individual, does not work. As the court asserted in plain terms '[t]he Trial Chamber does not rule out that those *circumstances* may have had some influence on the criminal behaviour of Darko Mrđa, although it does not accept that they were such that Darko Mrđa, even taking account of his age and low rank, would have had no alternative but to participate in the massacre of around 200 civilians.'[68] This straightforwardly rules out the defence of duress based on psychological grounds.[69] It should be noted that the fact that psychological, social environment-related coercion (which is linked to the actor rather than the act) is not accepted for this defence is further proof that duress is regarded as a justification rather than an excuse.[70] Even if one agrees that psychological oppression falls within the ambit of 'immediacy of the harm', a limit has been set in the sense that in 'situations in which international crimes are committed', 'some level of coercion of an offender by colleagues can often be expected'.[71] An exception to this understanding is the *Wetzling* Case in which the court conceded that the superior who was of 'cruel, brutal and fanatic character' 'constituted a permanent danger (*Dauergefahr*) for the three defendants', and thus, although he was not present at the execution sites, his character was playing on the minds of the defendants.[72] However, in this case it was not the general environment that was pressing on the perpetrator's mind but a particular individual from whom the threat emanated. The threat might have been continuous, but its source was clearly identifiable. In this case it might be argued that even though the coercer was not physically present he/she was operating on the person's mind.[73] This could be used in the case of child soldiers if a commander was of such character that they would constantly fear his reactions and behaviour.

In addition, it is disputed whether the immediacy link means that the harm must be inflicted at the time and scene of the commission of the offence. Whilst Bond and Fougere observe that 'where there truly were no alternatives available to the actor, it is irrelevant whether the threatened harm would have occurred five minutes or five hours or five days after the threat was issued since it was, by definition, inevitable',[74] case-law clearly rejects such a conception of the requirement of immediacy. The ICC's judgement in *Ongwen Confirmation of Charges* unambiguously underscores the temporal proximity between the threatened and the actual harm: '[t]he threat described by the Defence, *i.e.* the possibility of later disciplinary measures, was not imminent.'[75] If the court views immediacy as containing such a close temporal proximity, then it is unlikely that this defence would work for child soldiers since they are often punished later for refusing to carry out orders. The court seems to justify this stance by highlighting that subscribing to this stance would equate to 'provid[ing] blanket immunity to members of criminal organisations which have brutal systems of ensuring discipline as soon as they can establish that their membership was not voluntary'.[76] Institutionalised duress is not recognised by the law as the threat must be imminent.[77] In the light of the gruesome tactics used, especially by armed opposition groups, towards children, this legal position denies children who have committed international crimes the possibility to raise the defence of duress.

Overall, as immediacy is understood as necessitating a close link between the threat and the act as well as including a temporal proximity element, child soldiers cannot generally avail themselves of the defence of duress. It is accordingly left to courts to determine each case on a case-by-case basis, but it is nevertheless submitted here that this specific requirement needs to be refined in order to be applicable to child soldiers who commit crimes under international law.

4 Intention to Avert a Threat

The third requirement demands from the individual, who believes that the threat will be carried out unless he/she obeys the order, that his/her intention must ultimately be aimed at acting in such a manner as to attempt to avert the danger.[78] Whether the harm was indeed averted is irrelevant as what matters is that the person intended to do so.[79] The introduction of a subjective test,[80] 'the intention', has however been criticised, for it seems at odds with the very notion of duress[81] as duress is viewed as the compulsion to act in a certain manner. It seems that the creation of the 'intention' element aims at ensuring that there was some resistance to carrying out the unlawful act.

A meticulous analysis of previous case-law reveals that subjectivity is not unknown to this requirement of duress. In particular, two elements can be distinguished. Firstly, he/she must in a meaningful manner explain that he/she wishes to dissociate him/herself from the act.[82] If the person 'had any reasonable opportunity to extricate him [sic] from the coercive situation without committing the crime, either by resisting the coercer or by escaping'[83] then the defence of duress is unsupportable.[84] In other words, the perpetrator must indicate that he/she does not want to follow through with the offence after the threat was posed, and that his/her will does not coincide with the will of the person who is putting him/her under duress.[85] If he/she does not do so, even on the basis of a genuine 'there was no point in trying' attitude, then it conveys the impression that the individual did not wish to disengage him/herself from the act.[86] Similarly, words that 'sound like a comment only about the accomplishment of the operation, rather than a refusal to obey an order' cannot be considered as expressing an individual's dissociation of the act.[87] It is irrelevant whether or not the defendant had a motive for averting the specific threat. As the court in the *Einsatzgruppen* Case postulated, 'the motive is irrelevant if he killed willingly.'[88] Secondly, the intention of the perpetrator to avert the threat must be caused by the duress that the perpetrator is placed under, which in turn causes the perpetrator to commit a crime.[89] The perpetrator believes that it is impossible to disobey the order[90]: committing the crime is inescapable. To some extent, the question is therefore whether a child soldier realises that he/she can express a contrary opinion and disobey the order.[91] Child soldiers who have witnessed and experienced all forms of abuse and violence tend to have a distorted view of the power of their commanders[92] and so will believe that the threat will be executed.

It is contended that children 'are more likely to be influenced by peer groups to commit group crimes, and are more susceptible to weaknesses in their community'.[93] Research reveals that in peacetime substantial weight might be given by children, and especially juveniles, to peer perception as well as 'dominant social expectation' in the community in which they are living.[94] Moreover, it is recognised that 'juveniles are more susceptible to "*negative* influences and outside pressures, including peer pressure"'[95] and that 'resistance to peer influence [...] increase [sic] linearly from early to late adolescence.'[96] Whilst adults have the capacity, both physical and mental, to negotiate the terms of their personal engagement and to reject coercion and aggression,[97] children are in no such position. They tend to cave in easily to coercion.[98] Such behaviour is accentuated in times of conflict. Research shows that even adult '[p]erpetrators of international crimes violate international rules but often act in conformity with the social norms and values which are prevalent in that particular state at that particular time'.[99] For children, the situation is worse as they have been cut off from their communities and the armed opposition group becomes the sole society or family a child might know or remember. It is accepted that 'social processes within a group not only result in the pressure to conform but group members often desperately *want* to belong and thus want to comply.'[100] As a result, children are quick to resocialise.[101] These children will conform to the rules of that group and so will learn aggressive behaviour by observing and imitating others.[102] Violence is unwittingly normalised, rationalised and trivialised. As McKay explains, '[p]erpetrating violence and torture become normal and routine within a culture of violence that pervades every aspect of daily routines and activities.'[103] Having spent some time in the group also impacts on their mental health to the effect that children are at greater risk of increased engagement in risky and aggressive behaviour.[104] How can a child under such circumstances be in a position to express his/her discontent with the acts he/she is asked to carry out? How can one expect him/her to show any inclination to resist duress? What is more, in highly hierarchised societies where parents, relatives, as well as any adult, are perceived as persons of power, children respect their views, orders and values.[105] Children will apply moral concepts, albeit those of the group, in order to fit in, and will not test these concepts. Therefore, a child may not even realise that he/she is under peer and community pressure[106] and that he/she has embraced a flawed understanding of what is right and wrong.

Even research studies that show that children do not lose their moral compass in adverse conditions reveal that they might not actively challenge such concepts.[107] Their free will is factually constrained by their lived experience.[108] Although a child may be conscious of the doubtful morality of the act he/she has either little leeway to challenge the unlawful order or has developed mechanisms and strategies to manage, regulate and keep under control emotions[109] which prevent him/her from acting against the order. Understanding the general and complex background is primordial when ascertaining whether the child believed the threat would be carried out and so acted to avert the threat. Although general remarks can be made regarding the behaviour of child soldiers in such circumstances, each child will react differently and so a case-by-case determination is necessary when prosecuting a child soldier.

In this line, it is contended that '[i]n all conflicts, children can take, and some choose to take, an active role in supporting violence. Children make calculated decisions during armed conflict about how to access shelter, food, medicine, and best ways to keep themselves and their family members safe.'[110] In the LRA, 'good' behaviour was rewarded with the aforementioned elements, as well as with knowledge and information, escorts and spies for protection, sexual gratification, girls for domestic services and so on.[111] Similarly, the RUF used a system of allocation of rewards and promotion to strengthen solidarity and encourage absolute fealty and compliant behaviour.[112] These decisions are based on learning, knowing and complying with the rules of the group.[113] Honwana calls this 'tactical agency', 'a specific type of agency that is devised to cope with the concrete, immediate conditions of their lives in order to maximize the circumstances created by their military and violent environment'.[114] Similarly, Schmidt[115] as well as Fisher[116] acknowledge that children, as actors in a conflict, make rational choices. They make the best of poor situations and take decisions that they deem are most beneficial to them.[117] The crux of the concept of agency is that an 'individual could, at any phase in a given sequence of conduct, have acted differently'.[118] The agent has transformative capacity, 'the power to intervene or to refrain from intervention'.[119] If child soldiers have this capacity, then surely they can act in a way that they can avert the threat and so may have willingly obeyed the order in the sense that they went along with it and did not dissociate themselves from the act.

It is generally agreed that child soldiers can 'manipulate' situations in order to turn them into 'opportunities' for the sake of survival.[120] For example, some child soldiers attain positions of command in armed groups and become leaders by actively participating in the hostilities and committing some of the worst atrocities (e.g., killing civilians, punishing and executing fellow child soldiers, etc.).[121] Dominic Ongwen is currently standing trial at the International Criminal Court for the commission of crimes against humanity and war crimes while he was one of the commanders of the infamous Lord's Resistance Army (LRA) in Uganda. His case though, at first sight, is rather unique as he was only a little boy when he was abducted by the LRA[122]; however, Kwoyelo has a similar story.[123] Concomitantly, carrying out violent acts might enhance a child's 'sense of personal empowerment and heightened social status'.[124] This means that a child soldier who has been recruited for a longer time may be in a better position to avert the threat than a child soldier who has not gained the trust of the commander.[125] In other words, children who have become accustomed to the mechanics of an armed group might be in a safer position to ignore the threat, act against it or avert it, and thus not commit a crime. However, research also reveals that children who have been recruited for an extended period of time have been laced into violence[126] and have a higher propensity to kill,[127] as they are merely copying what they have learned during training.[128] In contrast, those who stayed in such groups for shorter periods of time kept 'their basic trust in human beings and social values more or less intact'.[129] As a result, due to this acculturation within the group and socialisation into violence[130]—the very fact that violence becomes a normal part of life[131]—the children who one might think are able to avert the threat are likely to commit atrocious acts without any second thoughts. In relation to the conflict in Sierra Leone, Maclure and Denov explain that 'the boys' agency was consummated as integral to the militarist structure of the RUF.'[132] Similarly Almohammad explains that the political agency of children recruited by ISIS was 'tied to the general realities and conditions of their daily lives'.[133] Additionally some child soldiers have grown up in a society marred by armed conflict. For example, an entire generation of children in South Sudan has internalised violence and learned that it is a common means to solve disagreements and disputes.[134] Given the circumstances, there is no other way of thinking possible.

Children in such a situation develop 'an adaptive capacity to cope with experiences associated with the war'.[135] Their existence is 'based on sheer survival'.[136] Some are better at adapting than others in the sense that 'there are important individual differences in the ways how people regulate their emotions and that some ways of regulating emotions may be more adaptive than others'.[137] Ongwen is sadly a live illustration of the child soldier's predicament: he lived most of his life in a ruthless armed opposition group and, as the Defence argued, '[h]is so-called rank was demonstrative of one thing: that he was surviving better than others while under duress.'[138] As Pangalangan summarises: 'Ongwen, having spent his formative years and adult life with the LRA, inculcates the disvalues of the same—a species of Social Darwinism where only the most fit survive.'[139] Interestingly, the Prosecution sought to shatter this inconvenient fact by stressing the criminal depravity and monstrosity of Ongwen as a person and highlighting his acquiescence and even genuine support for such crimes.[140] In his case, he 'shared the ideology of the LRA'[141] and was part of a system, thus nullifying a potential claim that he attempted to disassociate himself from the unlawful order(s). In this situation, there can be no intention to avert the threat as required by the defence of duress.

Yet, agency can also be understood in a different way. It is not a question of capacity or ability but one of possibility or real freedom,[142] and thus boils down to investigating 'to what extent we are able to act within a given context'.[143] Generally, in an armed conflict context, agency is always qualified; consent never absolute.[144] As Honwana stresses, whilst child soldiers are able to make at least tactical decisions, their choices are constrained by their weak position.[145] As a matter of fact, their choices are based on the '[limited] information they possess and their [limited] ability to weigh one choice against another'.[146] The decisions children make are oftentimes nothing but reactions to an identifiable, immediate event or threat rather than carefully weighed and processed views taking into consideration the (long-term) consequences of their actions.[147] In contrast, as Ongwen rose in the ranks of the LRA his agency was less and less curbed. In fact, it turned from a tactical to a strategic, albeit limited too, agency.[148] Branch points out that Ongwen was able to make his own decisions. After all, he tried to flee.[149] The same holds true of Thomas Kwoyelo.[150] This means that some children might be able to form opinions and make autonomous decisions, but this varies from child to child and must be taken into account when deciding on whether a child acted with the intention to avert the threat or simply embraced the order.

Furthermore, Brett and Specht importantly note that child soldiers make impulsive decisions (impulse control grows linearly from early to late adolescence),[151] and that there is a tendency among children 'to be rather opportunistic, taking immediate benefits seriously'.[152] Neuroscience also bolsters the belief that children's decision-making is 'more instinctive and directed by emotion ... than rational and considered'.[153] A sociological interpretation of the situation, that incorporates internal and external factors in the equation, yields similar results. Such children are not able to make truly autonomous decisions and hence cannot truly act to avert the threat since they mainly see the immediate 'benefit' of the situation of duress, they can save their lives if they execute the act required of them.

Accordingly, when determining the intention of the child soldier at the time of averting the threat, emphasis must be placed on his/her history and how it has impacted on his/her decision-making abilities, in addition to the fact that he/she may find it difficult to exercise control over reckless impulses.[154] Phrased in legal language, the question boils down to whether the child soldier, under the unique circumstances in which they found themselves, intended to avert the threat rather than accepted the threat outright. As shown, whilst some might have shown the intention to avert the threat, the majority will not.

5 Proportionality: Necessary and Reasonable—Greater Harm

In averting the threat, the person who claims duress must prove that his/her action was necessary, that is, it was the only possibility to eliminate the threat to his/her life or limb, and reasonable,[155] that is, it was appropriate to avert the danger and caused no disproportionate consequences.[156] To demand a reasonable course of action is again a typical feature of a justification defence,[157] as the key element is that society permits or tolerates certain conduct only because it is necessary and reasonable. On balance the act is a reasonable course of action given the circumstances unique to the case.[158] The test to determine duress in Article 31(1)(d) is glaringly similar to the test for proportionality in self-defence.[159] It is an objective proportionality test which includes the question whether a reasonable person would have given in to the threat.[160] According to this standard, the test is whether a person in a similar position would have acted in a similar manner.[161] Viewed as a justification, the defence of duress requires that the action be necessary and reasonable, and this must be distinguished from proving that the person is 'of reasonable firmness'.[162] If, on the other hand, the focus is on the actor and the defence is to be measured according to whether the specific individual was of reasonable firmness, then the defence of duress is regarded as an excuse.[163] As explained below, the case-law of international criminal tribunals supports the view that duress in its current form is a justification defence.

This legal constraint was unmistakably propounded by the ICC Trial Chamber in *Confirmation of Charges* of Ongwen as it not only questioned whether the acts were 'necessary (and reasonable) to avoid the alleged threat and could … satisfy the required intent of proportionality' but also provided vivid examples to illustrate acts that did not conform to the requirement. For example, as regards Ongwen being 'forced' to participate as a commander in attacks against civilians, the court noted that not only did he not take any action to reduce harm to the civilians, but he seemed to have done the opposite.[164] Whilst it must be remembered that the court is prosecuting Ongwen for acts committed as an adult, these cursory comments of the court give some insight into how the proportionality requirement might be interpreted in future cases.

Applied to children, it is contended that they are not likely to make the *right* decision because their definitions of 'necessary' and 'reasonableness' depend on their age and maturity, their education[165] and more generally their own searing experience. All these elements are also paramount in appreciating how easily a child transitions from an 'innocent' child to a child soldier.[166]

The (im)maturity of the child soldier will play a considerable role in determining whether he/she is able to adopt necessary and reasonable measures when shoehorned into a situation of duress. Children do not have the same maturity as adults, and it is for this reason that in most societies they are not allowed to marry, vote, consume alcohol and so on, all markers of adulthood, until they reach 18 years of age.[167] They lack the psychological capacity, as well as the experience, to make informed decisions,[168] and tend to make poor situational judgements.[169] Peacetime studies show that adolescents do 'not possess the same abilities [as adults] to act independently or appreciate the rights of others as an adult'.[170] As Grover explains, child soldiers might 'not appreciate how to minimize the pain suffered by the victim' and in fact, owing to inexperience, inflict more pain.[171] In the light hereof, requiring them to act in a reasonable and necessary manner makes very little sense. In the words of Lord Diplock (though in relation to a defence of provocation), 'to require old heads on young shoulders is inconsistent with the law's compassion of human infirmity'.[172]

In their formative years, which are crucial for laying down the foundations for judgement and awareness of morally acceptable norms,[173] child soldiers might have received little to no ethical/moral education. The 'steady hand of adult guidance and protection' that is so 'crucial in children's process of becoming human as they emerge from the state of incomplete personhood'[174] is basically absent. Amidst the armed conflict where disorder and violence are commonplace, where gratuitous acts and arbitrariness are the norm, children become accustomed to violence[175] and can lose touch with any concepts of morality.[176] It is widely recognised that the period of adolescence is a stressful period of transition between childhood and adulthood and that exposure to war disrupts such a transition.[177] Once they are in the armed group, they 'may mature rapidly in such an environment [but] they do so without moral and ethical guidance'.[178] Their entire environment is geared towards acting in a way that is totally devoid of moral values and may turn them into merciless killers,[179] 'a horde of insensate killers' as Faulkner calls them.[180] As a consequence it is argued that '[children's] ability to [...] exercise independent judgment to decide an appropriate course of action is fundamentally distorted by the circumstances of their involvement',[181] and so it seems inappropriate for the law to require child soldiers to act in a necessary and reasonable manner.

Empirical research, however, vehemently rejects such a damning picture of child soldiers doomed in an immoral maze created by armed groups. Psychologists, in particular, challenge this portrayal of child soldiers as 'pathological or irredeemable killers'.[182] Despite having been confronted with adverse conditions, children have developed and displayed prescriptive and generalisable moral concepts.[183] Further research unearths that children do display a sense of culpability after the armed conflict, thus indicating that some core values have remained,[184] but, owing to the circumstances prevailing at the time, prefer not to exhibit and/or apply them. Baines makes the point that sometimes children choose to lose their moral sensibilities or opt to suppress them for the sake of survival[185] or 'to gain a sense of power and control over their lives'.[186]

Even if a child knows that he/she needs to act in a way that is necessary and reasonable, the problem is that it is his/her skewed understanding of these concepts at the time of the commission of the crime that he/she will apply. This understanding fluctuates over time and is dependent on a variety of internal and external factors. Firstly, a child soldier's mental development is continuous. As Haer and Böhmelt point out, 'due to the fact that they are young, the effect of these events on children's psyches is magnified as they occur during a period when personalities are being formed and in which the brain and its functions are still in development.'[187] According to the cognitive theory prolonged exposure to such a situation will have an impact on a child's brain and central nervous system, thereby impacting on his ability to regulate his or her emotions and impulses.[188] Secondly, a child's maturity depends strongly on his/her surroundings,[189] as exposed by the social-ecological theory on human development which argues that a person's development is shaped by a variety of internal and external factors and processes.[190] This is especially true, for example, when a child is confronted with the realities of war and conflicting demands. As X in *Prosecutor v. X* explained: 'Because at that time the situation was very scared [sic] and we were ordered by Gabriel Kolo as our chefe [sic] of the village as [sic] acting also as a commander of the milisia Sakunar and I am [sic] young and afraid I didn't have a plan to kill him.'[191] The predominant view is that social factors, such as war, poverty, lack of education and various other factors, are some of the main determinative elements that cause child soldiers to commit atrocities.[192] Thirdly, many children are affected by an array of psychological disorders, such as high prevalence rates of symptoms of post-traumatic stress disorder, depression and anxiety and externalising problems.[193] Some of these symptoms are linked (directly or indirectly) to war exposure generally[194] whilst others relate to their own personal experienced life (e.g., killing an individual, being sexually assaulted)[195] or a combination thereof.[196] Undoubtedly, such disorders affect the ability of child soldiers to act rationally.[197] All this appears to negate the child's ability to know whether his/her action was necessary and reasonable even though he/she might be aware that it is morally wrong to commit a crime.[198] As Olusanya suggests with regard to adults, the notion of reasonableness should be understood in the context in which the crimes were committed: what was a 'reasonable' Hutu during the genocide, what was a 'reasonable' Serb during the conflict in the former Yugoslavia?[199] Simply put, what is a 'reasonable' child soldier in conflict-ridden Uganda, Sierra Leone, Liberia and so on?

What is more, the harm sought must be limited to what is necessary and the reaction of the person must not cause greater harm than that which he/she tried to avoid.[200] This requirement can be viewed as a stricter proportionality test: 'the actor causes a harm which is not merely reasonably proportional to, but actually less than the harm or evil threatened.'[201] In other words, 'the crime committed under duress must be, on balance, the lesser of two evils.'[202] The paradigmatic case (though of necessity) of *Dudley and Stephens* comes to mind—the lives of three individuals were saved by the killing of one.[203] Article 31(1)(d) of the ICC Statute however does not oblige the individual to choose the lesser of two evils, for it specifies 'provided that the person does not intend to cause a greater harm than the one sought to be avoided'. It means that it could be an 'equal' harm.[204] As Weigend illustrates, the test 'limits the scope of the defence to situations in which the actor takes a life to save a life (or several lives), or strikes out an eye in order to save one'.[205] The jurisprudence of the military tribunals set up to deal with crimes committed by Germans during WWII actually discloses that attention was paid to whether the harm threatened and the harm meted out were similar in terms of gravity.[206] The ICC could thus rely on these decisions to dismiss the lesser evil doctrine that is classic of justification defences.

Whilst the aforementioned 'necessary and proportional measures' test can be viewed as an objective requirement of balancing interests, the 'greater harm' test is deemed to be subjective by certain scholars[207] (some refer to it as the *dolus*)[208] as it takes into account the perpetrator's perception of the situation, and is characteristic of justification defences.[209] In essence, such a decision is a moral choice that is justified.[210] As explained earlier, striking such a balance could be too demanding to fulfil for child soldiers who grew up without a moral compass: they are unlikely to be able to do so correctly as children's 'ability to determine right from wrong [...] is fundamentally distorted by the circumstances of their involvement'.[211] Even if one espouses the approach that children are not completely sucked into a bleak moral vacuum, they might take a practical decision (which they know is wrong) adapted to the situation.[212] Thus, even those who are able to distinguish right from wrong might not make the *right* choice in the particular situation.

An additional challenge, as Ambos stresses, is that 'the underlying rationale of duress is not the balancing of competing legal interests but the criterion of *Zumutbarkeit* (could it fairly be expected that the person concerned resisted the threat?)'.[213] As a matter of fact, although the defence of duress is a justification and hence technically focussed on the act, it is based on the notion of the 'reasonable man'.[214] The greater harm threshold is truly linked to the actor and not the act.

To make matters worse, under such a conception, 'it might be proper for society to demand that the agent resist the threat even if this requires sacrificing her own life'.[215] Such a position was approved by the ICTY in *Erdemović* in as much as it ensconced a moral absolute in relation to the behaviour of individuals claiming duress.[216] This conception of duress in Anglo-American law has already been severely criticised in relation to adults for being unrealistic in its application and, more crucially, for failing to appreciate basic human instinct,[217] and the right of self-preservation that is recognised in liberal societies.[218] To require a child to behave like an adult who is also unlikely to resist certain threats is unwarranted. As Singer rightly notes, 'regardless of their crimes, those under eighteen are different from adults on a wide range of emotional, physical, social, political, and legal levels.'[219]

It is acknowledged that a court should diligently evaluate each situation on a case-by-case basis and ascertain whether the child soldier was at the time of the commission of the crime able to distinguish right from wrong, and make a rational decision. Yet, overall, it is highly unlikely that a child soldier will meet the dual requirements to act in a reasonable and necessary manner, as well as to weigh the harm which would result from not obeying the order as opposed to obeying the order.

6 Conclusion

The claim that, generally, child soldiers, if prosecuted for international crimes, can successfully avail themselves of the defence of duress is to some extent misguided. The application of the requirements of the duress plea to the situation of child soldiers in this chapter lays bare the limited possibilities for child soldiers to use the defence successfully. Highlighting children's agency, resilience and coping mechanisms shatter the hope that they can be considered as individuals acting under duress. This is partially due to the fact that duress is considered a justification and, hence, stringent conditions that focus more on the act than on the actor are attached to it. The act to be lawful requires a mature, well-levelled, almost heroic, actor. Even a nuanced approach to the predicament of child soldiers, viewed as much as victims as perpetrators, and an improved perception of children as tactical agents with constrained choices, perhaps lost in a moral maze, do not support the articulation of a supportable defence of duress. The specific situation of children, caught between the figure of the innocent victim and that of the monstrous perpetrator, does not fit the defence of duress.

In this light, it might be argued that a separate, special standard has to be applied to children, as children should not be regarded as little adults.[220] In other words the defence of duress should be of a different standard. Whilst Article 40 UNCRC recognises the special needs and circumstances of children facing justice, it does neither encourage nor oblige states to create a new set of defences for children or to interpret defences in a different manner. Even General Comment No. 10 on Children's Rights in Juvenile Justice makes no reference to defences at all.[221] That being said, the spirit of the Convention combined with Article 3 on the best interests of the child would warrant a child-friendly application of the defences. So far such an approach has not been adopted which means that overall, the current state of the law and its application do not augur well for children taking part in hostilities and facing prosecution. They are deemed culpable of international crimes.

Notes

1. Werle and Jessberger 2014, 240. See also Cassese et al. 2013, 218; Bassiouni 2013, 445.
2. See generally Ambos 2013, 348–356; Bassiouni 2013, 445.

3. See discussion of the importance of victims in Triffterer, Bergsmo and Ambos 2016, 7. See also Schabas 2016, 42–43; Kochhar and Hieramente 2016, 229–230.
4. Greenawalt 2011, 1111.
5. See ICC Statute 1998, Preamble.
6. See, for example, Schabas 2016, 637; Cryer et al. 2014, 398.
7. ICC *Ongwen* 2016c. See also Schabas 2016, 636–637.
8. ICC *Ongwen* 2016a.
9. For a discussion on the distinction between duress and necessity, see ICTY *Erdemović* 1997a, para. 14. See Eser 2016, 1149–1150.
10. It should be noted that whilst the requirements can be neatly spelled out in terms of the law their application is often intertwined and so factual elements used to understand the application of one requirement might be also pertinent for another requirement.
11. See discussion in Abebe and Bessell 2011, 767. This is also referred to as the biomedical model of childhood. Hinton 2008, 288–289; Derluyn et al. 2015, 30.
12. See Eser 2016, 1152; Ambos 2013, 359.
13. See Ambos 2013, 366.
14. UNCRC 1989, Art. 3.1 provides that '[i]n all actions concerning children, whether undertaken by public or private social welfare institutions, courts of law, administrative authorities or legislative bodies, the best interests of the child shall be a primary consideration.'
15. See Steinl 2017, 251–252. Stahn notes that '[i]nternational justice is underdeveloped in this regard. It lacks special measures for juvenile justice and sentencing.' Stahn 2019, 317.
16. See, for example, Dinstein 2000, 373–374; Ambos 2013, 357; Schabas 2016, 646; Werle and Jessberger 2014, 241.
17. Bassiouni 2013, 440; Cryer et al. 2014, 407; Ambos 2013, 357. The threat cannot merely exist in the perpetrator's mind but it must be objectively present. See Eser 2016, 1151.
18. '[I]f the job was not done to the satisfaction of the Germans, the consequences would have been no more severe than being put out of the job and resuming the life of an ordinary inmate.' *Enigster Yehezkel Ben Alish*, as cited in Bazyler and Tuerkheimer 2014, 213.
19. Anonymous 1956, 769–770.
20. 'Auch eine langandauernde Freiheitsentziehung kann aber eine ernste Beeinträchtigung der Gesundheit zur Folge haben und deswegen als Leibesgefahr angesehen werden.' Germany *Gestapo Informer* 1949, 201.
21. See Werle and Jessberger 2014, 241; Ambos 2013, 357. US courts martials for Prisoners of War (POWs) returning from the Korean war often

dismissed duress as a defence, despite the considerable ill-treatment suffered by the POWs. See Anonymous 1956.

22. Lafayette 2012–2013, 313. See Singer 2005, 71–72.
23. Young 2007, 20; Graf 2012, 952; Amone-P'Olak and Ovuga 2017, 18; Drumbl 2012, 80.
24. Veale 2006, 97; Happold 2005, 17; Singer 2005, 113.
25. Happold 2005, 17. See Singer 2005, 72–73.
26. Singer 2005, 113. See Ben-Ari 2009, 4; Wainryb 2011, 283.
27. Wessells notes that '[w]ar creates long-lasting wounds, both visible and invisible. Most conspicuous are the physical wounds. Less visible are the hidden wounds of the mind, heart, and soul.' See Wessells 2006, 126.
28. Trenholm et al. 2012, 220.
29. See Wessells 2006, 79; Fonseka 2001, 71; Nortje 2017, 191; Maclure and Denov 2006, 124; Grant 2016, 10–11; Almohammad 2018, 19.
30. Branch 2017, 42.
31. Maclure and Denov 2006, 126.
32. UNSG 2000, para. 32. See Maclure and Denov 2006, 129.
33. Yarbrough 2014, 534. See Twum-Danso 2003, 29 and 41; ICC *Ongwen* 2016c, paras 36–57.
34. Faulkner 2001, 499; Honwana 2000, 65.
35. Akakpo 2012, 39; Grant 2016, 9.
36. Happold 2005, 158. See Dinstein 2000, 373.
37. Cryer et al. 2014, 408. Ambos refers to a threat in terms of Article 31(1)(d) as a 'broader danger'. See Ambos 2013, 357.
38. Cryer et al. 2014, 408.
39. Ambos 2013, 357.
40. Eser 2016, 1149–1150; Ambos 2013, 357.
41. Bassiouni 2013, 440; Ambos 2013, 358.
42. US *Krupp et al.* 1948, 1438. See generally Bassiouni 2013, 440; Ambos 2013, 349 and 357; Dinstein 2000, 374.
43. See generally Werle and Jessberger 2014, 236–238 and 239; Ambos 2013, 356 and 359; Cryer et al. 2014, 404 and 408.
44. Smith 1982, 1197.
45. Dressler 1988–1989, 1340. See US *Krupp et al.* 1948, 1439; US *Einsatzgruppen* 1948, 480; Bassiouni 2013, 440; Yeo 2004, 355.
46. Yeo 2004, 362.
47. US *Einsatzgruppen* 1948, 480; Cassese et al. 2011, 473.
48. US *Einsatzgruppen* 1948, 411.
49. US *Einsatzgruppen* 1948, 483–484.
50. US *Einsatzgruppen* 1948, 468–469.
51. ICC *Katanga and Chui* 2008, para. 518.

52. ICC *Ongwen* 2016b, paras 25 and 35; ICC *Katanga* 2014, para. 1026. See Happold 2006, 70; Singh 2007, 233.
53. Freeland 2005, 304. Singer states that '[c]ombined with liberal amounts of terror and propaganda, impressionable children can rapidly begin to identify with causes they barely understand.' See Singer 2005, 72.
54. Murphy 2003, 70. See Huyghebaert 2009, 68. Wessells note that '[m]any children living in abusive situations see an armed group as providing a better "family" than the one they are living with.' Wessells 2006, 48.
55. ICC *Katanga and Chui* 2008, para. 518.
56. ICC *Lubanga* 2012, paras 883–889.
57. Trenholm et al. 2012, 212.
58. Derluyn et al. 2004, 861; Klasen et al. 2010, 576; Klasen et al. 2015, 184; Amone-P'Olak and Ovuga 2017, 18; Happold 2005, 10–11; Amone-P'Olak et al. 2015, 156; Almohammad 2018, 22. Siegrist notes that '[m]odern warfare has exposed children to the worst possible violence and abuse.' Siegrist 2006, 53.
59. As cited in Pangalangan 2018, 617–618. See Singer 2005, 88.
60. As cited in ICC *Ongwen* 2016b, para. 25.
61. Grant 2016, 8. Singer furthermore notes that '[t]he very process of recruitment and indoctrination are designed to bind the children to the group and, if this is not successful, prevent escape.' Singer 2005, 88.
62. Werle and Jessberger 2014, 241; Souris 2017, 330; Bantekas and Nash 2007, 64.
63. Maystre 2014, 992.
64. Bond and Fougere 2014, 491–500. Akakpo uses the French concept of 'états généraux de contrainte'. Akakpo 2012, 40.
65. Bond and Fougere 2014, 493.
66. ECCC *Duch* 2010, para. 555. See Cryer et al. 2014, 408.
67. Werle and Jessberger 2014, 241.
68. ICTY *Mrđa* 2004, para. 66 (emphasis added).
69. See Olusanya 2010, 54–55 (and accompanying footnotes) and 63.
70. Cassese et al. 2013, 215.
71. Cryer et al. 2014, 406.
72. Nemitz 2009, 972.
73. See Yeo 2004, 356 and 365.
74. Bond and Fougere 2014, 500 and discussion at 507–510.
75. ICC *Ongwen* 2016a, para. 153.
76. ICC *Ongwen* 2016a, para. 153.
77. Stahn 2019, 155.
78. Werle and Jessberger 2014, 243; Ambos 2013, 360; Tadros 2011, 223; US *Krupp et al.* 1948, 1443–1444. The person exposed to the threat can either be the perpetrator or someone else. This broad approach also

allows for the protection of third persons, while no special relationship is required between the perpetrator and the other person who is being threatened. Eser 2016, 1152.

79. Scaliotti 2001, 156; Ambos 2013, 360.
80. Krebs 2013, 407.
81. Scaliotti 2001, 156; Ambos 2013, 359-360; Eser 2016, 1154.
82. ICTY *Mrđa* 2004, para. 66.
83. Olusanya 2010, 56. See generally Alexander and Kessler Ferzan 2011, 264.
84. Eser 2016, 1152. See Yeo 1990, 44–45.
85. US *Krupp et al.* 1948, 1439; US *Flick et al.* 1947, 8. See Dinstein 1985, 234.
86. US *Einsatzgruppen* 1948, 482.
87. *Public Prosecutor v. Joni Marques & Ors* (*Lospalos* Case), as cited in Linton and Reiger 2001, 191.
88. US *Einsatzgruppen* 1948, 482.
89. Eser 2016, 1152. See Cassese et al. 2013, 215.
90. ECCC *Duch* 2010, para. 555.
91. Nylund states that: 'A consideration is required around whether children can really be tried against the standard of "know or should have known" about the criminal impact of activities that they were involved in when they are not yet able to fully form their knowledge.' Nylund 2016, 204.
92. Grover 2005, 233. Happold posits that child soldiers 'may develop a dependency relationship with their commanders and become inured to killing'. Happold 2005, 17.
93. Custer 2005, 470; Wessells 2006, 57; Happold 2005, 31; Fisher 2013, 73.
94. Fagan cited in Dore 2007–2008, fn 142; McDiarmid 2016, 332.
95. Dore 2007–2008, 1309 (emphasis added). See Lafayette 2012–2013, 318–319; Happold 2005, 14.
96. Achton Thomas 2013, 9.
97. Smeulers however argues that even adults struggle to make the right decisions. She explains that 'the environment in which perpetrators of international crimes operate seems to approve the crimes, and that is a decisive factor which turns many more people, even otherwise law-abiding people, into perpetrators.' Smeulers 2008, 980.
98. See Chapleau as cited in Akakpo 2012, 39.
99. Smeulers 2008, 974 and 978–981.
100. Smeulers 2008, 976. See Fisher 2013, 77.
101. Drumbl 2012, 80.
102. Haer and Böhmelt 2016, 412. See ICC *Ongwen* 2016b, para. 25; Trenholm et al. 2012, 220.

103. McKay 2005, 388.
104. Weierstall et al. 2012; Klasen et al. 2010, 579–580.
105. Manirakiza 2008–2009, 754; Grover 2005, 231 in relation to Rwanda.
106. See discussion on adults in Smeulers 2008, 977.
107. Posada and Wainryb 2008, 883 and 894.
108. McDiarmid 2016, 331; Fisher 2013, 68.
109. See discussion in Amone-P'Olak et al. 2007, 657; Trenholm et al. 2012, 314.
110. *See* Expert Group 2006, 3.
111. Baines 2009, 174. See Amone-P'Olak and Ovuga 2017, 18.
112. Maclure and Denov 2006, 128.
113. Souris 2017, 324.
114. Honwana 2005, 49. De Certeau defines a tactic as 'a calculated action determined by the absence of a proper locus'. See de Certeau 1984, 37.
115. Schmidt 2007, 60.
116. Fisher 2013, 65.
117. Fisher 2013, 68.
118. Honwana 2005, 48.
119. Honwana 2005, 48.
120. Baines and Boniface 2008, 10; Manirakiza 2008–2009, 737–738.
121. Twum-Danso 2003, 41; Baines and Boniface 2008, 6. Generally Hinton explains that 'children can manage hazards and misfortune, and influence their own fate and that of those around them'. Hinton 2008, 295.
122. See Nortje 2017, 187; Branch 2017, 28.
123. See generally Seelinger 2017; Bradfield 2017.
124. Maclure and Denov 2006, 121 and 129.
125. See, for example, Singer 2005, 72.
126. Souris 2017, 320.
127. Drumbl 2012, 88.
128. ICC *Ongwen* 2016b, para. 25.
129. Boothby and Thomson 2013, 743. Some child soldiers also normalise violence partly because they have no other option but to fight. See Brett and Specht 2004, 41.
130. See UNSG 1996, para. 48. See Amone-P'Olak and Ovuga 2017, 18.
131. Baines 2009, 166; Dickson-Gomez 2002, 350; Almohammad 2018, 5–6.
132. Maclure and Denov 2006, 125.
133. Almohammad 2018, 12.
134. Maxted 2003, 68. More generally, see Almohammad 2018, 6.
135. Amone-P'Olak and Ovuga 2017, 18.
136. Trenholm et al. 2012, 212.
137. Amone-P'Olak et al. 2007, 656–657.

138. ICC *Ongwen* 2016c, para. 4. See Drumbl 2016, 241-242; Pangalangan 2018, 628.
139. Pangalangan 2018, 629.
140. Branch 2017, 40–41.
141. ICC *Ongwen* 2016a, para. 154.
142. See discussion in Huyghebaert 2009, 67–68.
143. Vigh 2008, 11.
144. Branch 2017, 41.
145. Honwana 2000, 75–76.
146. Schmidt 2007, 60.
147. Honwana 2000, 75–76. See Quénivet 2013, 1106; Fisher 2013, 73 and 81. In peacetime it is argued that juveniles make decisions based on the 'best and immediate interests rather than an abstract code of norms that exists only outside the immediate context'. Fagan cited in Dore 2007–2008, fn 142.
148. See Baines 2009, 182; Drumbl 2012, 91.
149. Branch 2017, 41.
150. See Macdonald and Porter 2016.
151. Achton Thomas 2013, 9.
152. Brett and Specht 2004, 31.
153. McDiarmid 2016, 331.
154. Wessells 2006, 142.
155. Grant 2016, 12; Eser 2016, 1153. See also Ambos 2013, 359; Cryer et al. 2014, 408–409; Knoops 2003, 71; Krebs 2013, 408.
156. Werle and Jessberger 2014, 241; Eser 2016, 1153; Ambos 2013, 359. 'The test is similar, but not necessarily identical, to that of proportionality in self-defence.' Cryer et al. 2014, 408. See US *Krupp et al.* 1948, 1443, 1445 and 1446.
157. Robinson 1982, 219; Colvin 1990, 388; Joyce 2015, 639.
158. Colvin 1990, 399; Cassese et al. 2011, 479. See ICTY *Erdemović* 1997b, para. 82.
159. See Ambos 2013, 359; Cryer et al. 2014, 408; Eser 2016, 1153.
160. Ambos 2013, 359; Cryer et al. 2014, 408;
161. See Krebs 2013, 408–409.
162. UK *Howe* 1987, Lord Hailsham of St. Marylebone.
163. See Berman 2003, 65; Fletcher 2000, 831; Byrd 1987, 1308.
164. ICC *Ongwen* 2016a, para. 155. See discussion on whether Ongwen was reasonable in Grant 2016, 15.
165. Sadly, military life often presents the child soldier with the only hope of building a future due to a lack of education, exacerbated by war. See Wessells 2006, 49–50.
166. Achton Thomas 2013, 13.

167. McDiarmid 2016, 333. See Steinl 2017, 253; Cohn and Goodwin-Gill 1994, 7.
168. Dore 2007–2008, 1304 and 1309.
169. Fagan cited in Dore 2007–2008, fn 142.
170. Grossman 2007, 347.
171. Grover 2005, 233. See Steinl 2017, 253.
172. UK *Camplin* 1978, 717. See Singer 2005, 154.
173. Dore 2007–2008, 1304. See Singer 2005, 109.
174. Park 2014, 49.
175. Boyden 2003, 351; Boothby and Thomson 2013, 741. For a comprehensive discussion of the effects of violence on children, generally see Weaver et al. 2008, 96–112.
176. Coalition to Stop the Use of Child Soldiers 2001, 7; Dutli 1990, 421.
177. Amone-P'Olak et al. 2007, 656; Wainryb 2011, 283.
178. Souris 2017, 323. In relation to girl child soldiers, see Quénivet and Shah-Davis 2008, 122.
179. Quénivet 2014, 73.
180. Faulkner 2001, 499. For a critique of this stylised presentation of child soldiers, see Drumbl 2012, 89.
181. Custer 2005, 470. See generally Cohn and Goodwin-Gill 1994, 30–31; Trenholm et al. 2012, 220.
182. See discussion in Wainryb 2011, 275.
183. Posada and Wainryb 2008, 893–894.
184. See Boyden 2003, 354.
185. See Maclure and Denov 2006, 126.
186. Baines 2009, 178.
187. Haer and Böhmelt 2016, 413.
188. Wainryb 2011, 283.
189. Triffterer and Clark 2016, 1034; Eccles 1999, 31 and 33–34.
190. See Betancourt 2011, 308–309.
191. East Timor Tribunal *X* 2002, para. 59.
192. See Wessells 2006, 46–47; Singer 2005, 71; Murphy 2003, 62.
193. Derluyn et al. 2015, 33.
194. See Okello et al. 2013, 718–720; Amone-P'Olak et al. 2014, 425; Amone-P'Olak et al. 2007, 665.
195. Klasen et al. 2010, 576.
196. Amone-P'Olak et al. 2015, 163.
197. Happold 2005, 18.
198. See discussion in Posada and Wainryb 2008, 893–896 in relation to children asked about theft and acts of revenge.
199. Olusanya 2010, 72. More fundamentally, Mohamed explains '[a]cknowledging their humanity might be alarming; it forces us to reckon with the

idea that, if they are capable of committing these horrors, then perhaps we all might be able to do the same. At the same time, acknowledging the ordinary humanity of perpetrators is productive, because it forces us to examine the choices they made, and the paths that led them to commit their crimes.' Mohamed 2015, 1165.

200. ICC Statute, Art. 31(1)(d); Ambos 2013, 359; Dinstein 2000, 374.
201. Robinson 1982, 219. See US *Krupp et al.* 1948, 1446 that refers to 'a worse plight'. See Eser 2016, 1154.
202. ICTY *Erdemović* 1997a, para. 16. See Eser 2016, 1154.
203. UK *Dudley* 1884. See Bassiouni 2013, 442–443; Cryer et al. 2014, 408; Fletcher 2000, 823–825.
204. Joyce 2015, 640; Stahn 2019, 154.
205. Weigend 2012, 1224. See ICTY *Erdemović* 1997b, para. 81; Cassese et al. 2011, 478.
206. See Joyce 2015, 627.
207. Stahn 2019, 154.
208. Ambos 1999, 27.
209. Werle and Jessberger 2014, 243; Knoops 2008, 59–60. See also Ambos 2006–2007, 660; Weigend 2012, 1224; Heim 2013, 168.
210. Risacher 2013–2014, 1417; Dinstein 2000, 373.
211. Custer 2005, 470; Reis 1997, 752.
212. Posada and Wainryb 2008, 893–896.
213. Ambos 2002, 1037. See Eser 2016, 1154–1155; Fletcher 2007, 322.
214. Arenson 2014, 70. See Ambos 2013, 347 and 359.
215. Chiesa 2008, 757.
216. ICTY *Erdemović* 1997b, para. 80.
217. Arenson 2014, 78.
218. See Fichtelberg 2008, 24.
219. Singer 2005, 154; Happold 2005, 32; Cohn and Goodwin-Gill 1994, 23.
220. Singer 2005, 154. See McDiarmid 2006, 85–86.
221. United Nations Committee on the Rights of the Child 2007.

References

Abebe, T. and S. Bessell, 2011, 'Dominant Discourses, Debates and Silences on Child Labour in Africa and Asia', 32 *T.W.Q.* 765–786.

Achton Thomas, M., 2013, 'Malice Supplies the Age? Assessing the Culpability of Adolescent Soldiers', 44 *Cal.W.Int'l L.J.* 1–38.

Akakpo, L., 2012, '*Procureur c. X: les enseignements à tirer de la poursuite des enfants soldats pour crimes contre l'humanité*', 42 *R.G.D.* 9–56.

Alexander, L. and K. Kessler Ferzan, 2011, 'Beyond the Special Part', in Duff, R.A. and S.P. Green (eds), *Philosophical Foundations of Criminal Law* (OUP) 253–278.

Almohammad, A., 2018, *ISIS Child Soldiers in Syria: The Structural and Predatory Recruitment, Enlistment, Pre-training Indoctrination, Training, and Deployment*, International Centre for Counter-Terrorism, Research Paper, February 2018.

Ambos, K., 1999, 'General Principles of Criminal Law in the Rome Statute', 10 *Crim.L.F.* 1–32.

Ambos, K., 2002, 'Other Grounds for Excluding Criminal Responsibility', in Cassese, A., et al., *The Rome Statute of the International Criminal Court: A Commentary (Vol. I)* (OUP) 1003–1048.

Ambos, K., 2006–2007, 'Toward a Universal System of Crime: Comments on George Fletcher's *Grammar of Criminal Law*', 28 *Cardozo L.Rev.* 2647–2673.

Ambos, K., 2013, *Treatise on International Criminal Law: Volume I: Foundations and General Part* (OUP).

Amone-P'Olak, K. and E. Ovuga, 2017, 'The Influence of Types of War Experiences on Conduct Problems in War-Affected Youth in Northern Ugandan: Findings from the WAYS Study', 251 *Psychiatry Res.* 14–19.

Amone-P'Olak, K., et al., 2007, 'Adolescents Caught between Fires: Cognitive Emotion Regulation in Response to War Experiences in Northern Uganda', 30 *J.Adolesc.* 655–669.

Amone-P'Olak, K., et al., 2014, 'Postwar Environment and Long-Term Mental Health Problems in Former Child Soldiers in Northern Uganda: The WAYS Study', 68 *J.Epidemiol. Community Health* 425–430.

Amone-P'Olak, K., et al., 2015, 'War Experiences and Psychotic Symptoms among Former Child Soldiers in Northern Uganda: The Mediating Role of Post-War Hardships—The WAYS Study', 45 *S.Afr.J.Psychol.* 155–167.

Anonymous, 1956, 'Misconduct in the Prison Camp: A Survey of the Law and an Analysis of the Korean Cases', 56 *Colum.L.Rev.* 709–794.

Arenson, K.J., 2014, 'The Paradox of Disallowing Duress as a Defence to Murder', 78 *J.C.L.* 65–79.

Baines, E., 2009, 'Complex Political Perpetrators: Reflections on Dominic Ongwen', 47 *J.Mod.Afr.Stud.* 163–191.

Baines, E. and O. Boniface, 2008, 'Complicating Victims and Perpetrators in Uganda: On Dominic Ongwen', 7 *Justice and Reconciliation Project Field Note* (July) 1–19.

Bantekas, I. and S. Nash, 2007, *International Criminal Law* (3rd edn., Routledge).

Bassiouni, M.C., 2013, *Introduction to International Criminal Law* (2nd edn., Martinus Nijhoff).

Bazyler, M.J. and F.M. Tuerkheimer, 2014, *Forgotten Trials of the Holocaust* (NYUP).

Ben-Ari, E.A., 2009, 'Facing Child Soldiers, Moral Issues, and "Real Soldiering": Anthropological Perspectives on Professional Armed Forces', 37 *South African Journal of Military Studies* 1–59.

Berman, M.N., 2003, 'Justification and Excuse, Law and Morality', 53 *Duke L.J.* 1–77.

Betancourt, T.S., 2011, 'Developmental Perspectives on Moral Agency in Former Child Soldiers. Commentary on Wainryb', 54 *Human Development* 307–312.

Bond, J., and M. Fougere, 2014, 'Omnipresent Threats: A Comment on the Defence of Duress in International Criminal Law', 14 *Int.C.L.R.* 471–512.

Boothby, N. and B. Thomson, 2013, 'Long-Term Impacts of Involvement in Child Soldiering. Child Soldiers as Adults: The Mozambique Case Study', 22 *J.Aggress.Maltreat. Trauma* 735–756.

Boyden, B., 2003, 'The Moral Development of Child Soldiers: What Do Adults Have to Fear?', 9 *Peace Confl.* 343–362.

Bradfield, P., 2017, 'Reshaping Amnesty in Uganda: The Case of Thomas Kwoyelo', 15 *J.I.C.J.* 827–855.

Branch, A., 2017, 'Dominic Ongwen on Trial: The ICC's African Dilemmas', 11 *I.J.T.J.* 30–49.

Brett, R. and I. Specht, 2004, *Young Soldiers: Why They Choose to Fight* (Lynne Rienner).

Byrd, B.S., 1987, 'Wrongdoing and Attribution: Implications beyond the Justification-Excuse Distinction', 33 *Wayne L.Rev.* 1289–1342.

Cassese, A., et al., 2011, *International Criminal Law: Cases and Commentary* (OUP).

Cassese, A., et al., 2013, *Cassese's International Criminal Law* (3rd edn, OUP).

Chiesa, L.E., 2008, 'Duress, Demanding Heroism and Proportionality', 41 *Vand.J.Transnat'l L.* 714–773.

Coalition to Stop the Use of Child Soldiers, 2001, *Sexual Exploitation of Child Soldiers: An Exploration and Analysis of Global Dimensions and Trends.*

Cohn, I. and G.S. Goodwin-Gill, 1994, *Child Soldiers: The Role of Children in Armed Conflicts* (OUP).

Colvin, E., 1990, 'Exculpatory Defences in Criminal Law', 10 *O.J.L.S.* 381–407.

Cryer, C., et al., 2014, *An Introduction to International Criminal Law and Procedure* (3rd edn, CUP).

Custer, M., 2005, 'Punishing Child Soldiers: The Special Court for Sierra Leone and the Lessons to be Learned from the United States' Juvenile Justice System', 19 *Temp.Int'l & Comp.L.J.* 449–476.

de Certeau, M., 1984, *The Practice of Everyday Life* (UCP).

Derluyn, I., et al., 2004, 'Post-Traumatic Stress in Former Ugandan Child Soldiers', 363 *The Lancet* 861–863.

Derluyn, I., et al., 2015, 'Victims and/or Perpetrators? Towards an Interdisciplinary Dialogue on Child Soldiers', 15 *BMC Int. Health Hum. Rights* 28–40.

Dickson-Gomez, J., 2002, 'Growing up in Guerrilla Camps: The Long-Term Impact of Being a Child Soldier in El Salvador's Civil War', 30 *Ethos* 327–356.

Dinstein, Y., 1985, 'International Criminal Law', 20 *Isr.L.Rev.* 206–242.

Dinstein, Y., 2000, 'Defences', in McDonald, G.K. and O. Swaak-Goldman (eds), *Substantive and Procedural Aspects of International Criminal Law: The Experience of International and National Courts*, Volume I: Commentary (Kluwer) 371–388.

Dore, C.L., 2007–2008, 'What to Do with Omar Khadr? Putting a Child Soldier on Trial: Questions of International Law, Juvenile Justice, and Moral Culpability', 41 *J.Marshall L.Rev.J.* 1281–1320.

Dressler, J., 1988–1989, 'Exegesis of the Law of Duress: Justifying the Excuse and Searching for its Proper Limits', 62 *S.Cal.L.Rev.* 1331–1386.

Drumbl, M., 2012, *Reimagining Child Soldiers in International Law and Policy* (OUP).

Drumbl, M., 2016, 'Victims who Victimise', 4 *Lond.Rev.Int. Law* 217–246.

Dutli, M.T., 1990, 'Captured Child Combatants', 278 *I.R.R.C.* 421–434.

East Timor Tribunal *X*, 2002, *Prosecutor v. "X"*, East Timorese Public Administration, Dili District Court, Special Panel for Serious Crimes, Case No. 04/2002, 2 December 2002.

ECCC *Duch*, 2010, *Prosecutor v. Kaing Guek Eav* alias *Duch*, Extraordinary Chambers in the Courts of Cambodia, Judgment, Case No. 001/18-07-2007/ECCC/TC, 26 July 2010.

Eccles, J.C., 1999, 'The Development of Children Ages 6 to 14', 9 *The Future of Children* 30–44.

Eser, E., 2016, 'Article 31: Grounds for Excluding Criminal Responsibility', in Triffterer, O. and K. Ambos (eds), *The Rome Statute of the International Criminal Court: A Commentary* (3rd edn., Beck) 1125–1160.

Expert Group, 2006, Meeting of the United Nations Division for the Advancement of Women (DAW) in collaboration with UNICEF on the Elimination of All Forms of Discrimination and Violence Against the Girl Child, Florence, Italy, *The Girl Child and Armed Conflict: Recognizing and Addressing Grave Violations of Girls' Human Rights*, U.N. Doc. EGM/DVGC/2006/EP.12, 25–28 September 2006.

Faulkner, F., 2001, 'Kindergarten Killers: Morality, Murder and the Child Soldier Problem', 22 *T.W.Q.* 491–504.

Fichtelberg, A., 2008, 'Liberal Values in International Criminal Law: A Critique to *Erdemović*', 6 *J.I.C.J.* 3–19.

Fisher, K.J., 2013, *Transitional Justice for Child Soldiers. Accountability and Social Reconstruction in Post-Conflict Contexts* (Palgrave).

Fletcher, G.P., 2000, *Rethinking Criminal Law* (OUP).

Fletcher, G.P., 2007, *The Grammar of Criminal Law* (OUP).

Fonseka, F., 2001, 'The Protection of Child Soldiers in International Law', 2 *A.P.J.H.R.L.* 69–89.
Freeland, S., 2005, 'Child Soldiers and International Crimes—How Should International Law Be Applied?', 3 *N.Z.J.P.I.L.* 303–328.
Germany *Gestapo Informer*, 1949, *Gestapo Informer* Case, Oberlandsgericht Freiburg i. Br., Ss 64/48, Hoechstrichterliche Entscheidungen, Sammlung von Entscheidungen der Oberlandesgerichte und der Oberststen Gerichte in Strafsachen, Volume 2, 200–203, 17 February 1949.
Graf, R., 2012, 'The International Criminal Court and Child Soldiers: An Appraisal of the Lubanga Judgment', 10 *J.I.C.J.* 945–969.
Grant, N., 2016, *Duress as a Defence for Former Child Soldiers? Dominic Ongwen and the International Criminal Court*, International Crimes Database Brief 21, December 2016.
Greenawalt, A.K.A., 2011, 'The Pluralism of International Criminal Law', 86 *Ind.L.J.* 1063–1130.
Grossman, N., 2007, 'Rehabilitation or Revenge: Prosecuting Child Soldiers for Human Rights Violations', 38 *Geo.J.Int'l.L.* 323–362.
Grover, L., 2005, 'Trial of the Child Soldier: Protecting the Rights of the Accused', 65 *Z.a.ö.R.V.* 217–238.
Haer, R. and T. Böhmelt, 2016, 'Child Soldiers as Time Bombs? Adolescents' Participation in Rebel Groups and the Recurrence of Armed Conflict' 22 *Eur.J.Int.Relat.* 406–436.
Happold, M., 2005, *Child Soldiers in International Law* (MUP).
Happold, M., 2006, 'The Age of Criminal Responsibility for International Crimes under International Law', in Arts, K. and V. Popovski (eds), *International Criminal Accountability and the Rights of Children* (Asser Press) 69–84.
Heim, S.J., 2013, 'The Applicability of the Duress Defense to the Killing of Innocent Persons by Civilians', 46 *Cornell Int'l L.J.* 165–190.
Hinton, R., 2008, 'Children's Participation and Good Governance: Limitations of the Theoretical Literature', 16 *Int'l J. Child Rts* 285–300.
Honwana, A., 2000, 'Innocents et coupables: Les enfants-soldats comme acteurs tactiques', 80 *Politiques Africaines* 58–78.
Honwana, A., 2005, 'Innocent and Guilty: Child-Soldiers as Interstitial and Tactical Agents', in Honwana, A. and F. de Boeck (eds), *Makers and Breakers: Children & Youth in Postcolonial Africa* (James Currey) 31–52.
Huyghebaert, P., 2009, 'Les enfants dans les conflits armés: une analyse à l'aune des notions de vulnérabilité, de pauvreté et de "capabilités"', 2 *Mondes en développement* 59–72.
ICC *Katanga*, 2014, *Situation in the Democratic Republic of the Congo in the Case of the Prosecutor v. Katanga*, International Criminal Court, Judgment Pursuant to Article 74 of the Statute, Case No. ICC-01/04-01/07, 7 March 2014.

ICC *Katanga and Chui*, 2008, *Situation in the Democratic Republic of the Congo in the Case of The Prosecutor v. Katanga and Ngudjolo Chui*, International Criminal Court, Decision on the Confirmation of Charges, Case No. ICC-01/04-01/07, 30 September 2008.

ICC *Lubanga*, 2012, *Situation in the Democratic Republic of the Congo in the Case of the Prosecutor v. Lubanga Dyilo*, International Criminal Court, Judgment Pursuant to Article 74 of the Statute, Case No. ICC-01/04-01/06, 14 March 2012.

ICC *Ongwen*, 2016a, *Situation in Uganda in the Case of the Prosecutor v. Ongwen*, International Criminal Court, Decision on the Confirmation of Charges against Dominic Ongwen (Public Redacted), Case No. ICC-02/04-01/15, 23 March 2016.

ICC *Ongwen*, 2016b, *Situation in Uganda in the Case of the Prosecutor v. Ongwen*, International Criminal Court, Pre-Trial Brief on Behalf of Victims Represented by the Common Legal Representative, Case No. ICC-02/0-01/15, 6 September 2016.

ICC *Ongwen*, 2016c, *Situation in Uganda in the Case of the Prosecutor v. Ongwen*, International Criminal Court, Third Public Redacted Version of 'Defence Brief for the Confirmation of Charges Hearing', Filed on 18 January 2016 as ICC-02/04-01/15-404-Conf, Pre-Trial Chamber II, Case No. ICC-02/04-01/15, 25 May 2016.

ICC Statute, 1998, Statute of the International Criminal Court, U.N. Doc. A/CONF.183/9, (1998) 2187 UNTS 90.

ICTY *Erdemović*, 1997a, *Prosecutor v. Erdemović*, International Criminal Tribunal for the Former Yugoslavia, Judgment—Dissenting Opinion of Judge Cassese, Case No. IT-96-22-A, 7 October 1997.

ICTY *Erdemović*, 1997b, *Prosecutor v. Erdemović*, International Criminal Tribunal for the Former Yugoslavia, Judgment—Joint Separate Opinion of Judges McDonald and Vohrah, Case No. IT-96-22-A, 7 October 1997.

ICTY *Mrđa*, 2004, *Prosecutor v. Mrđa*, International Criminal Tribunal for the Former Yugoslavia, Judgment, Case No. IT-02-59-S, 31 March 2004.

Joyce, M., 2015, 'Duress: From Nuremberg to the International Criminal Court, Finding the Balance between Justification and Excuse', 28 *L.J.I.L.* 623–642.

Klasen, F., et al., 2010, 'Multiple Trauma and Mental Health in Former Ugandan Child Soldiers', 23 *J. Trauma. Stress* 573–581.

Klasen, F., et al., 2015, 'The Guiltless Guilty: Trauma-Related Guilt and Psychopathology in Former Ugandan Child Soldiers', 46 *Child Psychiatry Hum. Dev.* 180–193.

Knoops, G.A., 2003, *An Introduction to the Law of International Criminal Tribunals: A Comparative Study* (Transnational Publishers).

Knoops, G.A., 2008, *Defenses in Contemporary International Criminal Law* (Martinus Nijhoff).

Kochhar, S and M. Hieramente, 2016, 'Of Fallen Demons: Reflections on the International Criminal Court's Defendant', 29 *L.J.I.L.* 223–244.

Krebs, B., 2013, 'Justification and Excuse in Article 31(1) of the Rome Statute', 2 *C.J.I.C.L.* 382–410.

Lafayette E., 2012–2013, 'The Prosecution of Child Soldiers: Balancing Accountability with of Justice', 63 *Syracuse L.Rev.* 297–325.

Linton, S. and C. Reiger, 2001, 'The Evolving Jurisprudence and Practice of East Timor's Special Panels for Serious Crimes on Admissions of Guilt, Duress and Superior Orders', 4 *Y.I.H.L.* 167–212.

Macdonald, A. and H. Porter, 2016, 'The Trial of Thomas Kwoyelo: Opportunity or Spectre? Reflections from the Ground on the First LRA Prosecution', 86 *Africa* 698–722.

Maclure, R. and M. Denov, 2006, '"I Didn't Want to Die So I Joined Them": Structuration and the Process of Becoming Boy Soldiers in Sierra Leone', 18 *Terror. Political Violence* 119–135.

Manirakiza, P., 2008–2009, 'Les enfants face au système international de justice: à la recherche d'un modèle de justice pénale internationale pour les délinquants mineurs', 34 *Queen's L.J.* 719–768.

Maxted, J., 2003, 'Children and Armed Conflict in Africa', 9 *Social Issues* 51–72.

Maystre, M., 2014, 'The Interaction between International Refugee Law and International Criminal Law with Respect to Child Soldiers', 12 *J.I.C.J.* 975–996.

McDiarmid, C., 2006, 'What Do they Know? Child-Defendants and the Age of Criminal Responsibility: A National Perspective' in Arts, K. and V. Popovski (eds), *International Criminal Accountability and the Rights of Children* (Asser Press) 85–95.

McDiarmid, D., 2016, 'After the Age of Criminal Responsibility: A Defence for Children who Offend' 67 *N.I.L.Q.* 327–341.

McKay, S., 2005, 'Girls as "Weapons of Terror" in Northern Uganda and Sierra Leonean Rebel Fighting Forces', 28 *Stud.Confl.Terror.* 385–397.

Mohamed, S., 2015, 'Of Monsters and Men: Perpetrator Trauma and Mass Atrocity', 115 *Colum.L.Rev.* 1157–1216.

Murphy, W.P., 2003, 'Military Patrimonialism and Child Soldier Clientalism in the Liberian and Sierra Leonean Civil Wars', 46 *Afr.Stud.Rev.* 61–87.

Nemitz, J., 2009, 'Wetzling and Others', in Cassese, A. (ed), *Oxford Companion to International Criminal Justice* (OUP) 972–972.

Nortje, W., 2017, 'Victim or Villain: Exploring the Possible Bases of a Defence in the *Ongwen* Case at the International Criminal Court', 17 *Int.C.L.R.* 186–207.

Nylund, B.V., 2016, *Child Soldiers and Transitional Justice: Protecting the Rights of Children Involved in Armed Conflicts* (Intersentia).

Okello, J., et al., 2013, 'War-Related Trauma Exposure and Multiple Risk Behaviors among School-Going Adolescents in Northern Uganda: The Mediating Role of Depression Symptoms', 151 *J.Affect.Disord.* 715–721.

Olusanya, O., 2010, 'Excuse and Mitigation under International Criminal Law: Redrawing Conceptual Boundaries', 13 *New Crim.L.Rev.* 23–89.
Pangalangan, R.L.A., 2018, 'Dominic Ongwen and the Rotten Social Background Defense: The Criminal Culpability of Child Soldiers Turned War Criminals', 33 *Am.U.Int'l L.Rev.* 605–635.
Park, A.S.J., 2014, 'Constituting Omar Khadr: Cultural Racism, Childhood, and Citizenship', 8 *Int. Political Sociol.* 43–62.
Posada, R. and C. Wainryb, 2008, 'Moral Development in a Violent Society: Colombian Children's Judgments in the Context of Survival and Revenge', 79 *Child Development* 882–898.
Quénivet, N., 2013, 'The Liberal Discourse and the "New Wars" of/on Children', 38 *Brook.J.Int'l L.* 1053–1107.
Quénivet, N., 2014, 'Transitional and Generational Justice: Children Involved in Armed Conflict', in Szablewska, N. and S.-D. Bachmann (eds.), *Current Issues in Transitional Justice: Towards a More Holistic Approach* (Springer) 55–81.
Quénivet, N. and S. Shah-Davis, 2008, '"Girl Soldiers" and Armed Conflict in Africa', in Becker, M.S. and J.N. Schneider (eds), *Human Rights Issues in the 21st Century* (Nova Science Publishers) 103–132.
Reis, C., 1997, 'Trying the Future, Avenging the Past: The Implications of Prosecuting Children for Participation in Internal Armed Conflict', 28 *Colum. Hum.Rts.L.Rev.* 628–655.
Risacher, B.J., 2013–2014, 'No Excuse: The Failure of the ICC's Article 31 "Duress" Definition', 89 *Notre Dame L.Rev.* 1403–1426.
Robinson, P.H., 1982, 'Criminal Law Defenses: A Systematic Analysis', 82 *Colum.L.Rev.* 199–291.
Scaliotti, M., 2001, 'Defences before the International Criminal Court: Substantive Grounds for Excluding Criminal Responsibility—Part 1', 1 *Int.C.L.R.* 111–172.
Schabas, W.A., 2016, *The International Criminal Court: A Commentary on the Rome Statute* (2nd edn., OUP).
Schmidt, A., 2007, 'Volunteer Child Soldiers as Reality: A Development Issue for Africa', 2 *N.S.E.R.* 49–76.
Seelinger, K.T., 2017, 'Uganda's Case of Thomas Kwoyelo: Customary International Law on Trial', 8 *C.L.R.* 19–39.
Siegrist, S., 2006, 'Child Participation in International Criminal Accountability Mechanisms: The Case of the Sierra Leone Truth and Reconciliation Commission', in Arts, K. and V. Popovski (eds), *International Criminal Accountability and the Rights of Children* (Asser Press) 53–66.
Singer, P., 2005, *Children at War* (Pantheon Books).
Singh, D., 2007, 'When a Child is not a Child: The Scourge of Child Soldiering in Africa', 7 *A.H.R.L.J.* 206–224.
Smeulers, A., 2008, 'Punishing the Enemies of All Mankind', 21 *L.J.I.L.* 971–993.
Smith, J.C., 1982, 'Subjective or Objective—Ups and Downs of the Test of Criminal Liability in England', 27 *Vill.L.Rev.* 1179–1204.

Souris, R.N., 2017, 'Child Soldiering on Trial: An Interdisciplinary Analysis of Responsibility in the Lord's Resistance Army', 13 *Int.J.L.C.* 316–335.

Stahn, C., 2019, *A Critical Introduction to International Criminal Law* (CUP).

Steinl, L., 2017, *Child Soldiers as Agents of War and Peace: A Restorative Transitional Justice Approach to Accountability for Crimes under International Law* (Asser Press).

Tadros, V., 2011, 'Wrongdoing and Motivation', in Duff, R.A. and S.P. Green (eds.) *Philosophical Foundations of Criminal Law* (OUP) 206–227.

Trenholm, J., et al., 2012, 'Constructing Soldiers from Boys in Eastern Democratic Republic of Congo', 16 *Men and Masculinities* 203–227.

Triffterer, O. and R.S. Clark, 2016, 'Article 26: Exclusion of Jurisdiction over Persons under Eighteen', in Triffterer, O. and K. Ambos, *The Rome Statute of the International Criminal Court: A Commentary* (3rd edn., Beck) 1030–1036.

Triffterer, O., et al. 2016, 'Preamble', in Triffterer, O. and K. Ambos, *The Rome Statute of the International Criminal Court: A Commentary* (3rd edn., Beck) 1–13.

Twum-Danso, A., 2003, *Africa's Young Soldiers: The Co-Option of Childhood*, available at http://www.issafrica.org/uploads/Mono82.pdf (last visited 21 February 2018).

UK *Camplin*, 1978, House of Lords, [1978] AC 705.

UK *Dudley*, 1884, *R. v. Dudley and Stephens*, High Court of Justice, [1881-5] 14 QBD 273 DC, All ER.

UK *Howe*, 1987, *R. v. Howe and others*, House of Lords, [1987] 1 ALL ER 771.

UNCRC, 1989, United Nations Convention on the Rights of the Child, 1577 UNTS 3, 20 November 1989.

United Nations Committee on the Rights of the Child, 2007, *General Comment No. 10: Children's Rights in Juvenile Justice*, U.N. Doc. CRC/C/GC.10, 25 April 2007.

UNSG, 1996, *Promotion and Protection of the Rights of Children. Impact of Armed Conflict on Children*, U.N. Doc. A/51/306, 26 August 1996.

UNSG, 2000, *Report of the Secretary-General on the Establishment of a Special Court for Sierra Leone*, U.N. Doc. S/2000/915, 4 October 2000.

US *Einsatzgruppen*, 1948, *United States of America v. Ohlendorf (Einsatzgruppen)*, Military Tribunal, Opinion and Judgment, Case No. 9, 8–9 April 1948, available at http://www.worldcourts.com/imt/eng/decisions/1948.04.09_United_States_v_Ohlendorf.pdf (last visited 18 February 2019).

US *Flick et al.*, 1947, *United States of America v. Flick et al.*, Military Tribunal, Judgment, Case No. 48, 20 April–22 December 1947, available at http://www.worldcourts.com/imt/eng/decisions/1947.12.22_United_States_v_Flick2.pdf (last visited 19 February 2019).

US *Krupp et al.*, 1948, *United States of America v. Krupp et al.*, Military Tribunal, Opinion and Judgment, Case No. 10, 31 July 1948, available at http://www.

worldcourts.com/imt/eng/decisions/1948.07.31_United_States_v_Krupp.pdf (last visited 18 February 2019).
Veale, A., 2006, 'The Criminal Responsibility of Former Child Soldiers: Contributions from Psychology', in Arts, K. and V. Popovski (eds), *International Criminal Accountability and the Rights of Children* (Asser Press) 97–108.
Vigh, H., 2008, 'Crisis and Chronicity: Anthropological Perspectives on Continuous Conflict and Decline', 73 *Ethnos* 5–24.
Wainryb, C., 2011, '"And so they Ordered Me to Kill a Person": Conceptualizing the Impacts of Child Soldiering on the Development of Moral Agency', 54 *Human Development* 273–300.
Weaver C.M., et al., 2008, 'Violence Breeds Violence: Childhood Exposure and Adolescent Conduct Problems', 36 *Am.J.Community Psychol.* 96–112.
Weierstall, R., et al., 2012, 'When Combat Prevents PTSD Symptoms—Results from a Survey with Former Child Soldiers in Northern Uganda', 12 *BMC Psychiatry* 12–41.
Weigend, T., 2012, 'Kill or Be Killed. Another Look at Erdemović', 10 *J.I.C.J.* 1219–1237.
Werle, G. and F. Jessberger, 2014, *Principles of International Criminal Law* (3rd edn., OUP).
Wessells, M., 2006, *Child Soldiers: From Violence to Protection* (HUP).
Yarbrough, S., 2014, 'Amnesty or Accountability: The Fate of High-Ranking Child Soldiers in Uganda's Lord Resistance Army', 47 *Vand.J.Transnat'l L.* 531–568.
Yeo, S., 2004, 'Considerations of Time and Space in Duress', 16 *S.Ac.L.J.* 354–376.
Yeo, S.M.H., 1990, *Compulsion in the Criminal Law* (Law Book Company).
Young, A., 2007, 'Preventing, Demobilizing, Rehabilitating, and Reintegrating Child Soldiers in African Conflicts', 7 *Journal of International Policy Solutions* 19–24.

CHAPTER 4

Limits of, and Exclusions from, the Defence of Duress

1 Introduction

In addition to the requirements stipulated in Article 31(1)(d) of the ICC Statute that must be fulfilled to successfully raise the defence of duress, a number of limitations and exclusions are integrated into the defence of duress. Firstly, the threshold of duress required from soldiers or, more accurately expressed, individuals who have a special duty to assume danger is higher. Secondly, individuals must prove that they did not voluntarily put themselves in a situation that led to the exercise of duress. Indeed, under customary international law, it is also required that the situation leading to duress must not have been voluntarily brought about by the person coerced.[1] If they did, then they cannot claim duress.

The situation of child soldiers is unique. At first sight, they are deemed to be soldiers as they take a direct part in the hostilities and so the law would expect them to behave accordingly. If, as shown in Chap. 3, they already struggle to fulfil the elements of duress, it is highly unlikely that they will be able to meet stricter requirements. In contrast, as it is often maintained that children are unable to make autonomous, conscious decisions, it should be relatively easy to demonstrate that they have not put themselves in such a situation voluntarily. Yet, as indicated in Chap. 3, the reality is more complex and the application of the law reveals a more nuanced picture of child soldiering. This chapter demonstrates that both the limitation and the exclusion prevent child soldiers from invoking successfully the

W. Nortje, N. Quénivet, *Child Soldiers and the Defence of Duress under International Criminal Law*,
https://doi.org/10.1007/978-3-030-20663-5_4

defence of duress. That being said, this must be determined on a case-by-case basis even though generalisations can be attempted.

2 Cases of Special Duty to Assume Danger

Some of the case-law on duress seems to indicate that although an individual might meet the requirements of duress, this defence is unavailable to him/her because he/she is under a special legal obligation to accept the danger. Such limitation stems from the post-World War II *Gestapo Informer* Case[2] (i.e., based on German law) and to some extent the *Erdemović* Case.[3] It is noteworthy that current German criminal law still refers to this limitation.[4] The ICC Statute is however silent on the topic because several attempts at including it in the Statute were thwarted, and it seems that the drafters left it for the court to deal with it under Article 31(2).[5] If the judges decide to use this limitation, it is likely that they will rely on ICTY case-law (as the ICC usually does in a number of fields) and that this limitation might be applicable and applied to the case of child soldiers.

The perpetrator's position or function may mean that it is expected of him/her to be able to make the right decision and be less susceptible to duress.[6] For example, it is commonplace for members of the armed forces to find themselves in situations where a higher level of accepted risk constantly arises.[7] The application of this limitation to child soldiers appears, at first sight, to lead to a *cul de sac*. To start with, it should be emphasised that the application of the limitation seems restricted to 'soldiers' and not 'civilians'. Indeed, in the *Gestapo Informer* Case, the court explained that only some individuals, such as soldiers (*Soldaten*), are required to show a heightened reasonableness (*erhöhten Zumutbarkeit*).[8] In *Erdemović* the choice of the word 'soldier' by the majority also suggests that the ruling was limited to such individuals.[9] Are 'child soldiers' soldiers in that sense of the word? Does this limitation apply to members of armed opposition groups and not only to soldiers of classic (i.e., State) armed forces? So far these controversies have remained untested in the courts.

The ICTY explains that a special duty is created because '[s]oldiers, by the very nature of their occupation, must have envisaged the possibility of violent death in pursuance of the cause for which they fight'.[10] Generally, the point is that a person who has committed him/herself to a job that may lead to a loss of limb and life cannot extract him/herself on the basis that it is too much to ask of him/her to carry it out.[11] After all, so it is argued, soldiers agree to sacrifice their lives for the good of others. They accept the risk to their lives and to undertake actions that are dangerous and life-threatening.[12] Greenawalt explains that there is nevertheless a difference between thinking of the possibility of death and 'actually facing the precise sort of pressure that Erdemović faced'.[13] Wiener also disagrees with this standard, positing that '[t]here is a distinct difference between accepting great risk to one's life (like a soldier in a charge for example) and between positively agreeing to die (like a soldier jumping on a live grenade). Soldiers are expected to do the former, and are immortalized when they do the latter.'[14] Applied to the situation of child soldiers, it would imply that a child who volunteered to join the armed forces or an armed group is held to the standards that he/she must have considered the possibility of dying. This raises a number of questions relating to, for example, the voluntariness of children joining such forces and groups, the ability of a child to understand that his/her life will be at risk and that he/she is expected to assume the danger of armed conflict once he/she joins the armed forces. To place an expectation on a child to assume the danger in view of the push and pull factors, such as poverty and revenge[15] which are intrinsically linked to voluntary conscription, is inappropriate. Needless to say, children who are forced to join armed groups could not be expected to assume the danger in which they are forced to participate. Moreover, children might in fact not have a 'death concept'[16] or, put otherwise, the ability to assume danger or a situation that poses a danger to their lives. It is particularly interesting to note that the ICTY in *Erdemović* seems to have created an even higher threshold because soldiers have accepted to die, fighting for a 'cause'. If this standard is adopted, one may question whether a child is able to determine the worth of a cause to die for. Accordingly, this specific and narrow conception of a special duty appears inappropriate in relation to child soldiers.

Another common vindication for the existence of such a special duty requirement is because '[i]n specific dangerous situations, a higher degree of risk-taking is to be expected of soldiers who have been trained for life-threatening situations'.[17] As explained by the ICTY in the *Erdemović* Case, it can be expected that soldiers will react differently, as opposed to civilians, when faced with a situation of duress, especially if their own life is at stake.[18] They are expected to show a certain level of resistance to coercion.[19] Yee rather brutally explains that '[i]f a particular combatant cannot achieve such a level of resistance, it is his own fault and he cannot complain about being convicted of a crime of general intent. Perhaps such a person should not participate in armed conflicts'.[20] Yet, as Weigend points out, whilst it might be true that soldiers are trained to deal with warfare situations, the training does not mean that they are able to resist unlawful threats made by either superiors or other members of the armed forces.[21] Even if one accepts that soldiers are prepared for the hardships of war, including 'the occupational hazard of dying'[22] and resisting unlawful orders, every soldier will not have the same level of appreciation of the dangers of warfare or ability to refuse to act in an unlawful manner. Therefore, '[i]n determining the duty to assume danger, the perpetrator's position in the military hierarchy must be taken into account'.[23] In agreement with Judge Cassese, it can be contended that the lower the rank the greater the soldier's tendency to surrender to duress.[24] As the stories of Dominic Ongwen and Thomas Kwoyelo sadly illustrate, child soldiers can be found in any ranks, from foot soldiers to commanders.

Yet, should a child soldier be regarded as a soldier in the first place? Whilst it is acknowledged that many children are being trained by (usually) adult soldiers with a view to act like soldiers, the type of training they receive needs to be scrutinised to understand whether they can truly be considered as soldiers. Since training is meant to prepare an individual to fight in a conflict, it involves instilling a soldier's frame of mind and teaching combat skills and tactics.[25] After all, most child soldiers are placed in a situation where it is crucial for them to understand the dynamics and tactics of warfare in order to survive. Here, though, a distinction must be drawn between children in State armed forces and those in armed opposition groups.

It would be expected of those children who have joined a State's armed forces that the physical as well as mental training they receive is commensurate with elements, such as age, tasks to be carried out and so on, but this is not always the case.[26] Singer notes that 'States' training of child soldiers is typically highly institutionalised, consisting of running them through formal training programs that mimic those given to adults.'[27] This is undertaken in order to instil discipline and a lack of fear in the minds of the child soldiers. Consequently, child soldiers dare not disobey their commanders. Children in State forces are also often supplied with uniforms, food and remuneration.[28] For example, under the rule of Saddam Hussein, the Iraqi State forces regularly sent child recruits to military-style summer 'boot camps'.[29] During these camps, boys as young as ten were taught how to handle small arms, run through drills, and were subjected to political indoctrination.[30] Similar activities, embedded in the education system, were organised in Syria too.[31]

For those children who have joined or were forced to join an armed or rebel group, the nature and duration of the training is varied though it tends to be usually less institutionalised and shorter than that of State forces.[32] Not all children are trained to fight though they might be trained in war-related activities such as spying. For example, very young children are 'trained to become informers, by selling water and groundnuts on the streets'.[33] For those who are old enough to fight, training might be limited to handling and using a weapon[34] (or even less[35]) though it can also be fully fledged.[36] In some instances, the training includes combat-based education[37] and the rules of the military (including behaviour and discipline).[38] Children learn, for example, to stand to attention and salute.[39] It is typical for children in armed groups to be made to obey orders without questioning them,[40] and to obtain new identities during the recruitment and training phase.[41] In the Revolutionary United Front, combat names, such as Rambo, were commonplace.[42] Military clothing might be provided,[43] thus further forging a military identity. Wessells stresses that '[c]ombat-related identities move children even farther from the world of civilian children in their society, where norms against killing apply'.[44] Whilst it may be a norm to most children, child soldiers do not experience the joys of childhood.[45] Moreover, '[c]ombined with liberal amounts of terror and propaganda, impressionable children can rapidly begin to identify with causes they barely understand'.[46] This has a significant impact on the mental development of child soldiers who are left with little option but to obey the orders of the armed groups. Mental preparation for warfare is certainly not part and parcel of the training; rather, the aim is to break the children's wills,[47] and this might include brainwashing.[48] The ultimate goal is to ensure full commitment to the cause and blind loyalty and discipline and not to train them to assume danger.

Two conclusions can be drawn from this. Firstly, it is highly unlikely that children can be considered as trained soldiers and so, they should not be considered as individuals with a special duty to assume danger. Secondly, even in situations where it is acknowledged that they carry out military activities that are usually undertaken by 'fully fledged' soldiers to require them to have the same ability as an adult to assume danger makes little sense.[49] In this respect, it is suggested that child soldiers should be differentiated from adult soldiers and that this limitation to the invocation of the defence of duress simply be revised. The authors thus propose that there is an assumption that child soldiers do not fall within that limitation to the application of the defence of duress. This assumption can nonetheless be rebutted on a case-by-case basis.

3 Voluntary—Free of Fault

Although it is not expressly mentioned in the definition of duress as enshrined in the ICC Statute,[50] one of the constituent elements of duress is that the perpetrator is free of fault, that is, that he/she did not put him/herself in a situation whereby he/she was likely to be compelled to act in an unlawful manner.[51] It is also known as the doctrine of prior fault used in domestic settings,[52] or *culpa in causa*, that 'the actor has been blameworthy in bringing about his dilemma'.[53] In a rather abrupt way the ICC defended that '[d]uress is not regulated in the Statute in a way that would provide blanket immunity to members of criminal organisations which have brutal systems of ensuring discipline as soon as they can establish that their membership was not voluntary'.[54] It seems to confirm the extensive case-law of the IMT, post-World War II tribunals,[55] the Special Panel in East Timor,[56] the Extraordinary Chamber in the Courts of Cambodia and the ICTY: any person who willingly, voluntarily chose to become a member of a unit, organisation or group known for operating in contravention of international law will not be able to avail him/herself of the defence of duress:[57] '[o]ne who embarks on a criminal enterprise of obvious magnitude is expected to anticipate what the enterprise will logically lead to'.[58] In other words, voluntary exposure to the danger negates this ground of exclusion of criminal responsibility,[59] a view that chimes well with Article 9 of the Statute of the IMT of Nuremberg which presumed guilt on the basis of association.[60] Such a requirement makes perfect sense when an individual was fully aware of the kind of organisations he/she was willingly joining. For example, the Einsatzsgruppen were created with the specific aim of carrying out killings under the Nazi regime.[61] It would be difficult to deny knowing their purpose in the first place. Similarly, long-standing members of the NSDAP, the Nazi party, could not claim that they did not know of the programme of, and the methods employed by, the group.[62] Furthermore, a French court pointed out in the *Papon* Case that the defendant 'had, just upon taking his post, a clear, reasoned, detailed and continuous knowledge of the plan formed by the Nazis to kill these persons—which constitutes premeditation—although he might have been unaware of the specific conditions of their ultimate suffering and the technical means used to kill them'.[63] This might make less sense if the individual was not fully cognisant of the activities and aims of the organisation he/she joined. Allowing a defence of duress for a person who has consciously decided to join an armed group would send the wrong message.

The reality that a number of children present themselves for service in the armed forces and groups should not be brushed aside,[64] many join out of their own free will.[65] As Smith notes, 'Western audiences might then have been less surprised to learn that over half of the child soldiers joined a fighting force under no direct threat of violence. Some of the young population engaged in informal warfare, as others entered the informal economy—for lack of a better alternative.'[66] In the light hereof, the application of the above requirement means that if children consented to participate in the conflict, then their initial voluntariness[67] would remain valid throughout their recruitment. The automaticity between voluntariness in recruitment and lack of duress for specific acts, however, needs to be challenged as it does not fit the reality with which child soldiers are confronted.

Some scholars observe that 'where an adolescent has *genuinely* volunteered to join an armed group or national army, his or her ability to rely on the plea of duress must be treated no differently than if applied to an adult soldier'.[68] The authors fully subscribe to this view. The key point is to define the concept of 'voluntary'. Undoubtedly, the debate on how 'voluntary' and/or 'genuine' a child's voluntary recruitment to the armed forces or groups is, is a long-standing one. Suffice it to say that a variety of push and pull factors (e.g., poverty, peer and family pressure, need for food/water/clothing/shelter, need for personal security, revenge, patriotism, vulnerability, sense of duty towards the community) are present[69] amongst the 15- to 18-year-old children who join armed forces or groups. As Trenholm et al. explain, 'the modes of entry into the military [...] do not occur within a vacuum'[70] but are rather contingent on a number of both collective and individual social and cultural factors. What is more, as '[a]dolescence is undoubtedly a stage of unrest'[71] '[s]oldiering is often attractive to children because it provides meaning, identity, and options civilian life does not afford'.[72] This goes against the mainstream discourse 'which presents a homogenous view of forced, tortured and abducted conscripts'.[73] For the Special Representative of the Secretary-General for Children and Armed Conflict, the issue of 'voluntary recruitment' is moot, for she avers that in this limited, concrete context the line between voluntary and involuntary is legally irrelevant.[74] In its dissenting opinion, Judge Robertson of the Special Court for Sierra Leone explained:

> Children who 'volunteer' may do so from poverty (so as to obtain army pay) or out of fear—to obtain some protection in a raging conflict. They may do so as the result of psychological or ideological inducement or indoctrination to fight for a particular cult or cause, or to achieve posthumous glory as a 'martyr'. Any organization which affords the opportunity to wield an AK47 will have a certain allure to the young. The result will be to put at serious risk a life that has scarcely begun to be lived.[75]

Accordingly, voluntary enrolment should not be used to dismiss automatically a defence of duress invoked by a child soldier. It needs to be determined on a case-by-case basis.

Furthermore, it can be argued that children who voluntarily joined the armed forces or group did not realise that they would also behave in contravention of the law. 'The lure of ideology is particularly strong in early adolescence',[76] yet due to their lack of capacity to evaluate properly, such children do not realise that their decision to join an armed group, though based on an informed choice, may have unforeseen ramifications and costs.[77] The magnitude of the crimes committed by the group might be unknown to the children. Moreover or alternatively, as they have grown up in a war milieu, their understanding of violence and criminality might be skewed.[78] What is more, as Lafayette explains, a child's moral development will have changed between the time of the recruitment and the time of the commission of the crime.[79] Therefore, taking into account his/her voluntary recruitment in ascertaining a duress defence makes little sense.

A further question is, what happens once they are in the group and realise that they have made the wrong choice? Indeed, '[o]nce recruited, either voluntarily or forcibly, into a military regime, they are forced to fight, kill, steal food, and even forced into sexual submission'.[80] Case-law nonetheless provides an avenue to delink the defence of duress from voluntary recruitment. Indeed, in *Kvocka et al.* the ICTY, after noting that one of the defendants had claimed duress, observed that he had stayed with the group despite knowing how abusive the detention conditions were and had 'performed the tasks required of him efficiently, effectively, and indifferently'.[81] Put differently, if he had left the group and/or declined to carry out these tasks, the defence of duress might have been used successfully.[82] A similar stance can be discerned in the ICC which elucidated that this automaticity between being in a group known for its violent actions and the impossibility to raise the defence of duress could be broken if the individual, having realised the violent nature of the group, attempts to escape from the group.[83] Such an interpretation is based on Article 31(1)(d)(ii) of the Statute that refers to 'other circumstances beyond that person's control' (and which technically refers to the defence of necessity).[84] The very essence of this rule is that it should discourage an actor from complacently staying in a group and then relying on duress as a ground for excluding responsibility.[85]

In contrast, children who were forcefully recruited and made to participate in an armed conflict can use the defence of duress[86] (provided all the aforementioned elements are fulfilled). Limitations are nonetheless set here too. Indeed, as the *Ongwen* Case indicates, the perpetrator must show that he/she did not embrace the ideology of the group. For example, Ongwen is seen to have 'pursued extreme violence and sadism as a way to achieve power, status and influence within the LRA',[87] and to have been 'a willing participant in the implementation of the policy to attack the civilian population'.[88] As the legal counsel of the victims in the *Ongwen* trial submitted, he willingly stayed in the armed opposition group whose objectives and purposes he shared.[89] As Souris states, '[f]or those who spend their adolescent years inside armed groups and become hardened, thus carrying out atrocities no one ordered them to commit, duress is no longer as readily available'.[90] Based on this jurisprudence, if a child soldier stays in the group then he/she cannot claim that the circumstances of his/her stay were beyond his/her control.

The ICC does point out that it was possible to escape from the LRA. Some research studies indeed support such a claim. For example, Klasen et al. found that 81% of the children they had interviewed had escaped the rebel forces in Uganda.[91] However, a court also needs to appreciate that children are often in thrall to these groups, unable to withdraw from the group physically as they are unremittingly surrounded by members of the armed group, and their moves are, to some extent, monitored. Those caught trying to flee are either killed or told that their families would be punished[92] and their villages raided.[93] Often such punishments are witnessed by other children, and sometimes other children are even forced to administer the punishment. Even those in high position, such as Ongwen, might be scrutinised[94] and executed for disloyalty.[95] Fear of the consequences of trying to abscond is thus constantly on a child's mind.[96] Moreover, children are mentally unable to withdraw from the group that turned into a surrogate family,[97] and where they bonded with fellow children.

Research carried out in peacetime shows that 'group belonging provides young people with a sense of definition, purpose, meaning, worth and social control'.[98] So why would they want to leave the group? Used to a military hierarchy and life outside normal society, their commanders and peers remain the most noteworthy figures in their lives. Killing may also be the only way, or at least instrumental in some cases, to earn the respect of their peers.[99] Furthermore, they have no family or community to return to.[100] In other instances, spiritual[101] and political[102] indoctrination dissuades them from leaving the group.[103] Sadly, many child soldiers become willing participants in the heinous activities of the armed groups.[104] Asking them to 'escape' to later be able to invoke duress fails to acknowledge the environment in which they live and have grown up. The complexity of this conundrum is further explicated by research showing that children, in fact, recreate the social system in which they have been ensnarled: 'sheer survival compelled young males to become the agents of practices that reinforced and reproduced the system into which they had been coopted.'[105] They are as much victims as actors: even their individual agency is intimately linked to the structures of this system.[106]

The complexity of this issue is best illustrated by the following interview with a Burmese child soldier who was only seven years old when he was abducted:

> About 10 Burmese soldiers in uniform with guns came and said, "Come with us." "No, we are very young." "No, follow us," they said, "We will give you food, candy." We were young, we couldn't think much. We traveled by motorboat for three nights. When we reached the recruitment center in Rangoon, we talked with others about how they had come there—their parents had kicked them out of the house and they didn't know where to go. Like us, they were forced or kidnapped with promises of food and candy. The center was called Ye Nunt. We were very, very afraid about what we were going to tell our parents. I tried to communicate through letters. I stayed in Ye Nyunt for five years. We were told we couldn't go back home and that we would have to stay there. They threatened us to keep us from escaping. Some escaped and were sent to prison. Some were beaten. Some committed suicide. I know of five. One person drowned by driving a truck into a river.[107]

Although it may look as if this boy initially voluntarily joined the armed group, it is clear that he was lured into joining. It is not always possible for children to realise whether they are in a dangerous situation or not, whereas adults use a higher degree of caution.[108] Children are also easier to manipulate and are indoctrinated by armed groups.[109] Extensive research has furthermore indicated that child soldiers join armed groups due to a variety of factors mentioned above. These factors should not be swept under the carpet in an attempt to ignore the social factors leading up to the presumed voluntary recruitment of the child soldier. A query about the child soldier's voluntary recruitment must be preceded by an investigation into the history and circumstances of the child prior to recruitment. Accordingly, there is no legitimacy in the argument that if child soldiers voluntarily joined an armed group it means that they should take full responsibility for the consequences of their actions, because, firstly, they might not have 'voluntarily' joined the armed forces or groups, secondly they might not have realised the ramifications of their decision to join the forces/group and thirdly, they might not have had the mental strength and capacity to escape. Again, in this instance, the authors suggest that an assumption be made that children did not voluntarily join the group or if they did they could not extract themselves. However, a rebuttal of this assumption should be possible on a case-by-case basis.

4 Conclusion

Overall, both the limitation of, and the exclusion to, the defence of duress are clear impediments to a successful use of this defence by child soldiers. Yet, they are not only problematic to child soldiers but also adults. The strict application of the defence shows that even a child soldier, the archetypal victim-perpetrator, struggles to plead duress.

The authors submit that in the case of child soldiers, both with regard to the limitation of, and the exclusion to, the defence of duress an assumption should be made that child soldiers do not have a special duty to assume danger and do not 'voluntarily' join an armed group and that, if they do, they were unaware of the scale of the atrocities committed and/or could not escape from the group. These two assumptions can, however, be rebutted by proving that a child had, for example, been specifically trained to be a soldier or that he/she was well aware of the crimes perpetrated by the group, made no attempt to leave it, and ostensibly embraced its actions and ideology. This might be viewed as pleading for a special law on duress for child soldiers. It is not. It is only asking for the burden of proof to be reversed in the specific case of child soldiers.

Notes

1. Cassese et al. 2013, 216. See Eser 2016, 1152; Knoops 2003, 71; Cryer et al. 2014, 408; Ambos 2013, 357–358.
2. Germany *Gestapo Informer* 1949.
3. ICTY *Erdemović* 1997b.
4. See discussion in Wiener 2014, 96 and fn 113; Oellers-Frahm and Specht 1998, 408–409. Ambos posits that 'German military law provides for a specific provision in ss 6 of the Military Criminal Code (Wehrstrafgesetz-WStG) according to which fear of personal danger is no excuse if the soldier's duty requires the assumption of this danger'. See Ambos 2013, 347
5. Bond and Fougere 2014, fn 67; Scaliotti 2001, 153.
6. Yee 1997, 299; Grant 2016, 14.
7. Werle and Jessberger 2014, 244; Cryer et al. 2014, 408.
8. Germany *Gestapo Informer* 1949, 202.
9. ICTY *Erdemović* 1997b, para. 84.
10. ICTY *Erdemović* 1997b, para. 84.
11. Germany *Gestapo Informer* 1949, 202.
12. Robinson 2013, 150.
13. Greenawalt 2011, 1117–1118.
14. Wiener 2014, 115.
15. See, for example, UNSG 1996, paras 38–43; Happold 2005, 11–15.
16. Waschefort 2015, 48 referring to an interview he conducted with Radhika Coomaraswamy.
17. Werle and Jessberger 2014, 244; Yee 1997, 298; Oellers-Frahm and Specht 1998, 408.
18. ICTY *Erdemović* 1997b, para. 84.
19. Stahn 2019, 153.
20. Yee 1997, 298. See Oellers-Frahm and Specht 1998, 408.
21. Weigend 2012, 1236. See ICTY *Erdemović* 1997a, paras 12 and 50.
22. ICTY *Erdemović* 1997b, para. 84.
23. Werle and Jessberger 2014, 244. See Cryer et al. 2014, 408.
24. ICTY *Erdemović* 1997b, para. 51.
25. Okebukola 2014, 593.
26. For example, Iranian children were not given any real military training prior to deployment in the Iran-Iraq war. Elahi 1988, 260. See also discussion in Happold concerning the military recruitment of children under the age of 18. Happold 2005, 19–21.
27. Singer 2005, 77. See Okebukola 2014, 593; Happold 2005, 19–21.
28. Singer 2005, 71 and 77. See Happold 2005, 19.
29. Singer 2005, 77. For a brief discussion of the participation of child soldiers in the Iran-Iraq war, see Cohn and Goodwin-Gill 1994, 38–39.

30. Singer 2005, 70.
31. Almohammad 2018, 3.
32. Singer 2005, 79. Wessells also notes that 'the armed group deliberately uses violence as a means of achieving its objectives.' Wessells 2006, 57.
33. ICC *Lubanga* 2012, para. 788.
34. SCSL *Sesay* 2009, para. 1619; SCSL *Fofana and Kondewa* 2007, para. 676; ICC *Katanga and Chui* 2008, para. 255.
35. Kuper 2008, 12 as cited in Okebukola 2014, 597.
36. ICC *Lubanga* 2012, paras 802–803.
37. Almohammad 2018, 18.
38. ICC *Lubanga* 2012, para. 802.
39. ICC *Katanga* 2014, para. 1072.
40. See, for example, Briggs 2005, 47. Okebukola 2014, 595.
41. Souris 2017, 319. Schmidt 2007, 52. Wessells notes that 'children construct new identities as soldiers, internalizing their transition from civilians to combatants'. Wessells 2006, 81.
42. Other names that have been recorded include 'Blood Never Dry' and 'Bad Pay Bad'. See Singer 2005, 73. See more generally Drumbl 2012, 88–89.
43. ICC *Lubanga* 2012, paras 792 and 803.
44. Wessells 2006, 84.
45. See Davison 2004, 125; Singh 2007, 212.
46. Singer 2005, 72.
47. Wessells 2006, 58. See, for example, the training described in SCSL *Sesay* 2009, paras 1640–1641.
48. Okebukola 2014, 595; Singer 2005, 72–73; Almohammad 2018, 22.
49. Singer notes that 'children are obviously not the prototypical recruit'. See Singer 2005, 70.
50. Heim 2013, 180. As a result, the ICC is left to clarify the issue in its jurisprudence. See Ambos 2013, 357–358; Werle and Jessberger 2014, 243–244.
51. Arenson 2014, 79; Heim 2013, 170; Ambos 2013, 348. ICTY *Erdemović* 1997a, para. 50.
52. See Happold 2005, 158 and Happold 2002, 1171–1172 (with a brief application to child soldiers).
53. Weigend 2012, 1235.
54. ICC *Ongwen* 2016a, para. 153.
55. See Germany *Gestapo Informer* 1949, 201. Lippman also notes that 'the Tribunal held that a defendant may not plead duress if the illegal order was the logical and foreseeable extension of the policy of an organization which the defendant had voluntarily joined'. See Lippman 1992, 46.
56. *Public Prosecutor v. Joni Marques & Ors* (*Lospalos* Case), as cited in Linton and Reiger 2001, 191.

57. IMT and Post WWII: US Military Tribunal *Einsatzgruppen* 1948, 481–483 (which refers to IMT case-law). See discussions in Cassese et al. 2013, 216; Heim 2013, 170–171; ICTY *Erdemović* 1997a, para. 17. Special Panels in East Timor: East Timor Tribunal *Leki* 2001, 8–9. See Linton and Reiger 2001, 192; ECCC: ECCC *Duch* 2010, para. 557; ICTY: ICTY *Erdemović* 1997b, para. 84.
58. US Military Tribunal *Einsatzgruppen* 1948, 481. See also discussion in Ambos 2013, 348–349; Lippman 1992, 46.
59. Werle and Jessberger 2014, 148. For a similar view, see Nagle 2011, 1–58.
60. See discussion in Gilbert 2006, 155. However, association by guilt is now rejected under international criminal law. See discussions in Wright 1949; Danner and Martinez 2005; Tomuschat 2006.
61. US Military Tribunal *Einsatzgruppen* 1948, 479–482. See discussion in Joyce 2015, 627.
62. See US Military Tribunal *Milch* 1947, 40–41.
63. France, Cour d'appel de Bordeaux, *Papon* 1996, (translation by the authors): '[il] a eu, dès avant sa prise de fonctions, une connaissance claire, raisonnée, circonstanciée et continue du dessein formé par les nazis d'attenter à la vie de ces personnes, constitutif de préméditation, même s'il a pu demeurer dans l'ignorance des conditions exactes de leurs souffrances ultimes et des moyens techniques utilisés pour leur donner la mort.' See also *Touvier* as explained in ICTY *Erdemović* 1997a.
64. Park 2014, 332 and 338.
65. Derluyn et al. 2015, 36.
66. Smith 2011, 100.
67. For a discussion on the definition of 'voluntary', see Quénivet 2013, 1071–1077.
68. Achton Thomas 2013, 34. To some extent, she acknowledges that there is a grey area around the concept of 'voluntary' but limits it to instances where children have been manipulated or subjected to subtle pressures. See discussion in Swart and Hassen 2016, 471.
69. UNSG 1996, paras 38–43; Waschefort 2015, 47 and 49–52; Okebukola 2014, 592–593; Huyghebaert 2009, 66; Happold 2005, 11–15; Maxted 2003, 61; Almohammad 2018, 7; Trenholm et al. 2012, 211 and 220; ICC *Lubanga* 2012, para. 804; ICC *Katanga* 2014, para. 1053.
70. Trenholm et al. 2012, 222.
71. Dore 2007–2008, 1303. See Happold 2005, 11.
72. Wessells 2006, 4.
73. Trenholm et al. 2012, 205.
74. UNSR 2008. See Jamison 2005, 153; UNSG 1996, paras 34–36; Singh 2007, 210.

75. SCSL *Norman* 2004, para. 8.
76. UNSG 1996, para. 43.
77. See, for example, UNSR 2011, 10; West 2000, 188.
78. See Brett and Specht 2004, 9–14. See a contrario Posada and Wainryb 2008.
79. Lafayette 2012–2013, 306.
80. Hackenberg 2000, 422. See Njeru 2010, 33–34.
81. ICTY *Kvocka et al.* 2001, para. 457.
82. See East Timor Tribunal *Leki* 2001, 8.
83. ICC *Ongwen* 2016a, para. 154.
84. Grant 2016, 11; Risacher 2013–2014, fn 81; Dinstein 2000, 373. It should be noted that the Court seems to fail to distinguish between the requirements for duress and necessity that are clearly delineated by a disjunctive ('or') rather than a conjunctive ('and') word. Eser points out that '[a]mong the many compromises which had to be made in order to get this Statute accepted, paragraph 1 (d) is one of the least convincing provisions, as in an ill-guided and lastly failed attempt it tried to combine two different concepts: (justifying) "necessity" and (merely excusing) "duress"'. See Eser 2016, 1149–1150. For an alternative view which argues that the use of the word 'other' relating to the defence of necessity means that this condition also applies to duress, see Cryer et al. 2014, 408.
85. See discussion in Olusanya 2010, 56. UK *M'Growther* 1746, 14 ('it is incumbent on every man, who makes force his defence, to shew an actual force, and that he quitted the service as soon as he could'). M'Growther had claimed that he had been coerced into joining the rebels. The report on the case also briefly touches about 'the practicability or impracticability of an escape'.
86. Achton Thomas 2013, 34.
87. Drumbl 2016, 240.
88. ICC *Ongwen* 2016b, para. 27.
89. ICC *Ongwen* 2016b, paras 30–31. See Grant 2016; Drumbl 2015.
90. Souris 2017, 321.
91. Klasen et al. 2010, 576. See Amone-P'Olak et al. 2015, 156.
92. Tercier Holst-Roness 2006, 13. See Fonseka 2001, 72; Abbott 2000, 514–515; Davison 2004, 137.
93. Amone-P'Olak and Ovuga 2017, 18.
94. Grant 2016, 9–10.
95. Vincent Otti, Kony's deputy, was executed in 2007 and Kony 'came close to executing Ongwen on several occasions.' Grant 2016, 13; Drumbl 2015.
96. Maclure and Denov 2006, 123. See Schmidt 2007, 51.

97. Crane 2008, 12; Maclure and Denov 2006, 124–125. For a full picture, see Faulkner 2001, 495; Murphy 2003, 70.
98. Newman et al. 2007, 259.
99. Redress 2006, 7; Wessells 2006, 80.
100. Tercier Holst-Roness 2006, 13; Redress 2006, 7; Singh 2007, 209.
101. Baines 2009, 170. Some armed groups maintain that they are spiritually led which leads to the spiritual indoctrination of child soldiers. One of these groups is the LRA which is a spiritualist rebel group that calls itself the 'Army of God'. See Pham et al. 2008, 405.
102. Maclure and Denov 2006, 124; Schmidt 2007, 52. See also discussion by Wessells about political socialisation and its role within the voluntary recruitment of child soldiers. Wessells 2006, 52–54.
103. Olusanya 2010, 56–57; Redress 2006, 7; Nagle 2011, 11.
104. Souris 2017, 320. See Schmidt 2007, 60.
105. Maclure and Denov 2006, 130.
106. See Maclure and Denov 2006, 131; Park 2014, 339. See Schmidt 2007, 60–61.
107. UNICEF 2002, 21.
108. See, for example, Singh 2007, 211; Schmidt 2007, 60.
109. See, for example, Singer 2005, 70; Singh 2007, 211.

References

Abbott, A.B., 2000, 'Child Soldiers—The Use of Children as Instruments of War', 23 *Suffolk Transnt'l L.Rev.* 499–537.

Achton Thomas, M., 2013, 'Malice Supplies the Age? Assessing the Culpability of Adolescent Soldiers', 44 *Cal.W.Int'l L.J.* 1–38.

Almohammad, A., 2018, *ISIS Child Soldiers in Syria: The Structural and Predatory Recruitment, Enlistment, Pre-training Indoctrination, Training, and Deployment*, International Centre for Counter-Terrorism, Research Paper, February 2018.

Ambos, K., 2013, *Treatise on International Criminal Law: Volume I: Foundations and General Part* (OUP).

Amone-P'Olak, K. and E. Ovuga, 2017, 'The Influence of Types of War Experiences on Conduct Problems in War-Affected Youth in Northern Ugandan: Findings from the WAYS Study', 251 *Psychiatry Res.* 14–19.

Amone-P'Olak, K., et al., 2015, 'War Experiences and Psychotic Symptoms among Former Child Soldiers in Northern Uganda: The Mediating Role of Post-War Hardships—The WAYS Study', 45 *S.Afr.J.Psychol.* 155–167.

Arenson, K.J., 2014, 'The Paradox of Disallowing Duress as a Defence to Murder', 78 *J.C.L.* 65–79.

Baines, E., 2009, 'Complex Political Perpetrators: Reflections on Dominic Ongwen', 47 *J.Mod.Afr.Stud.* 163–191.

Bond, J. and M. Fougere, 2014, 'Omnipresent Threats: A Comment on the Defence of Duress in International Criminal Law', 14 *Int.C.L.R.* 471–512.

Brett, R. and I. Specht, 2004, *Young Soldiers: Why they Choose to Fight* (Lynne Rienner).

Briggs, J., 2005, *Innocents Lost: When Child Soldiers Go to War* (Basic Books).

Cassese, A., et al., 2013, *Cassese's International Criminal Law* (3rd edn., OUP).

Cohn, I. and G.S. Goodwin-Gill, 1994, *Child Soldiers: The Role of Children in Armed Conflicts* (OUP).

Crane, D., 2008, 'Prosecuting Children in Times of Conflict: The West African Experience', 15 *H.R.B.* 11–17.

Cryer, C., et al., 2014, *An Introduction to International Criminal Law and Procedure* (3rd edn., CUP).

Danner, A.M. and J.S. Martinez, 2005, 'Guilty Associations: Joint Criminal Enterprise, Command Responsibility, and the Development of International Criminal Law', 93 *C.L.R.* 75–169.

Davison, A., 2004, 'Child Soldiers: No Longer a Minor Incident', 12 *Willamette J.Int'l L. & Disp.Resol.* 124–157.

Derluyn, I., et al., 2015, 'Victims and/or Perpetrators? Towards an Interdisciplinary Dialogue on Child Soldiers', 15 *BMC Int. Health Hum. Rights* 28–40.

Dinstein, Y., 2000, 'Defences', in McDonald, G.K. and O. Swaak-Goldman (eds) *Substantive and Procedural Aspects of International Criminal Law: The Experience of International and National Courts*, Volume I: Commentary (Kluwer) 371–388.

Dore, C.L., 2007–2008, 'What to Do with Omar Khadr? Putting a Child Soldier on Trial: Questions of International Law, Juvenile Justice, and Moral Culpability', 41 *J.Marshall L.Rev.J.* 1281–1320.

Drumbl, M., 2012, *Reimagining Child Soldiers in International Law and Policy* (OUP).

Drumbl, M., 2016, 'Victims who Victimise', 4 *Lond.Rev.Int. Law* 217–246.

Drumbl, M.A., 2015, 'The Ongwen Trial at the ICC: Tough Questions on Child Soldiers', *Open Democracy*, 14 April 2015, available at https://www.opendemocracy.net/openglobalrights/mark-drumbl/ongwen-trial-at-icc-tough-questions-on-child-soldiers (last visited 2 September 2018).

East Timor Tribunal *Leki*, 2001, *Prosecutor v. Leki*, East Timorese Public Administration, Dili District Court, Special Panel for Serious Crimes, Case No. 5/2000, 11 June 2001, available at http://www.worldlii.org/tp/cases/TPSPSC/2001/7.pdf (last visited 2 September 2018) at 8.

ECCC *Duch*, 2010, *Prosecutor v. Guek Eav* alias *Duch*, Extraordinary Chambers in the Courts of Cambodia, Judgment, Case No. 001/18-07-2007/ECCC/TC, 26 July 2010.

Elahi, M., 1988, 'The Rights of the Child under Islamic Law: Prohibition of the Child Soldier', 19 *Colum.Hum.Rts.L.Rev.* 259–279.

Eser, E., 2016, 'Article 31: Grounds for Excluding Criminal Responsibility', in Triffterer, O. and K. Ambos (eds), *The Rome Statute of the International Criminal Court: A Commentary* (3rd edn., Beck) 1125–1160.

Faulkner, F., 2001, 'Kindergarten Killers: Morality, Murder and the Child Soldier Problem', 22 *T.W.Q.* 491–504.

Fonseka, F., 2001, 'The Protection of Child Soldiers in International Law', 2 *A.P.J.H.R.L.* 69–89.

France *Papon*, 1996, *Papon* Case, Cour d'appel de Bordeaux, Chambre d'accusation, Judgment No. 806, 18 September 1996, available at http://www.haguejusticeportal.net/Docs/NLP/France/Papon_acte_accusation_18_09_96.pdf (last visited 2 August 2018).

Germany *Gestapo Informer*, 1949, *Gestapo Informer* Case, Oberlandsgericht Freiburg i. Br., Ss 64/48, Hoechstrichterliche Entscheidungen, Sammlung von Entscheidungen der Oberlandesgerichte und der Oberststen Gerichte in Strafsachen, Volume 2, 200–203, 17 February 1949.

Gilbert, J., 2006, 'Justice Not Revenge: The International Criminal Court and the "Grounds to Exclude Criminal Responsibility"—Defences or Negation of Criminality?', 10 *I.J.H.R.* 143–160.

Grant, N., 2016, *Duress as a Defence for Former Child Soldiers? Dominic Ongwen and the International Criminal Court*, International Crimes Database Brief 21, December 2016.

Greenawalt, A.K.A., 2011, 'The Pluralism of International Criminal Law', 86 *Ind.L.J.* 1063–1130.

Hackenberg, M.L., 2000, 'Can the Optional Protocol for the Convention on the Rights of the Child Protect the Ugandan Child Soldier?', 10 *Ind.Int'l & Comp.L.Rev.* 417–455.

Happold, M., 2002, 'Excluding Children from Refugee Status: Child Soldiers and Article 1F of the Refugee Convention', 24 *Am.U.Int'l.L.Rev.* 1131–1176.

Happold, M., 2005, *Child Soldiers in International Law* (MUP).

Heim, S.J., 2013, 'The Applicability of the Duress Defense to the Killing of Innocent Persons by Civilians', 46 *Cornell Int'l L.J.* 165–190.

Huyghebaert, P., 2009, 'Les enfants dans les conflits armés: une analyse à l'aune des notions de vulnérabilité, de pauvreté et de "capabilités"', 2 *Mondes en développement* 59–72.

ICC *Katanga*, 2014, *Situation in the Democratic Republic of the Congo in the Case of the Prosecutor v. Katanga*, International Criminal Court, Judgment Pursuant to Article 74 of the Statute, Case No. ICC-01/04-01/07, 7 March 2014.

ICC *Katanga and Chui*, 2008, *Situation in the Democratic Republic of the Congo in the Case of the Prosecutor v. Katanga and Ngudjolo Chui*, International Criminal Court, Decision on the Confirmation of Charges, Case No. ICC-01/04-01/07, 30 September 2008.

ICC *Lubanga*, 2012, *Situation in the Democratic Republic of the Congo in the Case of the Prosecutor v. Lubanga Dyilo*, Judgment Pursuant to Article 74 of the Statute, Case No. ICC-01/04-01/06, 14 March 2012.

ICC *Ongwen*, 2016a, *Situation in Uganda in the Case of the Prosecutor v. Ongwen*, International Criminal Court, Decision on the Confirmation of Charges against Dominic Ongwen (Public Redacted), Case No. ICC-02/04-01/15, 23 March 2016.

ICC *Ongwen*, 2016b, *Situation in Uganda in the Case of the Prosecutor v. Ongwen*, International Criminal Court, Pre-trial Brief on Behalf of Victims Represented by the Common Legal Representative, Case No. ICC-02/0-01/15, 6 September 2016.

ICTY *Erdemović*, 1997a, *Prosecutor v. Erdemović*, International Criminal Tribunal for the Former Yugoslavia, Judgment, Case No. IT-96-22-A, Dissenting Opinion of Judge Cassese, 7 October 1997.

ICTY *Erdemović*, 1997b, *Prosecutor v. Erdemović*, International Criminal Tribunal for the Former Yugoslavia, Judgment, Case No. IT-96-22-A, Joint Separate Opinion of Judges McDonald and Vohrah, 7 October 1997.

ICTY *Kvocka et al.*, 2001, *Prosecutor v. Kvocka et al.*, International Criminal Tribunal for the Former Yugoslavia, Judgment, Case No. IT-98-30/1-T, 2 November 2001.

Jamison, M.A., 2005, 'Detention of Juvenile Enemy Combatants at Guantanamo Bay: The Special Concerns of Children', 9 *U.C.Davis J.Int'l L. & Pol'y* 127–170.

Joyce, M., 2015, 'Duress: From Nuremberg to the International Criminal Court, Finding the Balance between Justification and Excuse', 28 *L.J.I.L.* 623–642.

Klasen, F., et al., 2010, 'Multiple Trauma and Mental Health in Former Ugandan Child Soldiers', 23 *J. Trauma. Stress* 573–581.

Knoops, G.A., 2003, *An Introduction to the Law of International Criminal Tribunals: A Comparative Study* (Transnational Publishers).

Lafayette, E., 2012–2013, 'The Prosecution of Child Soldiers: Balancing Accountability with Justice', 63 *Syracuse L.Rev.* 297–325.

Linton, S. and C. Reiger, 2001, 'The Evolving Jurisprudence and Practice of East Timor's Special Panels for Serious Crimes on Admissions of Guilt, Duress and Superior Orders', 4 *Y.I.H.L.* 167–212.

Lippman, M., 1992, 'The Other Nuremberg: American Prosecutions of Nazi War Criminals in Occupied Germany', 3 *Ind.Int'l & Comp.L.Rev.* 1–100.

Maclure, R. and M. Denov, 2006, '"I Didn't Want to Die So I Joined Them": Structuration and the Process of Becoming Boy Soldiers in Sierra Leone', 18 *Terror. Political Violence* 119–135.

Maxted, J., 2003, 'Children and Armed Conflict in Africa', 9 *Social Issues* 51–72.

Murphy, W.P., 2003, 'Military Patrimonialism and Child Soldier Clientalism in the Liberian and Sierra Leonean Civil Wars', 46 *Afr.Stud.Rev.* 61–87.

Nagle, L.E., 2011, 'Child Soldiers and the Duty of Nations to Protect Children from Participation in Armed Conflict', 19 *Cardozo J.Int'l & Comp.L.* 1–58.

Newman, B.M., et al., 2007, 'Peer Group Membership and a Sense of Belonging: Their Relationship to Adolescent Behavior Problems', 42 *Adolescence* 241–263.
Njeru, S., 2010, 'Dealing with the Past: The Youth and Post-War Recovery in Southern Sudan', 10 *Afr.J.Confl.Resolut.* 29–50.
Oellers-Frahm, K. and B. Specht, 1998, 'Die *Erdemovic*-Rechtsprechung des Jugoslawientribunals: Probleme bei der Entwicklung eines internationalen Strafrechts, dargestellt am Beispiel des Notstands', 58 *Z.a.ö.R.V.* 389–414.
Okebukola, E.O., 2014, 'Training Children for Armed Conflict—Where Does the Law Stand?', 14 *Int.C.L.R.* 588–618.
Olusanya, O., 2010, 'Excuse and Mitigation under International Criminal Law: Redrawing Conceptual Boundaries', 13 *New Crim.L.Rev.* 23–89.
Park, A.S.J., 2014, 'Constituting Omar Khadr: Cultural Racism, Childhood, and Citizenship', 8 *Int. Political Sociol.* 43–62.
Pham, P.N., et al., 2008, 'The Lord's Resistance Army and Forced Conscription in Northern Uganda', 30 *Hum.Rts.Q.* 404–441.
Posada, R. and C. Wainryb, 2008, 'Moral Development in a Violent Society: Colombian Children's Judgments in the Context of Survival and Revenge', 79 *Child Development* 882–898.
Quénivet, N., 2013, 'The Liberal Discourse and the "New Wars" of/on Children', 38 *Brook.J.Int'l L.* 1053–1107.
Redress, 2006, *Victims, Perpetrators or Heroes? Child Soldiers before the International Criminal Court*, September 2006.
Risacher, B.J., 2013–2014, 'No Excuse: The Failure of the ICC's Article 31 "Duress" Definition', 89 *Notre Dame L.Rev.* 1403–1426.
Robinson, D., 2013, 'A Cosmopolitan Liberal Account of International Criminal Law', 26 *L.J.I.L.* 127–153.
Scaliotti, M., 2001, 'Defences before the International Criminal Court: Substantive Grounds for Excluding Criminal Responsibility—Part 1', 1 *Int.C.L.R.* 111–172.
Schmidt, A., 2007, 'Volunteer Child Soldiers as Reality: A Development Issue for Africa', 2 *N.S.E.R.* 49–76.
SCSL *Fofana and Kondewa*, 2007, *Prosecutor v. Fofana and Kondewa*, Special Court for Sierra Leone, Judgment, Case No. SCSL-04-14-T, 2 August 2007.
SCSL *Norman*, 2004, *Prosecutor v. Hinga Norman*, Special Court for Sierra Leone, Decision on Preliminary Motion Based on Lack of Jurisdiction (Child Recruitment), Case No. SCSL-04-14-AR72(E), Dissenting Opinion of Justice Robertson, 31 May 2004.
SCSL *Sesay*, 2009, *Prosecutor v. Hassan Sesay et al.*, Special Court for Sierra Leone, Judgment, Case No. SCSL-04-15-T, 2 March 2009.
Singer, P., 2005, *Children at War* (Pantheon Books).
Singh, D., 2007, 'When a Child is not a Child: The Scourge of Child Soldiering in Africa', 7 *A.H.R.L.J.* 206–224.

Smith, S.W., 2011, 'Youth in Africa: Rebels without a Cause but not without Effect', 31 *SAIS Review* 97–110.

Souris, R.N., 2017, 'Child Soldiering on Trial: An Interdisciplinary Analysis of Responsibility in the Lord's Resistance Army', 13 *Int.J.L.C.* 316–335.

Stahn, C., 2019, *A Critical Introduction to International Criminal Law* (CUP).

Swart, M. and S. Hassen, 2016, 'A Comparison Between the Position of Child Marriage 'Victims' and Child Soldiers: Towards a Nuanced Approach', 16 *A.H.R.L.J.* 458–475.

Tercier Holst-Roness, F., 2006, *Violence against Girls in Africa during Armed Conflicts and Crises*, Second International Policy Conference on the African Child: Violence against Girls in Africa, International Committee of the Red Cross, Addis Ababa, 11–12 May 2006.

Tomuschat, C., 2006, 'The Legacy of Nuremberg', 4 *J.I.C.J.* 830–844.

Trenholm, J., et al., 2012, 'Constructing Soldiers from Boys in Eastern Democratic Republic of Congo', 16 *Men and Masculinities* 203–227.

UK *M'Growther*, 1746, Commission for the Trial of the Rebels, (1746) Fost 13, 31 July 1746.

UNICEF, 2002, *Adult Wars, Child Soldiers: Voices of Children Involved in Armed Conflict in the East Asia and Pacific Region*, 2002, https://www.unicef.org/sowc06/pdfs/pub_adultwars_en.pdf (last visited 2 March 2019).

UNSG, 1996, United Nations Secretary General, *Promotion and Protection of the Rights of Children. Impact of Armed Conflict on Children*, U.N. Doc. A/51/306, 26 August 1996.

UNSR, 2008, Special Representative of the Secretary-General for Children and Armed Conflict, Written Submissions, Situation in the Democratic Republic of the Congo in the Case of *The Prosecutor v. Lubanga Dyilo*, Submitted in Application of Rule 103 of the Rules of Procedure and Evidence, Case No. ICC-01/04-01/06-1229-AnxA 18-03-2008 2/10 CB T, 17 March 2008.

UNSR, 2011, Special Representative of the Secretary-General for Children and Armed Conflict, *Children and Justice during and in the Aftermath of Armed Conflict*, Working Paper No. 3, September 2011.

US *Einsatzgruppen*, 1948, *United States v. Ohlendorf (Einsatzgruppen)*, Military Tribunal, Opinion and Judgment, Case No. 9, 8–9 April 1948, available at http://www.worldcourts.com/imt/eng/decisions/1948.04.09_United_States_v_Ohlendorf.pdf (last visited 18 February 2019).

US *Milch*, 1947, *United States v. Milch*, Military Tribunal, Judgment, Case No. 39, 20 December 1946—17 April 1947, available at http://www.worldcourts.com/imt/eng/decisions/1947.04.17_United_States_v_Milch.pdf (last visited 2 September 2018).

Waschefort, G., 2015, *International Law and Child Soldiers* (Hart).

Weigend, T., 2012, 'Kill or Be Killed. Another Look at *Erdemović*', 10 *J.I.C.J.* 1219–1237.

Werle, G. and F. Jessberger, 2014, *Principles of International Criminal Law* (3rd edn., OUP).
Wessells, M., 2006, *Child Soldiers: From Violence to Protection* (HUP).
West, H.G., 2000, 'Girls with Guns: Narrating the Experience of War of FRELIMO's "Female Detachment"', 73 *Anthropol.Q.* 180–194.
Wiener, N., 2014, 'Excuses, Justifications, and Duress at the International Criminal Tribunals', 26 *Pace Int'l L.Rev.* 88–131.
Wright, Q., 1949, 'International Law and Guilt by Association', 43 *A.J.I.L.* 746–755.
Yee, S., 1997, 'The *Erdemovic* Sentencing Judgement: A Questionable Milestone for the International Criminal Tribunal for the Former Yugoslavia', 26 *Ga.J.Int'l & Comp.L.* 263–309.

CHAPTER 5

Duress as an Excuse Defence for International Crimes

1 Introduction

The application of the defence of duress essentially viewed as a justification reveals that even child soldiers who are considered, by and large, as innocent victims caught in a violent conflict cannot successfully invoke duress. The likelihood of any adult doing so is even slimmer, and this certainly raises questions as to whether there is any point in offering a defence of duress that remains theoretical and impractical.

As the International Criminal Court (ICC) Statute is the product of a combination of common law and civil law systems,[1] and Article 31 has managed to bring together the two systems,[2] there is some room for manoeuvre regarding how the defence or, more accurately phrased, the ground to exclude criminal responsibility of duress can be interpreted. Against this backdrop, the authors propose to cast duress as an excuse rather than as a justification defence. The authors nonetheless concede that although it is not the ultimate answer, it seems to be the most suitable, bearing in mind that any solution to remedy the predicament of child soldiers' inability to invoke duress as a defence must (1) allow for the defence to negate and not only diminish culpability and (2) be applicable to all defendants and not only children.

Four reasons can be adduced to explain why duress understood as an excuse could be used by child soldiers: (1) it allows society to affirm that the conduct is not permitted; (2) it gives the court the opportunity to

W. Nortje, N. Quénivet, *Child Soldiers and the Defence of Duress under International Criminal Law*,
https://doi.org/10.1007/978-3-030-20663-5_5

focus on the actor rather than the act and thus deal 'sympathetically' with the child soldier phenomenon, thereby adopting a child-friendly interpretation of the law; (3) relatedly, because 'the nature of the crime and the proportionality of the act of the crime regulate the degree of sympathy we feel for the accused'[3] it keeps some notional sense of proportionality in the equation and (4) allows the tribunal to consider the 'defence' in all its variations, that is, as a ground excluding responsibility as well as a mitigating factor.

That being said, as the authors are conscious that the ICC will never judge the acts committed by child soldiers due to its jurisdictional limitation, they intend to discuss the law within a wider framework, beyond that of the narrow situation of child soldiers. In fact, the plight of child soldiers, both as victims and perpetrators, presents the unique opportunity to illustrate key problems relating to the application of the strict criteria of duress under international criminal law.

2 Understanding the Wrongful Conduct

A defence framed as an excuse, as opposed to a justification, assuredly indicates that a crime has been committed and that the international society does not tolerate such crimes. In the context of an excuse, the conduct is unlawful, but society understands that in the given circumstances the actor could not behave in a different manner and that it is not in the interests of society to punish the individual.[4] The point is not to endorse an individual's actions but to acknowledge the extreme situation in which he/she was placed. In other words, an excuse 'does not express society's approval of her act but only a certain degree of empathy'.[5] It still allows society, via judicial proceedings, to regard these acts with general opprobrium. Such a stance is vindicated by the fact that excuses focus on the actor rather than on the act. In this instance, 'a coerced actor is properly excused when her decision to engage in wrongful conduct finds sufficient understanding amongst the community to warrant an exemption from liability.'[6]

If duress is considered an excuse that 'negatives criminal culpability even though it does not wholly negative wrongfulness',[7] then the crimes perpetrated by children are treated for what they are, that is, war crimes, crimes against humanity and crimes of genocide, and all irrespective of the age of the perpetrator. These are acts plainly prohibited under international law, and perpetrators of such acts must be prosecuted.

Firstly, international treaties and customary law compel States to prosecute individuals who are alleged to have committed such crimes.[8] With regard to crimes committed in an international armed conflict, States are obliged to search for and prosecute individuals, be they members of the armed forces or private actors,[9] for grave breaches under Article 50 of the Geneva Convention I,[10] Article 51 of the Geneva Convention II,[11] Article 130 of the Geneva Convention III,[12] Article 147 of the Geneva Convention IV[13] and Article 85 of the Additional Protocol I.[14] There are further war crimes not listed in the grave breaches provisions. Whilst no similar treaty obligation relating to acts carried out in non-international armed conflicts exist, Rule 158 of the International Committee of the Red Cross (ICRC) Study on Customary International Humanitarian Law covers these situations as it specifies that 'states must investigate war crimes allegedly committed by their nationals or armed forces, or on their territory, and, if appropriate, prosecute the suspects. They must also investigate other war crimes over which they have jurisdiction and, if appropriate, prosecute the suspects', irrespective of the nature of the armed conflict.[15] Following from this, States have the duty to scrutinise alleged war crimes and, if appropriate, prosecute the suspects.[16] With regard to the crime of genocide, Article I of the 1948 Convention on the Prevention and Punishment of the Crime of Genocide unmistakeably stipulates that 'genocide [...] is a crime under international law' and that States Parties to the Convention must prosecute individuals who commit genocide.[17] Such duty to prosecute individuals suspected of genocide is further enshrined in Article IV of the Convention, and Article V obliges States to enact criminal legislation to punish such individuals. The caveat is the scope of the jurisdiction of States that remains territorial according to Article VI of the Convention. Whether a duty to prosecute crimes against humanity exists is the subject of lengthy academic debate, though most scholars seem to agree that it does, at least in relation to acts taking place in the territory of the State.[18] Additionally, the statutes as well as the jurisprudence of various international criminal and hybrid tribunals have strengthened the fight against impunity[19] for international crimes and paved the way to the establishment of the ICC.

Secondly, there is no immunity for such crimes,[20] they must be prosecuted even if an amnesty has been granted or if the perpetrator holds an official position. The International Criminal Court Statute, however, is silent on the matter whether individuals who receive national amnesty could still be prosecuted for the commission of crimes under international law.[21] In the Gaddafi Decision the ICC clearly stated that granting amnesties for serious acts was 'incompatible with internationally recognized human rights' as they prevented States from investigating, prosecuting and punishing perpetrators of international crimes.[22] The Court added that there was a 'strong, growing, universal tendency that grave and systematic human rights violations – which may amount to crimes against humanity by their very nature – are not subject to amnesties or pardons under international law'.[23] This further supports the view that customary international law has not yet developed in this regard.[24] That being said, numerous other international tribunals and domestic courts have stated in the past that amnesties should not be a bar to the prosecution of international crimes. For example, the Special Court for Sierra Leone stated that no amnesties can be granted for international crimes.[25] This position was recently reiterated by the Ugandan Supreme Court in *Kwoyelo*, a case involving a former child soldier.[26] Moreover, the statutes and the case-law of international criminal tribunals deny the applicability of immunities that inhere to one's official position,[27] for example, Head of State or Government.[28] This dates back to the IMT as Article 7 of the Charter enunciated that '[t]he official position of defendants, whether as Heads of State or responsible officials in Government Departments, shall not be considered as freeing them from responsibility or mitigating punishment'.[29] It was reiterated in the Nuremberg Principles,[30] and more contemporary examples include Article 7 of the ICTY Statute, Article 8 of the ICTR Statute, Article 6(2) of the Statute of the Special Court for Sierra Leone[31] and Article 27 of the ICC Statute which anchor the irrelevance of official capacity in the prosecution of alleged perpetrators of international crimes. The ICC has recently explained that '[i]t is of note that article 27(2) of the Statute is a clear provision in conventional law; but it also reflects the status of customary international law'.[32] As Ambos explains, '[t]his is one of the few provisions which has survived since Nuremberg without being substantially amended or challenged'[33] so that, as Scaliotti notes, '[s]ince the beginning of the PrepCom works broad consensus for the Statute to disallow any plea based on the official position of an accused was expressed'.[34] Both Charles Taylor and Slobodan Milošević[35] were hauled before the Special Court for Sierra Leone[36] and the ICTY,[37] respectively, the former having unsuccessfully relied on his official capacity as a bar to prosecution.[38]

Thirdly, apart from the ICC Statute that contains a *jurisdictional* clause relating to the age of perpetrators,[39] most international criminal tribunals' statutes are silent on the matter.[40] However, hybrid courts, such as the Special Court for Sierra Leone,[41] the War Crimes Chamber in the Court of Bosnia-Herzegovina[42] and the Special Panels for Serious Crimes in East Timor,[43] allow for the prosecution of individuals over the ages of 15, 14 and 12, respectively.[44] This demonstrates that age is no bar to the prosecution of individuals for international crimes.[45]

Consequently, international law mandates the prosecution of individuals accused of such offences and offers no immunity from prosecution. Therefore, duress cannot be a justification for international crimes, but it can be regarded as an excuse.

The knock-on effect of regarding duress as an excuse and acknowledging the fact that children commit crimes under international law which cannot be justified is that it would signal the end of a 'responsibility-free' age bracket of 15- to 18-year-old children viewed as innocent. At the moment, the ICC Statute 'sends the wrong message to those who are involved in the recruitment of children to participate as child soldiers'.[46] Also, it would discourage individuals from recruiting child soldiers on the basis that they can do their 'dirty work' whilst being free from prosecution.[47] After all, given that many children are forcefully recruited, the prosecution of a child soldier is often a trenchant testimony to the crimes of the armed group of which he/she was a part.

By considering duress as an excuse, a court would assuredly confirm these legal positions: the act is wrongful and must be condemned; yet the actor, that is, the child soldier, can be excused. 'We identify with the actor's dilemma, but we are repulsed by his actions'.[48] In this case, one needs to ascertain that the way the perpetrator acted 'is sufficiently comprehensible to warrant an exemption from punishment'.[49] The loaded question is, however: comprehensible to whom? Whilst in domestic criminal trials a jury, usually comprised of nationals and/or residents, represents the voice of society and thus its values, there is no such jury sitting in trials before international and hybrid criminal tribunals and it would be unrealistic to gather one.[50] Thus, the question is directed at the judges who will have to ascertain how society views the perpetrator. But the question is whose values do the judges represent? In international criminal tribunals, judges stem from a pool of individuals usually representing a variety of States and legal traditions. It is therefore important for international tribunals to have a balanced approach when selecting their judges. Consideration must be given as to whether the judges are versed in the various legal traditions of the cases they need to adjudge. In hybrid tribunals, some judges are nominated by the State where the crimes were committed,[51] and hence their values and morals might be closely related to the society that suffered at the hands of the perpetrators. Unfortunately, as defences are rarely ever used in international criminal trials and, moreover, no research has been carried out as to how a judge's societal background influences his/her views on the application of defences, it is impossible to gauge which values these judges incarnate and will apply. An alternative way to determine the moral yardsticks against which child soldiers should be judged in relation to the duress plea is to refer to the 'international community', all the more as international crimes are defined as attacks on humanity and as affronts to the international community as a whole.[52]

Still, can an attack on society in the form of a crime against humanity or an act of genocide ever be comprehended by society, whether national or international? After all, such perpetrators are viewed as ***hostis humani generis***, enemies of humankind.[53] Society tends to adopt an uncompromising view of such individuals; they are vilified.[54] As Chiesa underlines, '[a]n actor who chooses to save herself by wiping out a significant number of members of the community is unlikely to provoke sufficient feelings of understanding among the public to justify relieving her of criminal responsibility'.[55] One of the problematic issues is that understanding leads to forgiveness, and forgiveness might lead to amnesia.[56] The only potential recipients of such tonalities of compassion and clemency are likely to be children who are generally viewed as less culpable due to their immaturity. They essentially epitomise victimhood. At the national level, former child soldiers are nonetheless viewed with mixed feelings. Whilst some sections of the population might understand their actions, others believe they have gone too far. The reaction of the Acholi population to the prosecution of Kwoyelo is revealing in this regard: some view him as that innocent child forced to commit terrible crimes, whilst others consider that he has 'placed himself outside the moral jurisdiction of Acholi responses to wrongdoing'.[57] Judged at the national level, child soldiers might not be the recipients of much comprehension and so might not even be excused.

The situation is slightly different at the international level. Indeed, increasingly, the international community's view of child soldiers is that, although they might have been implicated in the worst crimes, 'they are to be regarded first and foremost as victims'.[58] A wide array of UN bodies have confirmed that 'children associated with armed groups should not be detained or prosecuted, but should be *primarily* treated as victims by virtue of their age and forced nature of their association'.[59] Likewise, though in slightly more nuanced terms, the non-legally binding Paris Commitments encourage States to consider children '*primarily* as victims of violations against international law and *not only* as alleged perpetrators'.[60] International society has, through the United Nations, NGOs and particular States, pushed towards viewing children as victims. In Drumbl's words, 'criminally prosecuting child soldiers … [is] increasingly… viewed as inappropriate and undesirable'.[61] According to this trend, it can be contended that international society is likely to comprehend a child soldier's behaviour. After all, if it foregoes prosecution it will even more readily acknowledge duress as an excuse in such instances. Out of compassion for the circumstances in which child soldiers lived the international society can acquit child soldiers whilst still recognising that their conduct is wrongful. The law would thereby show a certain measure of flexibility. If such a trend perdures on the international level, it is likely to seep into the national level to the effect that children are considered more as victims than perpetrators and so excused in their criminal behaviour.

3 Focus on the Actor

A second reason for approaching duress as an excuse is that the defence focusses on the actor rather than the act. The actor is excused because of the extreme pressure though the conduct as such is not deemed permissible.[62] It 'addresses the culpability of the actor as an issue separate from the character of the conduct'.[63] Claims of excuse point to the blameworthiness of the actor in the concrete situation. There is no moral virtue in the act (as indicated above, the act is unmistakably reprehensible), but the individual might show some moral virtue as a person. It is particularly revealing that some empirical studies show that some former child soldiers perceive themselves as perpetrators,[64] understanding the severity of the acts they have committed.[65] As Wainryb explains, they 'are grappling in problematic ways, with their actions and their sense of themselves as moral agents'.[66] Even in their own eyes, the line between victims and perpetrators is blurred. The duress excuse removes objectivity in ascertaining whether the act is reasonable, to focus on the peculiar situation and the peculiar characteristics of the perpetrator.

Duress is assuredly a context-based defence. Whereas it might be possible to view duress as a defence for contextually justified conduct, considered as an excuse it 'covers a wide range of contexts and conditions and it applies to claims of widely varying moral character'.[67] Accordingly, duress as an excuse puts at the heart of this discussion on child soldiers a more general inquiry into the person's 'real' autonomy, and thus assists in generating an improved understanding of the person's actions in the relevant context. More specifically, this allows taking into account: (1) the overall context in which the crimes are committed; (2) the unique, past experience of the person and (3) the lack of free will of the person. As Rosen explains, the '[e]xcuse theory allows the fact-finder to consider the whole individual and to evaluate whether, under the circumstances, her life experience enabled her to choose between criminal and noncriminal conduct'.[68] Whilst all these arguments relate to the situation of child soldiers as examined above and, as a result, unfurl the complexity of the child soldier phenomenon, they more generally put into relief the predicament of individuals, children and adults alike, who are both victims and perpetrators.

With regard to the 'range of contexts and conditions' experienced by the individual, inevitably the concrete background of the armed conflict must be taken into consideration as it places substantial burdens on human moral capacities. The omnipresence of a coercive and violent environment plays on the mind of the perpetrator[69] and the population at large.[70] In keeping with the human frailty doctrine,[71] a perpetrator should not be punished for acting in a way that most other individuals also would have chosen to.[72] Given the circumstances, the perpetrator's behaviour is not statistically abnormal.[73] In fact, '[m]ost perpetrators of international crimes are ordinary people in extraordinary circumstances, who have been gradually transformed into perpetrators through submission to an authoritarian leader, a genocidal ideology, or an oppressive regime'.[74] The question centres on what can be reasonably expected from someone in the given circumstances. As Judge Cassese rationalises, 'law is based on what society can reasonably expect of its members. It should not set intractable standards of behaviour which require mankind to perform acts of martyrdom, and brand as criminal any behaviour falling below those standards.'[75] It becomes, in fact, unreasonable to expect ordinary moral perception in extraordinary circumstances, even from a trained soldier.[76] Paphiti duly notes that 'to issue a blanket denial of the defense to soldiers is, with respect, going too far'.[77] The person has fallen victim to terrible circumstances[78] and is forgiven for not living up to the highest moral expectations. As the Judge stated in the *Goldstein* Case, 'do not judge your fellow-man until you have walked in his shoes'.[79]

This perspective is however not without glaring flaws. After all, pushed to its limits, appreciating and recognising the influence of the environment on individuals may lead to a presumption of non-responsibility.[80] The very purpose of the notion of individual criminal liability, which 'constitutes the bedrock of the international criminal justice system',[81] disappears under the mantle of the circumstances in which the crimes are committed. The collectivity and the environment, not the person, are deemed responsible. As Drumbl highlights with great lucidity in his article 'Victims who Victimise', it is often the environment in which individuals are put that enables crimes to be committed.[82] Using the example of the deportation and massacre of Armenians from a village in Turkey, Kurt poignantly demonstrates that international crimes do not happen in a vacuum; the support of the local population is critical in implementing a particular policy.[83] In situations of genocide, all fringes of the society take part in the crimes, transgressing all established age-, gender-, religion- and social status-related divisions.[84] Whilst this might be true, espousing such a view is dangerous. Indeed, whereas recognising a too broad defence of duress based on the environment might chime well with an understanding of humans as being frail, such stance completely dilutes and, in fact, negates the concept of personal responsibility. The importance of individual criminal responsibility and how it has revolutionised the enforcement of international law cannot be overemphasised.[85] The idea that individuals could be held responsible for mass atrocities was deliberated at the Nuremberg Trials, and it was decided that '[c]rimes against international law are committed by men, not by abstract entities, and only by punishing individuals who commit such crimes can the provisions of international law be enforced'.[86] What is more, '[i]nternational legal prescriptions are capable of imposing obligations directly on individuals, without the intermediary of the state wielding authority over such individuals'.[87] While the ICTY and the ICTR have fulfilled their duty to prosecute individuals who were involved in the respective situations, it is the ICC that has emerged as the primary legal response to the threats posed by individuals who commit crimes under international law, 'the ICC Statute [being] the core document of international criminal law today'.[88] The prosecution of Ongwen at the ICC confirms the notion that individuals who have allegedly committed crimes under international law will be prosecuted for such crimes, even though Ongwen was a child soldier before he became an adult soldier. The principle of individual criminal responsibility therefore stands as one of the success stories of the international criminal law discourse.

Context should not only be conceptualised as related to society and institutions at large but also as deeply personal and rooted in a person's lived experience. The background and experience of the individual will indubitably affect his/her moral character and accordingly his/her choices when faced with a situation of duress. Past experience will inform a person's decision to act in a certain manner, and, therefore, particular importance should be paid to the person's lived experience as such. The situation is particularly aggravated by the fact that almost all child soldiers suffer from post-traumatic stress-related symptoms[89] and the fact that they cannot properly process their experience.[90] 'In a sense, the phenomenon of child soldiers feeds upon itself. Each round of fighting creates a new cohort, traumatized by the war and bereft of hope and skills, who then become a potential pool and catalyst for the next spate of violence'.[91]

Albeit personal,[92] a child soldier's experience is sadly not uncommon, and similar experiences can be discerned.[93] 'Child soldiers are psychologically scarred due to the violent methods used by armed groups. These include indoctrination, forced intoxication and duress'.[94] Thus, when it is stated that Ongwen was 'a victim of circumstances and, these circumstances shaped his choices significantly. His motivations are a product of the context he lived in as a victim',[95] his predicament as a child soldier who was abducted at a young age in an armed conflict in Africa is a well-known one and does not need reiterating. His wrenching 'personal' experience is well-documented by copious, long-standing and excellent research in the area, and accordingly truly recognised.

However, readily welcoming such a point of view is somewhat erroneous too. It must be refined and nuanced as not all children fall victim to armed opposition groups. Indeed, some child soldiers might see their participation in armed conflict as a new lease on life, as many child soldiers are orphans prior to joining armed groups.[96] Such children might, in fact, have consciously chosen the path to violence: '[W]illingness to engage in violence could reflect the obligations of young people to ensure retribution for and restore honor to those individuals, groups, or beliefs that are cherished and have been defiled. Therefore, engagement in political struggle may in fact be an assertion of enhanced moral commitment and reasoning.'[97] Eventually, 'the chance to become a child soldier is a way to gain status, to gain a surrogate family, and to speak out amongst her male counterparts.'[98] Against all the odds, they may have strong moral competence[99] and may not be living without any moral compass at all.[100] As Park notes, 'children are capable of reasonable decision making and are political actors'.[101] Child soldiers might willingly commit particularly cruel acts when deployed in an operation far away from their commanders.[102] In this case, it becomes difficult to contend that children are simply obeying orders. From interviews carried out by Macdonald and Porter with persons who knew Kwoyelo as a child, it seems that he was exactly that type of child: 'his actions were not due to the "bad surroundings" of war but because essentially at his core he is rotten'.[103] Put plainly, a child's personal experience might be that of someone who has fully embraced the environment and who has not fallen victim to it.

It goes without saying that there is no one single profile of a child soldier, and that some are more responsible than others.[104] Owing to the fact that there is diversity in the children's 'capacity to exercise agency and to make independent choices'[105] and thus personal experience, it is contended that in all cases 'the assessment of a child's awareness of the choices open to him or her, whether to join the armed groups or to commit atrocities, should be undertaken critically, with due consideration to a child's vulnerability and limited understanding'.[106]

To avoid the danger of giving too much consideration to the general environment and a child's personal experience, it is more appropriate to combine them with the individual's inability to make any autonomous decision at the given time. Such a proposal would be more in accordance with some of the case-law of the post-World War II (WWII) trials as reviewed and synthesised by Joyce in his excellent article on duress,[107] and with the definition of duress as understood by some national criminal law systems.[108] Not only are the circumstances deemed coercive—in our case the general environment and the child's experience of the overall situation—but also the 'actor actually acted by reason of fear or compulsion arising from those coercive circumstances'.[109] As Joyce further elucidates, the case-law distinguishes between situations whereby a person is put in a difficult situation and others whereby 'a reasonable man would apprehend that he was in such imminent physical peril as to deprive him of freedom to choose'.[110] Undoubtedly the case-law of post-WWII trials accentuates more the importance of the mental state of the person rather than the act itself, thus viewing duress more as an excuse than a justification, and so adopting a less strict and conservative approach than the one espoused by the ICTY in *Erdemović*. It is the loss of actual freedom to choose how to act that is paramount in deciding, in the light of the coercive circumstances, whether there was indeed duress. 'Duress is an excuse that is premised on the idea that the actor is incapable of making a moral choice due to the overwhelming force of the threat [...]'.[111] As an excuse, duress 'speak[s] of circumstances that diminish or destroy the operation of the actor's free will such that concessions to human frailty require that the behaviour be forgiven'.[112]

The narrative is thus constructed around the concepts of autonomy and choice. To some extent this reverts to, and borrows ideas from, the discussion on voluntariness in Chap. 4, though the two must be distinguished as the former is about the will relating to joining the group and the latter about the will relating to carrying out the unlawful act.[113] In law, these are two separate legal requirements, and thus two different tests. If the individual committed the crime, there are two possible reasons why he/she acted in such a way: firstly, he/she went along with the principle behind the order he/she was given in the sense that he/she supports the principle and believes it to be right; secondly, he/she opposes the principle. The concepts of voluntariness and willingness centre on the divide between the first and second reason: did the defendant willingly accommodate the 'request' (rather than the threat)? For example, Flick and Weiss could not avail themselves of the defence of duress because they had 'approved of the principle behind the order'.[114] As Wall clearly explains, 'there is a *deliberate choice* between two alternatives and the movement of the limbs *originates within the agent*.'[115] The choice is free and deliberate.

Now, let's turn to the second reason. In contrast, discussing the autonomy of an individual is about splitting the second reason into three possible courses of action: (2.1) the person did not wish to show any resistance because it was the least difficult option; (2.2) the person showed resistance but on balance decided to protect his/her life or that of others dear to him/her; and (2.3) the person showed resistance and did not carry out the order (in which case he/she or his/her relatives might have paid the price with their lives). After all, in an excuse such as duress 'overwhelming external circumstances cause a mental pressure such that no reasonable person could resist it'.[116] The authors argue that the stress should be on 'free will' or *libre arbitre* in French law. The first option would, in the light of the post-WWII trials jurisprudence, fail the test and not be considered duress. The second option would, according to the *Erdemović* jurisprudence, fail the test too. In other words, only option three, that of sacrificing one's life, would be contemplated as duress. This makes little sense because it means that in the case where a person is threatened with his life duress can only be successfully pleaded if the person is dead (as the threat has been executed), in which case it cannot even be pleaded since there is no alleged criminal alive and no crime committed![117] As Robinson notes, 'a law that requires one to die in order to avoid censure is close to nonsensical.'[118] More crudely put, the application of this conception of duress shows that duress is a theoretical defence deprived of any concrete application in cases of international crimes involving the killing of a person.[119] Duress could potentially only be pleaded in cases where the threat was not executed or where the person's bodily integrity, rather than his/her life, was threatened. As a conclusion, the authors argue that the *Erdemović* jurisprudence must be set aside, and the law must allow for duress to be pleaded when the person shows resistance but owing to a lack of moral choice (there is no alternative) commits a crime to save his/her life or the individuals dear to him/her. However, the consequences of such a position need to be fully understood, and so, care must be exercised to avoid the law to be too broad-encompassing. Thus, the requirements of proportionality and not doing greater harm must be revised in accordance with these new elements.

4 Proportionality, and Not a Balance of Harms, Test

The idea that in the case of duress as a justification, we expect the person, as a moral agent, to take a stand and to sacrifice his/her own life or those of persons who are dear to him/her to preserve those of others is beyond a layperson's comprehension.[120] The argument of the sanctity of human life fails in view of the reality on the ground. As Weigend stresses, 'there [is no] [...] good reason for the law to demand or expect the sacrifice of a person's life, even if several others could thereby be saved.'[121] The application of this doctrine to child soldiers is even more incomprehensible. That society expects normal, reasonable individuals to show some level of resilience and resistance is understandable as this acts as a distinguishing factor between the above-mentioned reasons 2.1 (the person did not wish to show any resistance because it was the least difficult option) and 2.2 (the person showed resistance but on balance decided to protect his/her life or that of others dear to him/her); however, that it requires martyrdom is not.[122] As the Tribunal in the *Einsatzgruppen* Case explained in plain terms: '[l]et it be said at once that there is no law which requires that an innocent man must forfeit his life or suffer serious harm in order to avoid committing a crime which he condemns. The threat, however, must be imminent, real and inevitable. No court will punish a man who, with a loaded pistol at his head, is compelled to pull a lethal lever.'[123] Accordingly, the authors suggest that the requirement of proportionality be revised and the requirement of greater harm discounted.

The requirement of proportionality must be revised in the light of this new emphasis on the concept of autonomy and, more specifically, on the margin of autonomy of the individual. Risacher underlines that '[a]rguably an individual who is truly under duress does not intend to cause any harm since his free will and ability to make a moral decision has been overcome.'[124] As a consequence, he suggests that 'the proportionality requirement that currently limits the applicability of duress [...] be removed' on the basis that '[d]uress is an excuse, not a justification.'[125] He notably argues that '[b]y removing the proportionality requirement, the defense of duress would be restored as an excuse rather than a justification, and would better reflect principles of moral culpability and fundamental fairness.'[126] Whilst a person with some autonomy might indeed be able to act with some measure of proportionality, someone with little or no autonomy at all (and that is likely to be the case of a child soldier) will not. This approach chimes well with the approach espoused in civil law systems that negate responsibility in cases where the free will of a person was destroyed.[127] For example, in the *Papon* Case, the Appeal Court of Bordeaux declared that the pressures exercised on the defendant were not of such an intensity that they could be considered as a compulsion that had abolished the free will (*libre arbitre*) of Papon.[128] The principle of proportionality would be automatically fulfilled if the person had absolutely no free will, no possibility to act in any other way. After all, if the person 'lacked a fair opportunity to avoid acting unlawfully',[129] he/she had no choice at all.[130]

However, in contrast to Risacher, the authors do not suggest eliminating the proportionality requirement altogether as this would take away the distinguishing element between the aforementioned reason 2.1 and reason 2.2 to commit the act. Legal and policy considerations vindicate keeping the proportionality requirement. If it were to be discarded, then an individual might succumb too easily to the coercive environment.[131] For example, in *Touvier* the court pointed out that the defendant 'relie[d] unhesitatingly on the pressures exerted by the Germans to claim a state of necessity susceptible of constituting a justification'.[132] It might open a door to collusion and thereby encourage illegal behaviour. Also, 'society requires citizens to assume minimum obligations of solidarity toward their fellow citizens in order to make life in community possible'.[133] Rather, the authors propose that the proportionality requirement be diligently interpreted in the light of the realities of the environment at the time(s) of duress.

Generally, 'excuses will apply only when the wrongful conduct is substantially more attributable to coercive influences than to free will'.[134] In the former situation (reason 2.1) there is some, even if limited, choice, and the individual must make a moral choice and be able to *justify* that choice[135]; in the latter (reason 2.2), there is little or none and thus the individual must be *excused* for his/her act. If the individual had no more freedom than a pawn on a chessboard, then why punish him/her for acting the way he/she did?[136] As a matter of fact, the jurisprudence stemming from the post-WWII trials essentially focussed on whether the individual's free will had been constrained to such a level that punishing him/her would be considered unjust.[137] Ultimately, as Zahar and Sluiter emphasise, the individual is 'reduced to an instrument by means of which another person committed murder'[138] or any other unlawful act. The situation is particularly highlighted in the case of children who, it is submitted, are used by unscrupulous adults. After all, the claim put forward by many scholars and institutions dealing with the protection of children in armed conflict is that they are nothing more than pawns in an adult war.[139] As the Special Panel for East Timor acknowledged, the defendant, a minor, 'was like a tool on [sic] the hand of the true responsible for campaign of violence orchestrated against civilian population who was not following the autonomy within Indonesian [sic]'.[140] This requirement of proportionality viewed in the light of autonomy would ensure that a person who is able to make choices (e.g., Ongwen made certain choices including planning large-scale atrocities)[141] cannot avail themselves of the defence of duress. After all, he took advantage of the situation.

In light of the concrete situations in which international crimes are committed, the requirement of acting with a view to cause no greater harm than the harm threatened must be removed. This proposal is in conformity with the argument that duress is an excuse. 'The difference between justified and excuse necessity depends on whether the claim is that the criminal act led to a less evil outcome (and is therefore justified) or was the product of psychological coercion (and is therefore excused).'[142] In fact, the sanctity of human life argument used in the *Erdemović* Case is solidly grounded in the act and the circumstances around the act and not the mental state of the perpetrator.[143] Common law (and so contemporary international criminal law) expects 'a willingness to value the lives of others over one's own life, and to sacrifice one's own life, if necessary, for the good of another'.[144] Such an approach fails to understand human nature and is therefore nothing but a chimerical defence in cases where a person's life, or the life of a person dear to him/her, is at stake. Moreover, as mentioned before, applying this requirement to the situation of a child soldier who is still developing his/her ability to make important decisions is inconceivable. Child soldiers are more often than not also recruited into armed groups that instil fear in the children, which hampers the decision-making ability of such child soldiers. The child soldiers lose all sense of reality and the key point for them is not whom to kill or not to kill, but to survive at all costs.

As Chiesa notes, if duress is considered as an excuse then 'it would, as a general rule, be improper to limit its availability to cases where the actor chose the lesser evil'.[145] In his view, the fundamental question is 'whether the society could have reasonably required the defendant to overcome the coercion and resist the threats'.[146] This idea is probably best reflected in the German notion of *Zumutbarkeit* which questions what can be expected from someone in the given circumstances.[147] In English, this can be translated as 'fair expectability of defiance to psychological and physical compulsion',[148] or 'what a person can be fairly expected to put up with in the relevant circumstances'.[149] As Krebs explains, interpreting the concept of 'reasonable' in such a way allows for duress under Article 31(1)(d) to be classified as an excusatory defence.[150] The application of such a concept allows for a more nuanced approach towards duress, focussing on the individual and the surrounding circumstances, still keeping duress as an excuse and yet using some of the proportionality quality. In other words, is it fair to expect the individual to put aside his survival and self-preservation instincts? Refusing to act might be morally laudable but 'criminal law will not demand that we are all be heroes'.[151] Again, this bolsters the necessity to keep the proportionality element whilst removing the greater harm test as it allows distinguishing between those who (too) readily embrace the ideology of the group and commit crimes in the belief that they will move up the ranks and be empowered, and those who go along as they realise that there is no way they can disregard their 'duties', the difference between a 'Dominic Ongwen' child soldier and another child soldier.

The point nevertheless is not to give *carte blanche* to spineless individuals; the law still needs to discourage heinous crimes and protect civilians. Removing the 'greater harm' requirement and yet keeping the proportionality requirement as interpreted in the light of the principle of autonomy ensures that individuals are forced to consider whether and how they can act lawfully. As Bassiouni puts it more poignantly, duress is a 'concession to the instinct of human survival'.[152] Yielding to coercive threats that leave little or no choice to an individual might be wrongful but understandable. Therefore, the conduct should not be punished: it is excusable.

5 A Full Defence

The fourth benefit of interpreting duress as an excuse is that it discards the approach adopted by the ICTY in the *Erdemović* Case and which is prevalent in common law countries. Indeed, '[i]f duress is an excuse, the common law blanket rule excluding it as a defense to murder should be rejected. Granting an excuse to an actor who kills under coercion is not tantamount to recognizing that she had a right to kill her victim.'[153] If, as suggested above, the law does not require self-sacrifice then it should afford a full defence.[154]

The way the defences' provision is phrased under the ICC Statute enables the court to use any defence as a full, complete defence, finding the defendant not guilty. After all, it is, according to the language of the Statute, a ground for *excluding* criminal responsibility.[155] With this view, the court is well advised to consider duress as an excuse. As an excuse, the ICC would be able to use duress as a full defence, that is, a defence to crimes leading to the death of an individual, for example, direct attack on civilians or incidental effects of an attack on civilians. As sad as it is to say, some deaths are more excusable than others.

The additional advantage of allowing duress as an excuse means that it can be used both as a ground excluding responsibility *and* as a mitigating factor.[156] It is in this sense a defence in the broader understanding of the term. Although excuses tend to be dealt with at the sentencing stage, they are also exonerating defences. 'It is in fact a matter of policy whether a legal system grants a full excuse or merely reduces the penalty of a person who unlawfully commits an offence in a situation of particular strain.'[157] It is imperative to understand that an excuse defence affects the culpability of the individual and can lead to his/her acquittal. In contrast, a mitigating factor is only examined once the culpability of the individual has been established.[158] The ICC's Rules on Procedure and Evidence explicitly state that the ICC will take mitigating factors into account during sentencing including 'circumstances falling short of constituting grounds for exclusion of criminal responsibility, such as substantially diminished mental capacity or duress'.[159]

The authors argue that duress can be a complete excuse, go towards mitigation or do neither, and so the court could use the full panoply of possible levels of culpability and ensuing sentences. Bearing in mind the great variety of armed conflict-related, societal, collective and personal circumstances relating to duress, judges would be better equipped to respond adequately to the range of severity and types of coercion[160] levelled against alleged perpetrators under duress. For example, a situation where an individual has no free will, no autonomy at all, and has originally unambiguously rejected carrying out the act, might lead the judges to accept duress as a ground excluding responsibility, especially if, given the circumstances, the principle of proportionality has been respected. What is important in such an instance is that at the sentencing stage the court clearly indicates that this is an excuse and not a justification as it might otherwise send the wrong message: the act is wrong, the legal norm has been breached but the actor is excused and thus released from the consequences normally attached to such a violation.[161] A situation where, on the other hand, an individual has reluctantly killed a group of persons to save his/her own life as he/she has witnessed the killing of fellow soldiers refusing to execute a group of people, but has not clearly identified his/her opposition and has in the past gone along with similar orders, would give judges the opportunity to consider duress as a mitigating factor. Depending on the strength of the evidence provided by the defendant, the judges might also consider that in fact the alleged perpetrator had truly embraced the ideology of the group at the time, and was only at the time of the prosecution showing remorse and trying to rationalise his/her behaviour.[162] In this case, the judges might well feel that the person was not under duress at all, and that, it should not be considered even at the mitigation stage.

Furthermore, allowing the court flexibility in using duress as a ground for excluding responsibility and as a mitigating factor protects the rights of the defendant. The commission of murder as a crime under international law should therefore not be regarded as an offence that automatically excludes duress, since duress is a complete defence under international criminal law. Allowing defendants to raise duress for crimes under international law is paramount for the effective administration of international criminal justice. ‘It is not because the ICC deals with the most heinous crimes that persons accused must be recognised as culpable with no possibility to prove that their intention was not criminal.’[163] Whilst it is important to prosecute these crimes, it is similarly important to protect the rights of the defendant, which include the right to be presumed innocent until proven guilty. Article 66 of the ICC Statute unmistakably provides that ‘[e]veryone shall be presumed innocent until proved guilty before the Court in accordance with the applicable law’.[164] A different approach would clearly go against the current evolution of international criminal law and human rights law. Juveniles are afforded similar protection, as provided for by the United Nations Convention on the Rights of the Child (UNCRC).[165] The UNCRC has also made it clear that States Parties to the UNCRC must establish 'rules, regulations or protocols which enhance equal treatment of child offenders and provide redress, remedies and compensation'.[166] The Committee on the Rights of the Child also sets out a number of guidelines specifically geared towards the protection of the rights of juveniles who could possibly face prosecution for crimes under international law, while at the same time encourages States Parties to implement a juvenile justice policy in line with the UNCRC.[167] Importantly, the UNCRC provides that States Parties must guarantee that juveniles have access to legal representation which includes the preparation of a defence.[168]

All in all, child soldiers deserve special protection due to the unique circumstances during their recruitment. Including duress as a full defence under international law satisfies the rights of the international community which demands that defendants be prosecuted for such crimes, but at the same time protects the fair trial rights of the accused. The rights of the defendant, and in particular child soldiers, are limited by restricting the defence of duress as a justificatory defence. The authors consequently submit that the defence of duress should be a complete defence under international law.

6 Conclusion

The need to maintain that international crimes are crimes and that the perpetrators are prosecuted act in favour of viewing duress as an excuse. This ensures that the wrongfulness of the act is stressed whilst allowing for some compassion for the perpetrator. In this framework the whole 'package', that is, the context in which these crimes are committed, the past experience of the perpetrator and the limited or lack of autonomy and free will of the perpetrator, needs to be thoroughly examined on a case-by-case basis and properly understood, especially in relation to child soldiers. Whilst the authors argue that the defence of duress must be considered as an excuse, they contend that some element of proportionality must be retained, though it must be connected to the 'package'. An added benefit of duress as an excuse is that it enables the court to decide whether it is, in the specific context of the prosecution of an individual, a full defence or a mitigating factor if the individual falls short of fulfilling its requirements. The main advantage of revisiting duress as an excuse is that such a solution does not only benefit child soldiers but also adults. As previously stressed, the authors do not plead in favour of a special law of duress for children but for a better understanding of their situation.

Notes

1. Cassese et al. 2013, 6. See Ambos 2013, 56.
2. Gilbert 2006, 144; Schabas 2016, 636; Ambos 2013, 302.
3. Wall 2006, 739.
4. Joyce 2015, 637. See Ambos 2013, 305; Paciocco 2010, 243.
5. Weigend 2011, 1232; Cryer et al. 2014, 399.
6. Chiesa 2008, 745. Fletcher puts it differently and states that: '[t]he question should not be whether the actor can be fairly expected to resist human threats, but whether he can fairly expect to abstain from an act that seems required under the circumstances.' Fletcher 2000, 834.
7. Colvin 1990, 393. See discussion in Fletcher 1998, 83–85.
8. Ursini 2015, 1040 (in relation to the Geneva Conventions and genocide).
9. Sassòli 2002, 411–412.
10. Geneva Convention for the Amelioration of the Condition of the Wounded and Sick in Armed Forces in the Field 1949.
11. Geneva Convention for the Amelioration of the Condition of the Wounded, Sick and Shipwrecked Members of the Armed Forces at Sea 1949.
12. Geneva Convention Relative to the Treatment of Prisoners of War 1949.
13. Geneva Convention Relative to the Protection of Civilian Persons in Time of War 1949.
14. Protocol Additional to the Geneva Conventions of 12 August 1949, and Relating to the Protection of Victims of International Armed Conflicts (Additional Protocol I) 1977.
15. ICRC 2019. See discussions in Schmitt 2011, 44–48; Roht-Arriaza 1990, 465–467; Manirakiza 2008–2009, 736. Further, the statutes and the case-law of international criminal tribunals such as the ICTY, the ICTR, the SCSL and the ICC have jurisdiction over crimes perpetrated in international and/or non-international armed conflicts.
16. Akande 2012, 300; Cryer et al. 2014, 90; Roht-Arriaza 1990, 513.
17. Convention on the Prevention and Punishment of the Crime of Genocide 1948.
18. Hall and Ambos 2016, 155. See Schabas and Zeidy 2016, 786; Schabas 2016, 47.
19. For a definition of impunity, see UNSC 1997, 17.
20. See Cassese et al. 2013, 241–247; Horovitz et al. 2014, 227.

21. See discussion in Sadat 2006, 1022. Also, the ECCC stated in ECCC *Nuon et al.* 2011, para. 53, that 'the Chamber concludes that an emerging consensus prohibits amnesties in relation to serious international crimes, based on a duty to investigate and prosecute these crimes and to punish their perpetrators.' The crimes the Court refers to are genocide, torture and grave breaches of the Geneva Conventions. For other crimes, the ECCC argues that it is left to courts to evaluate amnesties.
22. ICC *Gaddafi* 2019, para. 77.
23. ICC *Gaddafi* 2019, para. 61.
24. Sadat 2006, 1022. For an opposing view, see Werle and Jessberger 2014, 88–89; Ambos 2013, 422–423.
25. SCSL *Kallon and Kamara* 2004. See Cassese et al. 2013, 244; Triffterer and Burchard 2016, 1052; Williams 2005.
26. Uganda *Kwoyelo* 2015. See Drumbl 2016, 238–239.
27. See discussion in Fournet 2008, 514–519; Cryer et al. 2014, 540; Ambos 2013, 411.
28. See Triffterer and Burchard 2016, 1052; Cryer et al. 2014, 540–541; Ambos 2013, 406–407.
29. Charter of the International Military Tribunal 1945; Charter of the International Military Tribunal for the Far East 1946. This was confirmed in the Nuremberg Judgement that proclaimed that '[t]he principle of international law which, under certain circumstances, protects the representatives of a state, cannot be applied to acts which are condemned as criminal by international law. The authors of these acts cannot shelter themselves behind their official position in order to be freed from punishment in appropriate proceedings'. *Re Goering* (1946) 13 ILR 203 (IMT) 221 as cited in Fournet 2008, 514. See also Ambos 2013, 413–414.
30. ILC 1950, Principle III.
31. SCSL Statute 2002.
32. ICC *Al-Bashir* 2019, para. 103.
33. Ambos 1999, 23.
34. Scaliotti 2002, 41. See Schabas 2016, 595.
35. For information on the case, see http://www.icty.org/case/slobodan_milosevic/4 (last visited 15 July 2018).
36. SCSL *Taylor* 2013.
37. In relation to Kosovo: ICTY *Milošević et al.* 2001; In relation to Croatia: ICTY *Milošević* 2001a; In relation to Bosnia-Herzegovina: ICTY *Milošević* 2001b.
38. SCSL *Taylor* 2004. For an analysis of the case, see Frulli 2004; Nouwen 2005; Frulli 2013.
39. In *Orić*, the ICTY opined that '[r]eference to Article 26 of the … Statute [of the ICC] is of no relevance as the age limit mentioned therein is only for jurisdictional purposes'. ICTY *Orić* 2006, fn 1177. See Drumbl 2012, 119.

40. See discussion in Drumbl 2012, 118.
41. SCSL Statute 2002, Art. 7. See Triffterer and Clark 2016, 1036.
42. See Criminal Code of Bosnia-Herzegovina, Arts 1(8) and 8.
43. UNTAET 2001.
44. Neither the Statute of the Extraordinary Chambers in the Courts of Cambodia nor the Statute of the Special Tribunal for Lebanon makes any reference to the age of the alleged perpetrator.
45. See discussion in Akakpo 2012, 30. See generally Quénivet 2017.
46. Freeland 2005, 324.
47. See Ursini 2015, 1034; Akakpo 2012, 24; Freeland 2005, 324.
48. Joyce 2015, 642.
49. Chiesa 2008, 762.
50. See Degan 2005, 55.
51. The Special Court for Sierra Leone has a mixed composition consisting of judges from Sierra Leone and international judges. For example, in SCSL *Kallon and Kamara* 2004, the three judges were Judge Renate Winter (Austria), Judge George Gelaga King (Sierra Leone) and Judge Emmanuel Ayoola (Nigeria).
52. Crimes under international law can be defined as the 'most serious crimes of concern to the international community as a whole'. ICC Statute 1998, Preamble. See Zimmermann 2016, 117; Cassese et al. 2013, 20; Schabas 2017, 75; Kittichaisaree 2001, 3.
53. See discussion in Mohamed 2015, 1213.
54. See Kochhar and Hieramente 2016, 231 and 243–244.
55. Chiesa 2008, 763–764.
56. Mohamed 2015, 1210.
57. Macdonald and Porter 2016, 710, but see discussion in whole article.
58. United Nations Secretary-General 2000, para. 7. See Nylund 2016, 201; Siegrist 2006, 55; Happold 2006, 76–81.
59. UNSR 2011, 27. See United Nations Committee on the Rights of the Child 2009, para. 72; Manirakiza 2008–2009, 722.
60. ICRC 2007, para. 11 (emphasis added).
61. Drumbl 2012, 103 and discussion 102–103.
62. Byrd 1987, 1301.
63. Colvin 1990, 389. See Robinson 1997, 81.
64. Klasen et al. 2015, 185–186. See Wessells 2006, 78–80; Fisher 2013, 82.
65. Iacono 2002, 450.
66. Wainryb 2011, 288.
67. Colvin 1990, 392. It is particularly interesting to note that Colvin suggests that defences be divided into three categories, one of which being 'defences of contextual permission' which allow for exculpation in cases of 'conduct which is reasonable in the sense that it might well be the conduct of a person displaying an ordinary level of concern for the welfare of others' (407).

68. Rosen 1986, 23.
69. See Bond and Fougere 2014, 498.
70. See Fisher 2013, 76–80.
71. See Paphiti 1999, 272.
72. Heim 2013, 169.
73. Dressler 1988–1989, 1363–1364.
74. Smeulers 2008, 973.
75. ICTY *Erdemović* 1997, para. 47. See Paphiti 1999, 272.
76. May, L., *Crimes against Humanity: A Normative Account* (New York: Cambridge University Press, 2005) as cited in Souris 2017, 330.
77. Paphiti 1999, 272.
78. Another way to look at this is to combine the defences of necessity and duress. See discussion in Bassiouni 2013, 441.
79. As cited in Ben-Naftali 2009, 696. See discussion in Singer 2013, 253.
80. Doris, J.M. and D. Murphy, 'From My Lai to Abu Ghraib: The Moral Psychology of Atrocity' 31 *Midwest Studies in Philosophy* (2007) 25–55 as cited in Souris 2017, 330.
81. Olusanya 2010, 69.
82. Drumbl 2016.
83. Kurt 2018. See discussion in Fisk 2018.
84. Dumas 2014, 79.
85. Greppi 1999; Werle and Jessberger 2014, 195. For a comprehensive overview of the difficulties faced with drafting the concept of individual criminal responsibility within the ICC Statute, see Schabas 2016, 561–564.
86. International Military Tribunal 1946, 221. See Werle and Jessberger 2014, 6.
87. Cassese et al. 2013, 3.
88. Werle and Jessberger 2014, 27.
89. Derluyn et al. 2004, 862–863; Klasen et al. 2015, 184–191. Generally, research demonstrates that perpetrators suffer from a variety of mental health problems. Mohamed 2015, 1163 and 1187.
90. Mohamed 2015, 1170.
91. Singer 2005, 109.
92. Huyghebaert 2009, 70; Drumbl 2015.
93. See Derluyn et al. 2004, 861; Nagle 2011, 2–3.
94. Nortje 2017, 196; Singer 2005, 88.
95. Baines and Boniface 2008, 10. See Baines 2009, 181.
96. Haer and Böhmelt 2016, 414; Coomaraswamy 2012, 159; Waschefort 2015, 49–52.
97. Boyden 2003, 356.
98. Valder 2014, 44. See Huyghebaert 2009, 62.

99. Lafayette 2012–2013, 306.
100. Sinha 2013, 588; Posada and Wainryb 2008.
101. Park 2014, 58.
102. See Drumbl 2012, 87–88.
103. Macdonald and Porter 2016, 712.
104. Akakpo 2012, 24.
105. Maclure and Denov 2006, 131.
106. Amnesty International 2000, 6–7. See Brett and Specht 2004, 9. Such a case-by-case assessment is not only warranted for children only but for a range of perpetrators. As Drumbl underlines, the false simplicity of setting a chronological age to the end of childhood yields the sad consequence of denying young adults whose physiological development is not finished the opportunity to be regarded as children. Drumbl 2014–2015, 626.
107. Joyce 2015, 626–630.
108. For example, the focus of the definition of duress under French law is on the force constraining the defendants' choice. French Criminal Code, Art. 122-2 states that '[a] person is not criminally liable who acted under the influence of a force or a constraint which they could not resist'. See discussion in Elliott 2000, 321; Wiener 2014, 95; Yee 1997, 296–297.
109. Joyce 2015, 629.
110. US *German High Command* 1947–1948. See Joyce 2015, 639.
111. Risacher 2013–2014, 1417; Wiener 2014, 124–125; Dinstein 2000, 373; Dinstein 1985, 2333.
112. Bond and Fougere 2014, 489. See also Knoops 2008, 49.
113. As Linton and Reiger stress, '[d]uress to join a group engaged in criminal activities and duress to commit a crime when part of that group requires its own evidence.' Linton and Reiger 2001, 197.
114. Joyce 2015, 628. US *Flick et al.* 1947, 8–9. See Lippman 1992, 87.
115. Walls 2006, 737.
116. Knoops, 'The Diverging Position of Criminal Law Defences before the ICTY and the ICC: Contemporary Developments', in Doria, J., et al. (eds), *The Legal Regime of the International Criminal Court: Essays in Honour of Professor Igor Blishchenko* (Brill, 2009) 779–794, 783 as cited in Weigend 2011, fn 56.
117. See relevant discussion by Ambos 2013, 361–362.
118. Robinson 2013, 150.
119. Ambos states that 'the remaining question is no longer whether duress/necessity can be invoked in the case of a killing of innocent persons at all, but rather what the specific requirements of such a defence are and how, from a theoretical point of view, it is to be clarified'. Ambos 2013, 363.
120. See Paphiti 1999, 272.

121. Weigend 2011, 1228. Similarly, The English Law Commission held that 'it is not only futile, but also wrong, for the criminal law to demand heroic behaviour. The attainment of a heroic standard of behaviour will always count for great merit; but failure to achieve that standard should not be met with punishment by the State'. See Legislating the Criminal Code: Offences Against the Person and General Principles 1993, para. 30.11. See Naylor 2006, 27. For an opposing view, see Dinstein 2000, 375, who states that 'neither ethically nor legally can the life of the accused be regarded as more valuable than that of another human being (let alone a number of human beings).'
122. See, for example, Carr 1991, 173; Smith 1989, 94.
123. US *Einsatzgruppen* 1948, 480. See Risacher 2013–2014, 1422. Similarly, in *Priebke* the Court explained that 'no person could have expected Priebke to act as a hero and to sacrifice his own life in order to avoid participating in the inhumane execution'. ICTY *Erdemović* 1997, fn 68 (translation by Cassese). The original reads as follows: 'in tale ipotesi, infatti, nessuno avrebbe potuto pretendere dal PRIEBKE un comportamento eroico ed il sacrificio della propria vita per evitare di concorrere in una disumana esecuzione.' Italy *Priebke* 1955, para. 9.2. See Dinstein 2000, 374.
124. Risacher 2013–2014, 1417. Knoops echoes this statement by stating that 'an accused is considered not to be criminally responsible for his/her acts only if the conduct was the result of factors preventing him or her from exercising his or her free will, which factors are in most events external to the person, such as is the case with duress'. See Knoops 2008, 54.
125. Risacher 2013–2014, 1405.
126. Risacher 2013–2014, 1421. See also Ambos 2013, 364.
127. See Risacher 2013–2014, 1408; Akakpo 2012, 43; Yee 1997, 297.
128. 'il ne ressort pas de l'instruction que les pressions ainsi faites ont été d'une telle intensité qu'elles aient pu constituer une contrainte ayant aboli le libre arbitre de Maurice PAPON.' France *Papon* 1996.
129. Dressler 1988–1989, 1365. See also Fletcher who states that '[t]here is no criminal liability without blameworthy wrongdoing.' Fletcher 1998, 85.
130. See Heim 2013, 169.
131. In an excuse, 'the relevant question is whether the particular actor can fairly be blamed for having succumbed to overwhelming pressure'. Rosen 1986, 23.
132. *Touvier* Case, Cour d'Appel de Versailles, 1ère chambre d'accusation, 2 June 1993, AN-647AP93 as cited in ICTY *Erdemović* 1997, fn 68 (translation by Cassese). See Bassiouni 2013, 447.
133. Chiesa 2008, 767.

134. Rosen 1986, 22. See UK *Hudson* 1971; Fletcher 2000, 831.
135. Risacher 2013–2014, 1417.
136. See Fisher 2013, 66.
137. See Joyce 2015, 626–627.
138. Zahar and Sluiter 2008, 429.
139. See for example discussion in Dumas 2014, 81 on children being used as tools in Rwanda. Fisher 2013, 64.
140. East Timor Tribunal *X* 2002, para. 57.
141. Nortje 2017, 198. See Baines 2009, 179–180.
142. Cassese et al. 2013, 215. See discussion in Smith 1989, 95.
143. Risacher 2013–2014, 1425. See discussion in Ambos 2013, 354.
144. Ehrenreich Brooks 2002–2003, 873. See also Werle and Jessberger 2014, 242; Smith 1989, 94.
145. Chiesa 2008, 753.
146. Chiesa 2008, 753. See ICTY *Erdemović* 1997, para. 47; Ehrenreich Brooks 2002–2003, 876; Brooks 2016, 211.
147. See Germany *Gestapo Informer* 1949, 202. See Fletcher 1998, 83.
148. Burchard 2009, 693.
149. Krebs 2013, 409; Ambos 1999, 28.
150. Krebs 2013, 409.
151. Happold 2003, 1163.
152. Bassiouni, M.C., *Crimes against Humanity in International Criminal Law* (Springer) 439 as cited in Achton Thomas 2013, 30.
153. Chiesa 2008, 753.
154. Greenawalt 2011, 1118.
155. Grant 2016, 18. See Ambos 2013, 302.
156. Grant 2016, 19. See Ambos 2013, 303–304; Carr 1991, 161. For a critique of the ICTY's lack of distinction between excuses and mitigating circumstances, see Olusanya 2010, 41–47; Cryer et al. 2014, 506–507.
157. Weigend 2011, 1233.
158. See Pruitt 2014, 152.
159. ICC Rules of Procedure and Evidence 2013, Rule 145 (2)(a)(i). See Cryer et al. 2014, 506–507.
160. Warburton explains that whether duress is used as a ground for excluding responsibility or as a mitigating factor depends on the nature of the coercion. Warburton 2003, 83.
161. Berman 2003, 5.
162. For a list of factors that could be considered by the ICC, see Cryer et al. 2014, 507.
163. Gilbert 2006, 144.
164. Generally, see Roberts 2012; Cryer et al. 2014, 439–440; Ambos 2013, 312–313; Schabas 2016, 1006–1007.

165. UNCRC, Art. 40(2)(b)(i).
166. United Nations Committee on the Rights of the Child 2007, para. 10.
167. United Nations Committee on the Rights of the Child 2007, para. 4.
168. United Nations Committee on the Rights of the Child 2007, paras 49–50.

References

Achton Thomas, M., 2013, 'Malice Supplies the Age? Assessing the Culpability of Adolescent Soldiers', 44 *Cal.W.Int'l L.J.* 1–38.

Akakpo, L., 2012, '*Procureur c. X*: les enseignements à tirer de la poursuite des enfants soldats pour crimes contre l'humanité', 42 *R.G.D.* 9–56.

Akande, D., 2012, 'The Effect of Security Council Resolutions and Domestic Proceedings on State Obligations to Cooperate with the ICC', 10 *J.Int'l Crim. Just.* 299–324.

Ambos, K., 1999, 'General Principles of Criminal Law in the Rome Statute', 10 *Crim.L.F.* 1–32.

Ambos, K., 2013, *Treatise on International Criminal Law: Volume I: Foundations and General Part* (OUP).

Amnesty International, 2000, *Child Soldiers. Criminals or Victims?*, AI Index: IOR 50/02/00, December 2000.

Baines, E., 2009, 'Complex Political Perpetrators: Reflections on Dominic Ongwen', 47 *J.Mod.Afr.Stud.* 163–191.

Baines, E. and O. Boniface, 2008, 'Complicating Victims and Perpetrators in Uganda: On Dominic Ongwen', 7 *Justice and Reconciliation Project Field Note* (July) 1–19.

Bassiouni, M.C., 2013, *Introduction to International Criminal Law* (2nd edn., Martinus Nijhoff).

Ben-Naftali, O., 2009, 'Goldstein (Cr. C. 93/52) *Attorney General v. Goldstein*, Israel, District Court, Tel-Aviv, 15 July 1953, unpublished', in Cassese, A. (ed.), *Oxford Companion to International Criminal Justice* (OUP) 696–696.

Berman, M.N., 2003, 'Justification and Excuse, Law and Morality', 53 *Duke L.J.* 1–77.

Bond, J. and M. Fougere, 2014, 'Omnipresent Threats: A Comment on the Defence of Duress in International Criminal Law', 14 *Int.C.L.R.* 471–512.

Boyden, B., 2003, 'The Moral Development of Child Soldiers: What Do Adults Have to Fear?', 9 *Peace Confl.* 343–362.

Brett, R. and I. Specht, 2004, *Young Soldiers: Why They Choose to Fight* (Lynne Rienner).

Brooks, R., 2016, *How Everything Became War and the Military Became Everything* (Simon and Schuster Paperbacks).

Burchard, C., 2009, 'Gestapo Informer Case', in Cassese, A. (ed.), *Oxford Companion to International Criminal Justice* (OUP) 693.

Byrd, B.S., 1987, 'Wrongdoing and Attribution: Implications beyond the Justification—Excuse Distinction', 33 *Wayne L.Rev.* 1289–1342.

Carr, C.L., 1991, 'Duress and Criminal Responsibility', 10 *Law and Philosophy* 161–188.

Cassese, A., et al., 2013, *Cassese's International Criminal Law* (3rd edn., OUP).

Charter of the International Military Tribunal, 1945, in Agreement for the Prosecution and Punishment of the Major War Criminals of the European Axis (London Agreement), 82 UNTS 280, 8 August 1945.

Charter of the International Military Tribunal for the Far East, 1946, Special Proclamation by the Supreme Commander for the Allied Powers at Tokyo, TIAS No. 1589, 19 January 1946.

Chiesa, L.E., 2008, 'Duress, Demanding Heroism and Proportionality', 41 *Vand.J.Transnat'l L.* 714–773.

Colvin, E., 1990, 'Exculpatory Defences in Criminal Law', 10 *O.J.L.S.* 381–407.

Convention on the Prevention and Punishment of the Crime of Genocide, 1948, General Assembly Resolution 260 A (III), 9 December 1948.

Coomaraswamy, R., 2012, 'Protecting Children in Situations of Armed Conflict: Interview with Radhika Coomaraswamy', 4 *Journal of Human Rights Practice* 155–163.

Criminal Code of Bosnia Herzegovina, available at http://www.sudbih.gov.ba/files/docs/zakoni/en/krivicni_zakon_3_03_-_eng.pdf (last visited 1 August 2019).

Cryer, C., et al., 2014, *An Introduction to International Criminal Law and Procedure* (3rd edn., CUP).

Degan, V.-D., 2005, 'On the Sources of International Criminal Law', 4 *Chinese J.I.L.* 45–83.

Derluyn, I., et al., 2004, 'Post-traumatic Stress in Former Ugandan Child Soldiers', 363 *The Lancet* 861–863.

Dinstein, Y., 1985, 'International Criminal Law', 20 *Isr.L.Rev.* 206–242.

Dinstein, Y., 2000, 'Defences', in McDonald, G.K. and O. Swaak-Goldman (eds) *Substantive and Procedural Aspects of International Criminal Law: The Experience of International and National Courts*, Volume I: Commentary (Kluwer) 371–388.

Dressler, J., 1988–1989, 'Exegesis of the Law of Duress: Justifying the Excuse and Searching for its Proper Limits', 62 *S.Cal.L.Rev.* 1331–1386.

Drumbl, M., 2012, *Reimagining Child Soldiers in International Law and Policy* (OUP).

Drumbl, M., 2014–2015, 'Children, Armed Violence and Transition: Challenges for International Law and Policy', 43 *Ga.J.Int'l. & Comp.L.* 623–627.

Drumbl, M., 2016, 'Victims who Victimise', 4 *Lond.Rev.Int. Law* 217–246.

Drumbl, M.A., 2015, 'The Ongwen Trial at the ICC: Tough Questions on Child Soldiers', *Open Democracy*, 14 April 2015, available at https://www.opendemocracy.net/openglobalrights/mark-drumbl/ongwen-trial-at-icc-tough-questions-on-child-soldiers (last visited 2 September 2018).

Dumas, H., 2014, 'Enfants victimes, enfants tueurs. Expériences enfantines (Rwanda, 1994)', 2 *Vingtième Siècle. Revue d'histoire* 75–86.

East Timor Tribunal *X*, 2002, *Prosecutor v. 'X'*, East Timorese Public Administration, Dili District Court, Special Panel for Serious Crimes, Case No. 04/2002, 2 December 2002.

ECCC *Nuon et al.*, 2011, *Prosecutor v. Nuon et al.*, Extraordinary Chambers in the Courts of Cambodia, Decision on IENG Sary's Rule 89 Preliminary Objections (Ne Bis In Idem and Amnesty and Pardon), Case No. 002/19-09-2007-ECCC/TC, D51/15, 3 November 2011.

Ehrenreich Brooks, R., 2002–2003, 'Law in the Heart of Darkness: Atrocity & Duress', 43 *Va.J.Int'l J.* 861–888.

Elliott, C., 2000, 'A Comparative Analysis of Defences in English and French Criminal Law', 8 *Eur.J.Crime Cr.L.Cr.J.* 319–326.

Fisher, K.J., 2013, *Transitional Justice for Child Soldiers. Accountability and Social Reconstruction in Post-conflict Contexts* (Palgrave).

Fisk, R., 2018, 'Whether Armenia, the Nazis or Isis—If You're Going to Commit Genocide, You Can't Do it Without the Help of Local People', *The Independent*, 24 May 2018, available at https://www.independent.co.uk/voices/armenia-genocide-nazi-germany-poland-isis-looting-war-a8367071.html (last visited 17 July 2018).

Fletcher, G.P., 1998, *Basic Concepts of Criminal Law* (OUP).

Fletcher, G.P., 2000, *Rethinking Criminal Law* (OUP).

Fournet, C., 2008, 'When the Child Surpasses the Father—Admissible Defences in International Criminal Law', 8 *Int.C.L.R.* 509–532.

France *Papon*, 1996, *Papon* Case, Cour d'appel de Bordeaux, Chambre d'accusation, Judgment No. 806, 18 September 1996, available at http://www.haguejusticeportal.net/Docs/NLP/France/Papon_acte_accusation_18_09_96.pdf (last visited 2 August 2018).

Freeland, S., 2005, 'Child Soldiers and International Crimes—How Should International Law Be Applied?', 3 *N.Z.J.P.I.L.* 303–328.

French Criminal Code, available at https://www.legifrance.gouv.fr/affichCodeArticle.do?cidTexte=LEGITEXT000006070719&idArticle=LEGIARTI000006417214 (last visited 10 March 2019).

Frulli, M., 2004, 'The Question of Charles Taylor's Immunity: Still in Search of a Balanced Application of Personal Immunities?', 4 *J.Int'l Crim.Just.* 1118–1129.

Frulli, M., 2013, 'Piercing the Veil of Head-of-State Immunity: The Taylor Trial and Beyond', in Jalloh, C.C. (ed.), *The Sierra Leone Special Court and Its Legacy. The Impact for Africa and International Criminal Law* (CUP) 325–339.

Geneva Convention for the Amelioration of the Condition of the Wounded and Sick in Armed Forces in the Field, 1949, 75 UNTS 31, 12 August 1949.

Geneva Convention for the Amelioration of the Condition of the Wounded, Sick and Shipwrecked Members of the Armed Forces at Sea, 1949, 75 UNTS 85, 12 August 1949.

Geneva Convention Relative to the Protection of Civilian Persons in Time of War, 1949, 75 UNTS 287, 12 August 1949.

Geneva Convention Relative to the Treatment of Prisoners of War, 1949, 75 UNTS 135, 12 August 1949.

Germany *Gestapo Informer*, 1949, *Gestapo Informer* Case, Oberlandsgericht Freiburg i. Br., Ss 64/48, Hoechstrichterliche Entscheidungen, Sammlung von Entscheidungen der Oberlandesgerichte und der Oberststen Gerichte in Strafsachen, Volume 2, 200–203, 17 February 1949.

Gilbert, J., 2006, 'Justice Not Revenge: The International Criminal Court and the "Grounds to Exclude Criminal Responsibility"—Defences or Negation of Criminality?', 10 *I.J.H.R.* 143–160.

Grant, N., 2016, *Duress as a Defence for Former Child Soldiers? Dominic Ongwen and the International Criminal Court*, International Crimes Database Brief 21, December 2016.

Greenawalt, A.K.A., 2011, 'The Pluralism of International Criminal Law', 86 *Ind.L.J.* 1063–1130.

Greppi, E., 1999, 'The Evolution of Individual Criminal Responsibility under International Law', 835 *I.R.R.C.* 531–553.

Haer, R. and T. Böhmelt, 2016, 'Child Soldiers as Time Bombs? Adolescents' Participation in Rebel Groups and the Recurrence of Armed Conflict', 22 *Eur.J.Int.Relat.* 406–436.

Hall, C.K. and K. Ambos, 2016, 'Article 7: Crimes Against Humanity', in Triffterer, O. and K. Ambos (eds), *The Rome Statute of the International Criminal Court: A Commentary* (3rd edn., Beck) 144–294.

Happold, M., 2003, 'Excluding Children from Refugee Status: Child Soldiers and Article 1F of the Refugee Convention', 24 *Am.U.Int'l L.Rev.* 1131–1176.

Happold, M., 2006, 'The Age of Criminal Responsibility for International Crimes under International Law', in Arts, K. and V. Popovski (eds), *International Criminal Accountability and the Rights of Children* (Asser Press) 69–84.

Heim, S.J., 2013, 'The Applicability of the Duress Defense to the Killing of Innocent Persons by Civilians', 46 *Cornell Int'l L.J.* 165–190.

Horovitz, S., et al., 2014, 'The International Criminal Court', in Shany, Y. (ed.), *Assessing the Effectiveness of International Courts* (OUP) 223–252.

Huyghebaert, P., 2009, 'Les enfants dans les conflits armés: une analyse à l'aune des notions de vulnérabilité, de pauvreté et de "capabilités"', 2 *Mondes en développement* 59–72.

Iacono, M., 2002, 'The Child Soldiers of Sierra Leone: Are they Accountable for their Actions in War?', 26 *Suffolk Transnat'l L.Rev.* 445–467.

ICC *Al-Bashir*, 2019, *Prosecutor v. Al-Bashir*, International Criminal Court, Judgment in the Jordan Referral re A-Bashir Appeal, Case No. ICC-02/05-01/09 OA2, 6 May 2019.

ICC *Gaddafi*, 2019, *Prosecutor v. Gaddafi*, International Criminal Court, Decision on the 'Admissibility Challenge by Dr. Saif Al-Islam Gadafi pursuant to Articles 17(1)(c), 19 and 20(3) of the Rome Statute', Case No. ICC-01/11-01/11, 5 April 2019.

ICC Rules of Procedure and Evidence, 2013, ICC-ASP/1/3 and Corr.1, available at https://www.icc-cpi.int/iccdocs/pids/legal-texts/rulesprocedureevidenceeng.pdf (last visited 10 March 2019).

ICC Statute, 1998, Statute of the International Criminal Court, U.N. Doc. A/CONF.183/9, (1998) 2187 UNTS 90.

ICRC, 2007, *The Paris Commitments to Protect Children from Unlawful Recruitment or Use by Armed Forces or Armed Groups*, consolidated version, February 2007, *available at* http://www.icrc.org/eng/assets/files/other/the-paris-commitments.pdf (last visited 1 August 2018).

ICRC, 2019, Study on Customary International Humanitarian Law, available at https://www.icrc.org/customary-ihl/eng/docs/v1_cha_chapter44_rule158 (last visited 31 July 2018).

ICTY *Erdemović*, 1997, *Prosecutor v. Erdemović*, International Criminal Tribunal for the Former Yugoslavia, Judgment, Case No. IT-96-22-A, Dissenting Opinion of Judge Cassese, 7 October 1997.

ICTY *Milošević*, 2001a, *Prosecutor v. Milošević*, International Criminal Tribunal for the Former Yugoslavia, Initial Indictment, Case No. IT-01-50-I, 8 October 2001.

ICTY *Milošević*, 2001b, *Prosecutor v. Milošević*, International Criminal Tribunal for the Former Yugoslavia, Initial Indictment, Case No. IT-01-51-I, 22 November 2001.

ICTY *Milošević et al.*, 2001, *Prosecutor v. Milošević et al.*, International Criminal Tribunal for the Former Yugoslavia, Initial Indictment, Case No. IT-99-37-I, 22 May 1999, First Amended Indictment, 29 June 2001 and Second Amended Indictment, Case No. IT-99-37-PT, 16 October 2001.

ICTY *Orić*, 2006, *Prosecutor v. Orić*, International Criminal Tribunal for the Former Yugoslavia, Judgment, Case No. IT-03-68-T, 30 June 2006.

ILC, 1950, *Principles of International Law Recognized in the Charter of the Nürnberg Tribunal and in the Judgment of the Tribunal*, International Law Commission, 1950, available at http://legal.un.org/ilc/texts/instruments/english/draft_articles/7_1_1950.pdf (last visited 10 March 2019).

International Military Tribunal, 1946, 'Judgment, Nuremberg, 1 October 1946', 41 *A.J.I.L.* 172–306.

Italy *Priebke*, 1955, *Priebke* Case, Military Tribunal, Ordinanza del Giudice per l'Udienza Preliminare presso il Tribunale Militare di Roma, 7 December 1995, available at http://www.asser.nl/upload/documents/DomCLIC/Docs/NLP/Italy/Priebke_OrderPreliminaryAudience_7-12-1995.pdf (last visited 2 September 2018).

Joyce, M., 2015, 'Duress: From Nuremberg to the International Criminal Court, Finding the Balance between Justification and Excuse', 28 *L.J.I.L.* 623–642.
Kittichaisaree, K., 2001, *International Criminal Law* (OUP).
Klasen, F., et al., 2015, 'The Guiltless Guilty: Trauma-Related Guilt and Psychopathology in Former Ugandan Child Soldiers', 46 *Child Psychiatry Hum.Dev.* 180–193.
Knoops, G.A., 2008, *Defenses in Contemporary International Criminal Law* (Martinus Nijhoff).
Kochhar, S. and M. Hieramente, 2016, 'Of Fallen Demons: Reflections on the International Criminal Court's Defendant', 29 *L.J.I.L.* 223–244.
Krebs, B., 2013, 'Justification and Excuse in Article 31(1) of the Rome Statute', 2 *C.J.I.C.L.* 382–410.
Kurt, Ü., 2018, 'Theatres of Violence on the Ottoman Periphery: Exploring the Local Roots of Genocidal Policies in Antep', (Online) *J. Genocide Res.* 1–21.
Lafayette, E., 2012–2013, 'The Prosecution of Child Soldiers: Balancing Accountability with Justice', 63 *Syracuse L.Rev.* 297–325.
Legislating the Criminal Code: Offences Against the Person and General Principles (Law Com. No. 218, 1993), available at http://www.lawcom.gov.uk/app/uploads/2015/06/lc218.pdf (last visited 17 March 2019).
Linton, S. and C. Reiger, 2001, 'The Evolving Jurisprudence and Practice of East Timor's Special Panels for Serious Crimes on Admissions of Guilt, Duress and Superior Orders', 4 *Y.I.H.L.* 167–212.
Lippman, M., 1992, 'The Other Nuremberg: American Prosecutions of Nazi War Criminals in Occupied Germany', 3 *Ind.Int'l & Comp.L.Rev.* 1–100.
Macdonald, A. and H. Porter, 2016, 'The Trial of Thomas Kwoyelo: Opportunity or Spectre? Reflections from the Ground on the First LRA Prosecution', 86 *Africa* 698–722.
Maclure, R. and M. Denov, 2006, '"I Didn't Want to Die So I Joined Them": Structuration and the Process of Becoming Boy Soldiers in Sierra Leone', 18 *Terror. Political Violence* 119–135.
Manirakiza, P., 2008–2009, 'Les enfants face au système international de justice: à la recherche d'un modèle de justice pénale internationale pour les délinquants mineurs', 34 *Queen's L.J.* 719–768.
Mohamed, S., 2015, 'Of Monsters and Men: Perpetrator Trauma and Mass Atrocity', 115 *Colum.L.Rev.* 1157–1216.
Nagle, L.E., 2011, 'Child Soldiers and the Duty of Nations to Protect Children from Participation in Armed Conflict', 19 *Cardozo J.Int'l & Comp.L.* 1–58.
Naylor, M., 2006, 'Resistance Is Futile: Duress as a Defence to Intentional Killing', 2 *C.S.L.R.* 24–32.
Nortje, W., 2017, 'Victim or Villain: Exploring the Possible Bases of a Defence in the *Ongwen* Case at the International Criminal Court', 17 *Int.C.L.R.* 186–207.
Nouwen, S., 2005, 'The Special Court for Sierra Leone and the Immunity of Taylor: The Immunity Defence Continued', 18 *L.J.I.L.* 645–669.

Nylund, B.V., 2016, *Child Soldiers and Transitional Justice: Protecting the Rights of Children Involved in Armed Conflicts* (Intersentia).

Olusanya, O., 2010, 'Excuse and Mitigation under International Criminal Law: Redrawing Conceptual Boundaries', 13 *New Crim.L.Rev.* 23–89.

Paciocco, D.M., 2010, 'No-One Wants to Be Eaten: The Logic and Experience of the Law of Necessity and Duress', 56 *C.L.Q.* 240–293.

Paphiti, A.S., 1999, 'Duress as Defence to War Crimes Charges', 38 *Mil.L.Rev.* 247–298.

Park, A.S.J., 2014, 'Constituting Omar Khadr: Cultural Racism, Childhood, and Citizenship', 8 *Int. Political Sociol.* 43–62.

Posada, R. and C. Wainryb, 2008, 'Moral Development in a Violent Society: Colombian Children's Judgments in the Context of Survival and Revenge', 79 *Child Development* 882–898.

Protocol Additional to the Geneva Conventions of 12 August 1949, and Relating to the Protection of Victims of International Armed Conflicts (Additional Protocol I), 1977, 1125 UNTS 3, 8 June 1977.

Pruitt, W.R., 2014, 'Aggravating and Mitigating Sentencing Factors at the ICTR: An Exploratory Analysis', 14 *Int.C.L.R.* 148–176.

Quénivet, N., 2017, 'Does and Should International Law Prohibit the Prosecution of Children for War Crimes?', 28 *E.J.I.L.* 433–455.

Risacher, B.J., 2013–2014, 'No Excuse: The Failure of the ICC's Article 31 "Duress" Definition', 89 *Notre Dame L.Rev.* 1403–1426.

Roberts, R.C.E., 2012, 'The Lubanga Trial Chamber's Assessment of Evidence in Light of the Accused's Right to the Presumption of Innocence', 10 *J.Int'l Crim.Just.* 923–943.

Robinson, D., 2013, 'A Cosmopolitan Liberal Account of International Criminal Law', 26 *L.J.I.L.* 127–153.

Robinson, P.H., 1997, *Structure and Function in Criminal Law* (OUP).

Roht-Arriaza, N., 1990, 'State Responsibility to Investigate and Prosecute Grave Human Rights Violations in International Law', 78 *C.L.R.* 449–513.

Rosen, C.J., 1986, 'The Excuse of Self-Defense: Correcting a Historical Accident on Behalf of Battered Women Who Kill', 36 *Am.U.L.Rev.* 11–56.

Sadat, L.N., 2006, 'Exile, Amnesty and International Law', 81 *Notre Dame L.Rev.* 955–1036.

Sassòli, M., 2002, 'State Responsibility for Violations of International Humanitarian Law', 87 *I.R.R.C.* 401–434.

Scaliotti, M., 2002, 'Defences before the International Criminal Court: Substantive Grounds for Excluding Criminal Responsibility—Part 2', 2 *Int.C.L.R* 1–46.

Schabas, W.A., 2016, *The International Criminal Court: A Commentary on the Rome Statute* (2nd edn., OUP).

Schabas, W.A., 2017, *An Introduction to the International Criminal Court* (5th edn., CUP).

Schabas, W.A. and M.E. Zeidy, 2016, 'Article 17: Issues of Admissibility', in Triffterer, O. and K. Ambos (eds), *The Rome Statute of the International Criminal Court: A Commentary* (3rd edn., Beck) 781–831.

Schmitt, M., 2011, 'Investigating Violations of International Law in Armed Conflict', 2 *Harvard National Security Journal* 31–84.

SCSL *Kallon and Kamara*, 2004, *Prosecution v. Kallon and Kamara*, Special Court for Sierra Leone, Decision on Challenge to Jurisdiction: Lomé Accord Amnesty, Case Nos SCSL-2004-15-AR72(E) and SCSL-2004-16-AR72(E), 13 March 2004.

SCSL Statute, 2002, Statute of the Special Court for Sierra Leone, Enclosure to the Report of the Secretary–General on the Establishment of a Special Court for Sierra Leone, U.N. Doc. S/2000/915, 2178 UNTS 138, 16 January 2002.

SCSL *Taylor*, 2004, *Prosecutor v. Taylor*, Special Court for Sierra Leone, Decision on Immunity from Jurisdiction, Case No. SCSL-03-01-I-59, 31 May 2004.

SCSL *Taylor*, 2013, *Prosecutor v. Taylor*, Special Court for Sierra Leone, Judgment, Case No. SCSL-03-01-A, 26 September 2013.

Siegrist, S., 2006, 'Child Participation in International Criminal Accountability Mechanisms: The Case of the Sierra Leone Truth and Reconciliation Commission', in Arts, K. and V. Popovski (eds), *International Criminal Accountability and the Rights of Children* (Asser Press) 53–66.

Singer, I.M., 2013, '*Reductio ad absurdum*: The *Kapo* Trial Judgements' Contribution to International Criminal Law Jurisprudence and Customary International Law', 24 *Crim.L.F.* 235–258.

Singer, P., 2005, *Children at War* (Pantheon Books).

Sinha, G.A., 2013, 'Child Soldiers as Super-Privileged Combatants', 17 *I.J.H.R.* 584–603.

Smeulers, A., 2008, 'Punishing the Enemies of All Mankind', 21 *L.J.I.L.* 971–993.

Smith, J.C., 1989, *The Hamlyn Lectures: Justification and Excuse in the Criminal Law* (40th series, Stevens and Sons).

Souris, R.N., 2017, 'Child Soldiering on Trial: An Interdisciplinary Analysis of Responsibility in the Lord's Resistance Army', 13 *Int.J.L.C.* 316–335.

Triffterer, O. and C. Burchard, 2016, 'Article 27: Irrelevance of Official Capacity', in Triffterer, O. and K. Ambos (eds), *The Rome Statute of the International Criminal Court: A Commentary* (3rd edn., Beck) 1037–1055.

Triffterer, O. and R.S. Clark, 2016, 'Article 26: Exclusion of Jurisdiction over Persons under Eighteen', in Triffterer, O. and K. Ambos (eds), *The Rome Statute of the International Criminal Court: A Commentary* (3rd edn., Beck) 1030–1036.

Uganda *Kwoyelo*, 2015, *Uganda v. Kwoyelo*, Supreme Court, Constitutional Appeal No. 1 of 2012, 8 April 2015.

UK *Hudson*, 1971, *R. v. Hudson*, House of Lords, [1971] 2 All E.R. 244 (Crim. App.).

UNCRC, 1989, United Nations Convention on the Rights of the Child, 1577 UNTS 3, 20 November 1989.

United Nations Committee on the Rights of the Child, 2007, *General Comment No. 10: Children's Rights in Juvenile Justice*, U.N. Doc. CRC/C/GC.10, 25 April 2007.

United Nations Committee on the Rights of the Child, 2009, *Consideration of Reports Submitted by States Parties under Article 44 of the Convention. Concluding Observations: Democratic Republic of Congo*, U.N. Doc. CRC/C/COD/CO/2, 10 February 2009.

UNSC, 1997, United Nations Sub-Commission on Prevention of Discrimination and Protection of Minorities, *The Administration of Justice and the Human Rights of Detainees—Question of the Impunity of Perpetrators of Human Rights Violations (Civil and Political)*, Revised Final Report Prepared by Mr. Joinet pursuant to Sub-Commission Decision 1996/119, Annex II (Set of Principles for the Protection and Promotion of Human Rights through Action to Combat Impunity), U.N. Doc. E/CN.4/Sub.2/1997/20/Rev.1, 2 October 1997.

UNSG, 2000, United Nations Secretary-General, *Report on the Establishment of a Special Court for Sierra Leone*, U.N. Doc. S/2000/915, 4 October 2000.

UNSR, 2011, Special Representative of the Secretary-General for Children and Armed Conflict, *Children and Justice during and in the Aftermath of Armed Conflict*, Working Paper No. 3, September 2011.

UNTAET, 2001, Regulation 2001/25 on the Amendment of UNTAET Regulation No. 2000/11: On the Organization of Courts in East Timor and UNTAET Regulation No. 2000/30: On the Transitional Rules of Criminal Procedure, United Nations Transitional Administration in East Timor, U.N. Doc. UNTAET/REG/2001/25, 14 September 2001.

Ursini, B., 2015, 'Prosecuting Child Soldiers: The Call for an International Minimum Age of Criminal Responsibility', 89 *St John's L.Rev.* 1023–1048.

US *Einsatzgruppen*, 1948, *United States of America v. Ohlendorf (Einsatzgruppen)*, Military Tribunal, Opinion and Judgment, Case No. 9, 8–9 April 1948, available at http://www.worldcourts.com/imt/eng/decisions/1948.04.09_United_States_v_Ohlendorf.pdf (last visited 18 February 2019).

US *Flick et al.*, 1947, *United States of America v. Flick et al.*, Military Tribunal, Judgment, Case No. 48, 20 April–22 December 1947, available at http://www.worldcourts.com/imt/eng/decisions/1947.12.22_United_States_v_Flick2.pdf (last visited 19 February 2019).

US *German High Command*, 1947–1948, *United States of America v. von Leeb and Thirteen Others*, Military Tribunal, Judgment, Case No. 72, 30 December 1947–28 October 1948, available at http://www.worldcourts.com/imt/eng/decisions/1948.10.28_United_States_v_von_Leeb.pdf (last visited 10 March 2019).

Valder, K., 2014, 'A Stolen Childhood: A Look into the World of Female Child Soldiers and the Initiatives Targeting the Ending of the Practice', 7 *Alb. Gov.L.Rev.* 34–55.

Wainryb, C., 2011, '"And so they Ordered Me to Kill a Person": Conceptualizing the Impacts of Child Soldiering on the Development of Moral Agency', 54 *Human Development* 273–300.

Wall, I.R., 2006, 'Duress, International Criminal Law and Literature', 4 *J.I.C.J.* 724–744.

Warburton, I.-G., 2003, 'The Commandeering of Free Will: Brainwashing as a Legitimate Defense', 16 *Capital Defense Journal* 73–97.

Waschefort, G., 2015, *International Law and Child Soldiers* (Hart).

Weigend, T., 2011, 'Germany', in Heller, K.J. and M.D. Dubber (eds), *The Handbook of Comparative Criminal Law* (SUP) 252–287.

Werle, G. and F. Jessberger, 2014, *Principles of International Criminal Law* (3rd edn., OUP).

Wessells, M., 2006, *Child Soldiers: From Violence to Protection* (HUP).

Wiener, N., 2014, 'Excuses, Justifications, and Duress at the International Criminal Tribunals', 26 *Pace Int'l L.Rev.* 88–131.

Williams, S., 2005, 'Amnesties in International Law: The Experience of the Special Court for Sierra Leone', 5 *H.R.L.Rev.* 271–309.

Yee, S., 1997, 'The *Erdemovic* Sentencing Judgement: A Questionable Milestone for the International Criminal Tribunal for the Former Yugoslavia', 26 *Ga.J.Int'l & Comp.L.* 263–309.

Zahar, A. and G. Sluiter, 2008, *International Criminal Law* (OUP).

Zimmermann, A., 2016, 'Article 5: Crimes within the Jurisdiction of the Court', in Triffterer, O. and K. Ambos (eds), *The Rome Statute of the International Criminal Court: A Commentary* (3rd edn., Beck) 111–126.

CHAPTER 6

Conclusion

Child soldiers are mainly regarded as victims of crimes under international law. However, one should not lose sight of the fact that they are also the perpetrators of such crimes. Consequently, child soldiers have been prosecuted for their involvement in the commission of international crimes. Yet, the fact that they face numerous challenges during their recruitment, as well as time with the armed forces or armed opposition groups including being indoctrinated, manipulated and forced to kill civilians, does not mean that they will automatically be viewed as innocent and thus acquitted of the charges.

In academic literature, duress, as defined in Article 31 of the ICC Statute,[1] is the defence which is the most referred to when discussing available defences to child soldiers. Against this background, the book explores whether child soldiers would indeed be successful in raising the defence of duress and be acquitted for their crimes. A careful, systematic application of the various elements of the defence of duress however shows that child soldiers are generally unlikely to meet the stringent requirements of this defence. Previous studies have already highlighted issues of concerns relating to the defence of duress, but these are exponentially accrued in the case of child soldiers. The authors argue that the defence of duress must be so interpreted as to pay heed to the personal and social circumstances of child soldiers as well as the overall context in which they live. At the moment, too little attention is given to the (extra)ordinary circumstances of their crimes. The definition of duress as enshrined in the ICC Statute is,

W. Nortje, N. Quénivet, *Child Soldiers and the Defence of Duress under International Criminal Law*,
https://doi.org/10.1007/978-3-030-20663-5_6

as it stands, not amenable to the situation of child soldiers and, should it be used in national courts, it would simply leave child soldiers unable to raise the defence of duress. It is therefore submitted that the provision should be adapted to be successfully invoked by child soldiers.

Further, the limits of and exclusions from the defence of duress are inappropriate in relation to child soldiers. Child soldiers cannot generally be viewed as trained soldiers on which a special duty is conferred. Yet, this assumption might be rebutted on a case-by-case basis. With regard to the inability of a defendant to claim duress if he/she has joined a group he/she knew was of a criminal nature, the authors argue that there should be an assumption that it does not apply to child soldiers. However, this assumption should be rebuttable since some children make the conscious choice to join and stay in the group despite being able to leave it.

In its current form, duress under international law is viewed as a justification and thus extremely difficult to invoke successfully. The authors suggest that the defence be recast as an excuse in light of their findings relating to its application to child soldiers. This would ensure that whilst the international society condemns the acts as crimes and child soldiers are cognisant of the criminality of their acts, compassion and empathy can be shown towards them. Moreover, an excusatory defence allows the court to focus on the actor rather than on his/her actions, thereby developing a better understanding of the personal, social and societal situation of child soldiers. Although an excuse does not necessitate the alleged perpetrator to have acted in a proportionate manner, the authors argue that a proportionality test should be maintained and the balance of harms test be removed. Also, duress could be used as a complete defence excluding responsibility as well as a mitigating factor at the sentencing stage, giving courts more flexibility. Nonetheless, even if duress is viewed as an excuse and courts are casting a child-friendly eye on child soldiers, the defence of duress might still be out of reach for many child soldiers.

As unpalatable as it might be, defences should be available to alleged perpetrators of international crimes as they should be afforded the highest level of human rights, including fair trial rights. While it is important to prosecute individuals for the commission of such heinous crimes, it is similarly important to ensure that the accused is aware that he/she might have a defence which may exclude criminal responsibility. Also, an alleged perpetrator who raises the defence of duress expects his or her claim to be regarded with the necessary respect and legitimacy by the ICC.[2] It is argued that the legitimacy and future of international criminal law would be seriously jeopardised if the role of defences was to be ignored and left undeveloped by international courts and tribunals. The development of duress as a ground for excluding criminal responsibility can largely be attributed to vital jurisprudence on the matter, such as *Erdemović*.[3] However, it is important that academic scholars, jurists and national and international courts alike do not focus solely on this judgement but question and challenge it so that in the application of Article 31 of the ICC Statute more attention is paid first, to the fact that the latter allows for duress to be used as a complete defence and second, to the circumstances in which such heinous crimes are committed. The future development of the defence of duress will depend in large part on how Article 31 of the ICC Statute is interpreted and whether judges create further jurisprudence on the matter. The case of *Ongwen*[4] at the ICC is one such case where the Court might have the opportunity to provide invaluable jurisprudence on the existence and status of duress as a ground that excludes criminal responsibility. It is essential that States Parties, that are most likely to prosecute child soldiers, have recourse to a provision that provides clarity on the question as to whether child soldiers can raise the defence of duress for crimes committed under international law.

The case against Ongwen at the ICC might also be the catalyst that ignites another crucial debate, that of the dual status of individuals as both victims and perpetrators. Child soldiers clearly epitomise this seemingly oxymoronic dyad. They find themselves caught in the darkest places on the earth, stranded at the extreme edge of human behaviour and emotion. They are in constant danger and are transformed from 'innocent civilians' into 'merciless soldiers'.[5] No child deserves to be indoctrinated, drugged, raped, forced to loot and kill and subjected to any other similar heinous act. The violations from which they suffer have a profound effect on their development and play an undeniable role in them acting the way they do. Also, one should not forget that they not only are moulded and exploited once they have been recruited but also faced daunting challenges prior to recruitment, including poverty, war and a lack of education. Their plight is often overseen or misunderstood by their own societies, communities and families. That being said, these child soldiers can still be held responsible for their involvement in the commission of crimes under international law. Their prosecution, especially on the national level, would illuminate their situation to such an extent that the population might realise that the children, like the rest of the population, were also victims, thereby smoothing the rehabilitation process.[6] To simply regard a child soldier as just another perpetrator on the basis of the crimes that he or she has committed is neither feasible nor welcome and due recognition must be given to the circumstances to which the child was subjected in order to objectively adjudicate whether the child acted under duress or not. In addition, each case is different, and so a case-by-case analysis is required before any conclusions can be arrived at. No general conclusions can be drawn just on the basis that an alleged perpetrator was a child soldier at the time of the commission of the crime. After all, a criminal trial is about ***individual*** liability.

Furthermore, the approach adopted in this book towards alleged perpetrators claiming the defence of duress could be applied to any adult in a similar position. Thus, the authors argue that this research has a wider significance than the narrow 'set' of children looked at.

Firstly, duress as an excuse empowers courts into recognising that the victim-perpetrator dichotomy in relation to international crimes fails to describe the reality. At the moment, the focus on victims in clear, elemental opposition to perpetrators[7] has created an irremediable division between the two that even a former child soldier like Ongwen seems to be unable to bridge.[8] The problem is that a 'justice system that aims to distinguish between victims and perpetrators loses its legitimacy if it simply ignores the environmental complexities that may significantly effect [sic] individual decision-making in the societies within which it operates'.[9] Unfortunately, international criminal courts tend to fail to understand generally these complex realities and too often reduce them to dichotomies of good victims and evil perpetrators, recognition and denial, guilt and innocence.[10] National courts should not fall in this trap. The international criminal justice project, as opposed to the narrow set of international criminal institutions, should not be only about the victims but should give a voice to all (social) actors and so present a more nuanced and refined picture of the context surrounding the commission of international crimes. A deliberate agenda to distinguish between the victim and the perpetrator also violates the presumption of innocence of the perpetrator. It is a customary international law principle that every accused is presumed innocent until proven guilty, even those accused who have been charged with crimes under international law. A better understanding of the challenges faced by individuals in armed conflict would greatly help the court apply the defence of duress in such a way that it becomes an effective, rather than an abstract, defence.

Secondly, in applying the defence of duress as an excuse, courts could pay more attention to the circumstances in which international crimes are committed to understand why a person acted in a certain way. This would enlighten as well as offer a more nuanced understanding of the complexity of perpetratorship. A court would be able to show the humanity of both the victims and the perpetrators, and the international criminal law project would be able 'to declare the commonness, the ordinariness, the humanness, of the people who commit these horrific crimes.'[11] The human factor of the perpetrator, in addition to the circumstances under which he or she acted, would not be sidelined in favour of the prosecution of such perpetrators. As Mohamed claims, international criminal courts and tribunals tend to highlight perpetrators' particular and unique deviance[12] and criminal depravity.[13] This is especially the case in relation to the ICC because, owing to the principle of complementarity[14] and the threshold of gravity,[15] it is bound to charge and prosecute individuals who are alleged to have committed innumerable heinous crimes. In contrast, other international and hybrid courts have not applied these principles and so have, much alike national courts, dealt with low-ranking individuals. Thus, it is not only the ICC that faces serious challenges when it comes to the progressive realisation of the rights of accused, but also the discourse of international criminal law in general. Those individuals who commit international crimes are more often than not judged before they are adjudged to have committed an offence. The legitimacy of the international criminal justice project is at stake when a defendant enters the courtroom already deemed guilty. It is submitted that the ICC, being the first permanent international court, should be at the forefront of protecting the rights of the accused and developing general principles of criminal law, in particular the defences or grounds excluding criminal responsibility, since the international jurisprudence on defences is underdeveloped. That being said, international criminal tribunals, as well as domestic courts, should not refrain from delivering quality judgments that include jurisprudence on defences. Individual criminal responsibility requires the law to regard each and every individual who commits an offence to be held individually responsible for that offence and should neither differentiate nor discriminate against an offender on the basis that he/she is alleged to have committed a crime under international law as opposed to a less serious crime. The fact is that '[w]hereas international crimes are indeed extraordinary in their level of heinousness, the men and women who commit them are very much ordinary.'[16] Erdemović is very much one of them, one of these individuals on trial, 'someone we can recognize—almost accidentally, against our urges—as human, a man rather than a monster'.[17] A judicial system that does not allow for the defence of duress to be raised successfully clearly fails to recognise the humanity of perpetrators of international crimes.

Also, a need exists to understand the environmental complexities of international crimes and the sphere within which individuals engage.[18] Certain social, political and economic contexts indubitably shape and promote the commission of international crimes as they foster an environment of forceful compliance.[19] Although the individual might be autonomous, the level of his or her agency is determined by the socio-political environment. As Branch illustrates '[i]n situations like the war in Uganda, in which longstanding violence has been deeply incorporated into societies, in which people must live under and try to make meaningful lives within local and global structures of violent constraint, consent is never absolute, and agency is always entangled and qualified.'[20] More generally seeing the individual 'as the locus of responsibility has shifted attention away from the societal causes that contributed to his deviance' and such causes include 'illiteracy, poor job opportunities, and poverty'.[21] The individual cannot be separated from society, especially if that individual is a child. Yet, it is this very society that expects a certain conduct under certain circumstances.[22] Fletcher notes that 'in a society with little tolerance for human nature as it is, one would expect to find little room for excuses.'[23] As a result, Fisher contends that 'the fact that an act was committed as part of a collective wrongdoing rather than against a backdrop of a well-ordered and peaceful environment [...] affects how acts of atrocity and their perpetrators ought to be judged.'[24] In relation to groups more specifically, it is argued that duress is rather common in situations where crimes are committed within a group activity, particularly where individuals are left with no other option but to remain within the confines of the groups. Here, it might be argued that the perpetrator is a means rather than an end; he or she is being used in a societal system that does not enable him or her to act otherwise. As Wiener suggests, the ICC could 'follow in the footsteps of the NMTs and refuse to hold responsible individuals who are inculpable because they had no choice but to commit the crimes because of duress'.[25] After all, once the theoretical and almost technical legal gaze of the defence of duress is removed, one can see in plain eyesight the complexity of the issue and especially that of perpetratorship.

At a more fundamental level, as Yee explains, '[t]he substantive law issue relating to the defence of duress takes on philosophical proportions. It is essentially the question of how much we can expect of humanity. Such a question obviously deserves a great deal of soul-searching.'[26] And such soul-searching goes beyond the plight of child soldiers.

Notes

1. ICC Statute 1998.
2. In addition, the Preamble of the ICC Statute proclaims that the States parties to the Statute are '[r]esolved to guarantee lasting respect for and the enforcement of international justice'. ICC Statute 1998.
3. ICTY *Erdemović* 1997.
4. ICC *Ongwen* 2016.
5. See Wessells 2006, 57; Crane 2008, 12.
6. Amann 2011–2012, 184. See Wessells 2004, 513. Such a process can also be reached via truth and reconciliation commissions (see UNICEF 2010 and Siegrist 2006, 58–59).
7. Kochhar and Hieramente 2016, 243 and 230.
8. See discussion in Drumbl 2012, 91.
9. Bond and Fougere 2014, 511. See Cryer et al. 2014, 406.
10. Rauschenbach 2018, 295.
11. Mohamed 2015b, 1169.
12. Mohamed 2015a, 1651–1652; Mohamed 2015b, 1209.
13. Branch 2017, 40.
14. ICC Statute 1998, Art. 1.
15. ICC Statute 1998, Art. 17(1).
16. Olusanya 2010, 88.
17. Mohamed 2015b, 1162.
18. See Cryer et al. 2014, 406.
19. Fisher 2013, 77.
20. Branch 2017, 41.
21. Kochhar and Hieramente 2016, 227.
22. Fletcher 1998, 83.
23. Fletcher 1998, 83.
24. Fisher 2013, 62–63; see 77 and 80.
25. Wiener 2014, 131. See also Fletcher 1998, 83.
26. Yee 1997, 307. See also Ambos 2013, 361.

References

Amann, D.M., 2011–2012, 'Calling Children to Account: The Proposal for a Juvenile Chamber in the Special Court for Sierra Leone', 29 *Pep.L.Rev.* 167–185.

Ambos, K., 2013, *Treatise on International Criminal Law: Volume I: Foundations and General Part* (OUP).

Bond, J. and M. Fougere, 2014, 'Omnipresent Threats: A Comment on the Defence of Duress in International Criminal Law', 14 *Int.C.L.R.* 471–512.

Branch, A., 2017, 'Dominic Ongwen on Trial: The ICC's African Dilemmas', 11 *I.J.T.J.* 30–49.

Crane, D.M., 2008, 'Prosecuting Children in Times of Armed Conflict: The West African Experience', 15 *H.R.B.* 11–17.

Cryer, C., et al., 2014, *An Introduction to International Criminal Law and Procedure* (3rd edn., CUP).

Drumbl, M., 2012, *Reimagining Child Soldiers in International Law and Policy* (OUP).

Fisher, K.J., 2013, *Transitional Justice for Child Soldiers. Accountability and Social Reconstruction in Post-conflict Contexts* (Palgrave).

Fletcher, G.P., 1998, *Basic Concepts of Criminal Law* (OUP).

ICC *Ongwen*, 2016, *Situation in Uganda in the Case of Prosecutor v. Ongwen*, International Criminal Court, Decision on the Confirmation of Charges against Dominic Ongwen (Public Redacted), Case No. ICC-02/04-01/15, 23 March 2016.

ICC Statute, 1998, Statute of the International Criminal Court, U.N. Doc. A/CONF.183/9, (1998) 2187 UNTS 90.

ICTY *Erdemović*, 1997, *Prosecutor v. Erdemović*, International Criminal Tribunal for the Former Yugoslavia, Judgment, Case No. IT-96-22-T, 7 October 1997.

Kochhar, S. and M. Hieramente, 2016, 'Of Fallen Demons: Reflections on the International Criminal Court's Defendant', 29 *L.J.I.L.* 223–244.

Mohamed, S., 2015a, 'Deviance, Aspiration, and the Stories We Tell: Reconciling Mass Atrocity and the Criminal Law', 124 *Yale L.J.* 1628–1689.

Mohamed, S., 2015b, 'Of Monsters and Men: Perpetrator Trauma and Mass Atrocity', 115 *Colum.L.Rev.* 1157–1216.

Olusanya, O., 2010, 'Excuse and Mitigation under International Criminal Law: Redrawing Conceptual Boundaries', 13 *New Crim.L.Rev.* 23–89.

Rauschenbach, M., 2018, 'Individuals Accused of International Crimes as Delegitimized Agents of Truth', 28 *Int.Crim. Justice Rev.* 291–316.

Siegrist, S., 2006, 'Child Participation in International Criminal Accountability Mechanisms: The Case of the Sierra Leone Truth and Reconciliation Commission', in Arts, K. and V. Popovski (eds), *International Criminal Accountability and the Rights of Children* (Asser Press) 53–66.

UNICEF, 2010, *Children and Transitional Justice. Truth-Telling, Accountability and Reconciliation*, UNICEF Innocenti Research Centre and Human Rights Program.

Wessells, M., 2004, 'Psychosocial Issues in Reintegrating Child Soldiers', 37 *Cornell Int'l L.J.* 513–525.

Wessells, M., 2006, *Child Soldiers: From Violence to Protection* (HUP).

Wiener, N., 2014, 'Excuses, Justifications, and Duress at the International Criminal Tribunals', 26 *Pace Int'l L.Rev.* 88–131.

Yee, S., 1997, 'The *Erdemovic* Sentencing Judgement: A Questionable Milestone for the International Criminal Tribunal for the Former Yugoslavia', 26 *Ga.J.Int'l & Comp.L.* 263–309.

Index[1]

[1] Note: Page numbers followed by 'n' refer to notes.

W. Nortje, N. Quénivet, *Child Soldiers and the Defence of Duress under International Criminal Law*,
https://doi.org/10.1007/978-3-030-20663-5

The manufacturer's authorised representative in the EU is Springer Nature Customer Service Centre GmbH, Europaplatz 3, 69115 Heidelberg, Germany. If you have any concerns regarding our products, please contact ProductSafety@springernature.com

Printed and bound by CPI Group (UK) Ltd, Croydon, CR0 4YY

30/09/2026

02225260-0014